Chasing Belief

Chasing Belief

Engaging Transformative Spirituality

WAYNE L. KREFTING

WIPF & STOCK · Eugene, Oregon

CHASING BELIEF
Engaging Transformative Spirituality

Wipf & Stock
An Imprint of Wipf and Stock Publishers
199 W. 8th Ave., Suite 3
Eugene, OR 97401

www.wipfandstock.com

PAPERBACK ISBN: 978-1-6667-3047-0
HARDCOVER ISBN: 978-1-6667-2206-2
EBOOK ISBN: 978-1-6667-2207-9

09/09/21

To Peggy, companion and steady keel on our journey together

Preface

Everything turns to ashes, everything whatsoever . . . whatever was great in my eyes upon earth, whatever small and contemptible, all without exception will fall back into dust.

—ROMANO GUARDINI, ITALIAN-BORN GERMAN CATHOLIC PRIEST, AUTHOR, AND ACADEMIC[1]

Growing up, Ash Wednesday was always a strange day to me. My Catholic friends would come to school with crosses painted on their foreheads in black ashes. I had no idea what the point was until much later. I do not even recall when, as a Lutheran, that tradition began in my own denomination. I do remember as an adult, though, the Ash Wednesday imposition of the ashes with the words, "You are dust, and to dust you shall return" (Gen 3:19).

Those words at first had a fairly chilling and, if not sinister, at least disconcerting resonance to them. Death, the reference was obviously to death. Not just any death, but my own, personal, individual, particular demise.

Death.

The words uttered at funerals in the cemetery, "Ashes to ashes, dust to dust, earth to earth." We commend this body to the ground. All in all, this phrase was a pretty overt punctuation point. And a reminder for those present, with an ear to hear, of their own eventual fate: we as creatures of earth, coming from the earth, walking the earth, will one day return to its soil.

How often are we reminded of that mortality in daily life, a continual series of Wednesdays smeared with ashes. The taste of ashes in our mouth: the ashes of broken promises, of failed hope, of the broken, forgotten, frightened, homeless, insecure, hopeless suffering ones among us both near and far left vulnerable to the depredations of the world due to our lack of compassion or even notice. Even as I write these words we are in the middle

1. Guardini, *Sacred Signs*, 18.

of a global pandemic which we are struggling to understand as large numbers of people die. Against this horror are those who deny the reality of this disease or find it inconvenient to their economic and social lives. These too are characteristics of those particular Wednesday ashes that mark the tenuousness of our lives.

Death is one of the foundational mysteries at the root of all religions. Death brings the question of meaning and morality in life into sharp focus. What was the point of it all? What justice, what sense of fairness or balance is there in the world? What becomes of all things of life that must pass away? Do they pass away into nothingness, into oblivion? Or, do they pass to another realm, become a part of something larger beyond our perceived existence?

Today for many in the Judeo-Christian-Islamic faiths, the answer, carried over from earlier times, is a literal paradise or heaven, a realm unknown but concrete described in the words of Scripture. This literal understanding of "after life" or "life after" has taken root in popular culture, too, in works such as movies *It's a Wonderful Life, What Dreams May Come, Defending Your Life*, the television show *The Good Place*, and a host of other films with heaven, angels, hell, or related themes. These literal interpretations of heaven (and hell) as real physical spaces are, to many, a bedrock of belief.

How does such a physical place to which the faithful go square with the biblical admonition that we are dust and to dust we will return?

The answer for many is found in "resurrection," a reconstitution physically of a body at some point or in a literal understanding of and belief in "the soul" as distinguished from "the body." The soul has come to be interpreted as a separate component of self contained (or trapped for some) within the physical body. The soul is the immortal self which carries on after the physical body dies. The immortal soul/self is what the physical body puts in jeopardy because the physical is broken, sinful, or otherwise at odds with "God's will." In either case, that answer has involved a continued personal history post-death.

Growing up, I mainly didn't think too deeply about any of this. But slowly and surely, as a child of the twentieth century, these answers became more and more problematic. My educational experiences presented a modern scientific understanding at odds with those beliefs. Trying to reconcile the subsequent effect on philosophical, metaphysical, and theological understandings of reality that I discovered in my university and seminary education made those easy "answers" of childhood religion untenable. The meanings and connections (and disconnections) between such knowledge and traditional spirituality created, to put it mildly, an intellectual and emotional dissonance.

Two factors in growing up played an important early role in this. My family had a wide generational spread and they were also highly educated, directed toward science and teaching. I never knew my father's father (who was born in 1856 and died long before I was born), but I had aunts, uncles, and cousins who were old enough to be my grandparents. With such a large elder family group death was not so distant. Even in life, pondering how these older people on the far side of life from me could also have undergone some of the same types of events, or even ones unique to them and their times beyond my understanding, made me curious about the notion of personhood—"who we are, what makes us, us." From the science and teacher family milieu came the easy step to ask what stood behind this personhood, what was the nature of the reality in which we all lived?

Although my family was religious, being Lutheran there was a reticence to engage in metaphysical discussion. Better were the political debates that engaged parents and their siblings. Perhaps this was the "age" in which they grew up. Or, perhaps, it was (and still is) the disconnected nature of our modern, scientific life in which the "spiritual," the metaphysical, is split off from our normal existence in a unreflective and dualistic parsing of life into non-interacting facets of life.

Both of these strands met in the mortality of these beloved older family members. How was one to reconcile the religious teaching of my youth and the scientific knowledge that my family and my education saw as fundamental to moving and living in this world? Religion and spirituality become most meaningful in the face of death, of the unknown. The knowledge that one day we will no longer exist to move among both the beauty and the tragedy of this world thrusts the issue of meaning squarely in our face. How does one find anything meaningful in the horror and insanity that coexists with life's beauty?

That the explanations are tied to fantastic stories from an ancient time only confounds the problem. How do you understand, from a modern point of view, the sun in the book of Joshua standing still in the sky, or Jesus climbing aboard a cloud and lifting off like a booster rocket into . . . outer space? Or, any number of other biblical stories that seem so out of step with the world in which we live. The language that points to "heaven" somewhere up, in the "vault of heaven," someplace in the . . . galaxy . . . the universe . . . some other dimension? There comes a time when the language, concepts, and explanations become nonsensical. And yet there is "something" there, "something" that the materialistic, scientific point of view cannot address— love and compassion toward others, the will to good, the will to evil, pain and suffering, the meaning of life. Neither the "old religion" nor the "new science" seemed prepared to deal with any of this.

Like many others today, I found myself "chasing belief." Past university days, through two seminary degrees, that search continued as a part of my life experience, whether in social work, the arts, family, or the communities of people in which I live and move. Reading. Thinking. Trying to understand this deepest of human experiences and its meaning for me.

Faith, in general terms, is a trust in underlying principles of our existence. Belief is the acknowledgment that such principles exist and have power. But that acknowledgment and subsequent trust engenders unhealthy consequences when disconnected from the reality and lived experience of our world.

The dissonance I experienced is not uncommon, and such a disconnect has fateful consequences for not only our spiritual life but our political and cultural life as well. Though the latter are not the purview of this book, they are nonetheless related. Perhaps this question is uniquely American, growing out of a problematic relationship American religion has with science, pluralism, technology, in short modern life. Perhaps. But I think the matter goes much deeper.

This issue is deeply embedded not only in American history and religious reflection but is central to the larger historical events and movements of the second half of the twentieth century. History and religion are deeply intertwined.

The fact that the changes wrought by scientific explorations have not had a marked impact on the reflective life of "the woman or man on the street" is not necessarily their fault. There really has been a failure of religious institutions (of all stripes), of churches, of theological schools to educate their respective communities on how to interpret and reinterpret religious faith in light of modern science. Of course, the scientific community, in not paying attention its own ontological and hermeneutical foundations, has contributed to the confusion and disconnect. Better to wall off controversial or confrontational areas than to give due consideration.

But even as mainstream seminaries and religious education teach the need for a metaphoric understanding of traditional language, that instruction rarely translates into the communications relayed by spiritual leaders. These metaphors do hold a truth, just not the literal one. Teasing out the meanings of these metaphors is what theology in our time should do. So often, however, the argument is left in the hands of those from both religious and anti-religious reductionist groups who view things from a literal perspective. Though theologians and philosophers may decry the anti-intellectualism and the nonreflective nature of what those groups hold as truth, for the most part religious and spiritual communities are left with a muddle.

Time to take seriously the implications of the metaphorical nature of religious scriptures.

The old familiar forms of conscious thought have gone as far as they can go and it is time to create new, transformed concepts emerging, as it were, from a chrysalis of crisis to a paradigm that thinks and believes both scientifically and religiously. The first part of this book is meant to "harrow" the ground, to turn over, break up the "old models" and thought patterns, to pull "weeds" of preconceptions, both in religious language and ideas and in the evolution of our scientific understanding of the world. In this way we can prepare for the seeds of new ideas, ways of looking at the world, to be planted.

The ground from which a metaphysical basis for existence can find meaningful content, I believe, is in a sense of the underlying, interconnectedness of all reality which not only underlies religious sensibilities but also is a part of our modern, quantum understanding of the universe. Life, as we are coming to understand it, has a complexity with resulting implications for both physical biology and metaphysical concepts. What we perceive grossly through our unaided senses differs markedly from what is actually happening in the particle or quantum realm. At the same time, though our mind and thought is not affected by each individual particle making up our physicality (as an organism we could not develop the ability of orderly thought if this were not the case, and orderly thought is the basis of perception and observation), we are made up of individual cells that in themselves operate as an integrated democracy of sub-lives (cells) whose additive nature produces a unity consciousness.

As will become evident in later chapters, I find it fruitful in understanding this interconnectedness, this interdependency, to look beyond Western intellectual concepts to Eastern, and more specifically Buddhist, insights.

As I reference Buddhism and Buddhist thought later in this volume, it is important to recognize that "Buddhism" covers quite a broad range of spiritual thought and practice, no less than such a reference to "Christian" would also encompass a wide variety of religious frameworks. Although many concepts considered are expressed across the variety of Buddhism, the particular Buddhist "lens," if you will, which my discussion uses is the Mahayana branch in Zen Buddhism, specifically that of the Kyoto (Japan) School. This is not to deny such approaches as the Hua-yen (Mahayana, Chinese) Buddhism or even the Taoist and other especially Chinese traditions. I personally find the Zen approach of the Kyoto School most helpful in creating a transformed understanding of spirituality that is the goal of this work.

While I do not seek to appropriate one tradition to another nor attempt to create a correspondence of one tradition to another, nonetheless I believe that the various human expressions seek to uncover, to describe, to partake in the same mystery, the Truth if you will, that lies at the heart of existence, that gives meaning to the cosmos.

The question of language and theology for this reconceptualization, or really transformation, is not whether this rethinking of the divine is understood differently from church orthodoxy (frankly, I am sure it is in a number of ways) but whether this conception is so different as to remove it from its most basic and fundamental claims, the deeper principles at play underlying the tradition's attitude toward the divine—the deeper intentions.

Certainly the picture painted here is different from tradition, and beyond the conception of the forebears of the Christian tradition. But it is important not to exaggerate those differences, either. Conceptual representation and revelation are not the same thing, and cultural context is important to the honest representation so that present-day attitudes, understandings, toward science, divinity, and humanity are also considered.

Changes in understandings of biblical texts, exegesis, are not only a present-day concern but present in Scripture itself. For one to argue that all theological understanding is contained within and set by Scripture is to misunderstand the basic documents. A fresh consideration of divine and human nature cannot be ruled out on the basis of either Scripture or tradition.

Interestingly, the Reformers also had diverse and not always consistent views on theological formulations they were presenting. Such diverse personalities as Luther, Wesley, Zinzendorf, Brenz, and Gerhard, all expressed a kenotic (from "kenosis," "self-emptying," or a renunciation of divine nature; discussed more fully in later chapters) viewpoint in one form or another even if not in the same terms as modern kenotic theology.[2]

The point here is that changes in intellectual climate make necessary changes in theological presentation, even if not consistent with past practice. Even a conservative reading of biblical texts and church teachings is, at best, ambiguous and ambivalent with regard to a kenotic interpretation, even one as radical perhaps as presented here.

Ultimately, even this task is not one that can be definitively completed, since the world grows, evolves, "actualizes," and we incorporate new knowledge of the cosmos of which we are an intricate part. Whatever formulations are made must stand up to the critical engagement and scrutiny of the mind.

---

2. For an extended discussion of the European kenotic tradition, see Brown, *Divine Humanity*.

As will be evident throughout, thinking is not the only framework within which human beings operate. "Experience" plays no less a role in the formation of identity as it does a source of material for thinking and reflection. The mistake is in segregating thought and experience into isolated compartments, ranking one above the other, and designating them as merely materialistic biological processes.

The choice of "Spirit" as the word used in this work in place of "God" for reconceptualizing the divine might have been, if not unconscious, at least a subconscious recognition of a deeper truth expressed here. "Spirit" in Hebrew, *ruach*, רוח, is expressive of "wind," "breath," a movement which in the latter case fills with life as it empties, breathes out.

I breathe; you breathe. In and out. Filling and emptying, separate motions but so deeply interconnected that they are one motion, one action. Breath—its presence signals life, its lack is deadly. The flow of breath is holy. The "breath of God," *ruach*, Spirit, pours out life in Genesis, in Ezekiel, to cite only two examples. Spirit empties into creation to create and sustain life and is in turn filled with the possibilities actualized—self-emptying, self-giving, self-limiting.

Chasing Belief is not written as a finished theological work. My interest was not with the logic or essence of theological thought so much as with a consideration of modern lived, experienced existence. Thus I did not attempt a defense or apologia of specific creedal tenets. The disconnect between the "words of faith," the theological constructions, and our existential questioning, though often intellectually avoided or denied, has actually created an inability of the religious or spiritual language to make sense.

The task in *Chasing Belief* is to find a way toward meaningful expression of spirituality—spiritual experience—in the modern context. I believe that God (Spirit) disclosed in Christ is not a "new" thing suddenly created or appearing, but a clarification, a statement of "re-revelation," if you will, of what the divine has always been. Finding an intelligible ground for that discussion—a metaphysic—and the "tools" to excavate that ground was and still is the continuing task.

In the end, my intention here is to bring benefit to your life. Your efforts in this process of understanding the reality of our world will be a benefit as the potential for your own realization and awareness.

Chapter 1

Every day the sun rises and the sun sets, but the world always goes on without stopping, without taking notice of life's suffering and pain.

This truth is often masked by our preoccupation with the present moment, our distraction by a passing event, our egocentric view of life, and a habitually uncritical appraisal of our existential position in the universe. The inconceivable immensity of that cosmos in its limitless dimension, and the overwhelming power, majesty, and indifference of nature, the natural world in which we live, are too much to comfortably contemplate.

The world may be, as Shakespeare once wrote in *As You Like It*, a stage and we mere players who upon our exit may engender applause at our passing. But more often in the course of human affairs and natural history the action has been brutal and "the rest is silence," to steal from *Hamlet*.

The psalmist gave voice to this sense of existential minuteness with a sense of humility: "When I look at your heavens, the work of your fingers, the moon and the stars, that you have established; what are human beings that you are mindful of them, mortals that you care for them?" (Ps 8:3–4).

The truth too often psychically hidden from view is that the "cosmos," by whatever name we choose—"nature," the "universe," "the world"—pays no attention to us and to what are the momentous events in our lives. Thousands killed in war, dozens slaughtered by a crazed person, hundreds swept away by flood, disease, earthquake, or famine. Still the seasons change. Tempestuous seas sweep the oceans. The sun rises; the moon sets. Another day.

A friend, a beloved, a stranger dies. And yet the world turns, scant notice, if any, taken.

The result is a "moral terror [at] the indifference of the cosmos to our personal fates, exemplified most dramatically in our inevitable personal oblivion."[1] Blaise Pascal, the seventeenth-century French philoso-

---

1. Raymo, *When God Is Gone*, 120.

pher, described his anguish at being suspended between the infinite and nothingness, and equally remote from both: "When I consider the short duration of my life, swallowed up in the eternity before and after, the little space which I fill, and even can see, engulfed in the infinite immensity of spaces of which I am ignorant, and which know me not, I am frightened. . . . The eternal silence of these infinite spaces alarms me."[2]

Of course even amid the fear there is beauty, so defined by whatever we have as present cultural markers. We celebrate, or mourn, those key moments. But there is no escaping the truth of ever-present suffering and the marginality of our existence within the universe. In the face of this suffering and the neutrality, if not seeming unconcern, of the world in which we find ourselves it is only natural to ask, "Why?"

We quest for meaningfulness in our lives, our suffering, the ambiguous mixture of beauty and horror all around us. This is the genesis of all religion: to make sense of mortality and morality in an indifferent universe, to discover a sure footing that will provide a basis for morality, and through it all the wonderment at those "infinite immensity of spaces" in which our "short duration" dwells.

Answers abound, of course. Look around at the multifarious religious and faith institutions, or even the now numerous anti-religious groups. Each one will insist on the veracity of their "truth" and the "blindness" of others. Are they all true? Are they all false? Is there just "one way" among them that holds the key?

How do we grapple with, how do we explicate, how do we understand the journey we all travel? Where are hope and peace to be found among fear and alienation? I do not believe this is a journey with an end; that would imply complete understanding which is not possible for a finite being in a universe, possibly infinite, definitely contingent. I cannot say whether or not the path outlined here will be your path. But I believe that we as sentient beings must put aside our petty though seemingly insurmountable differences to recognize the commonality that we all share as we cling to this mote of dust floating in the vastness of the cosmos.

The impetus for this exploration comes from a long-standing belief that religious language as expressed by various modern-day communities, whether using traditional and archaic expressions, or jargon "updated" to a present-day sensibility, does not make sense. Too often theological language and the language of everyday religious expression seem divorced from the reality of the physical world in which we live. Our understanding of "how things work," incomplete as it is in terms of modern science, is at odds with

2. Pascal, *Pensées*, 28.

literal interpretations of religious metaphors, and often with the metaphors themselves. There is, I believe, a need for credible language and conceptuality about spirituality in the seats of power as well as in the ghettoes of oppression.[3]

The core message of all the world's great religions is an invitation to consider a vision of existence, something important and of ultimate significance that conveys something comprehensible and trustworthy about the world. The question is how, or perhaps whether, such a vision can be made intelligible and meaningful in a contemporary setting. Theological language today, most especially in the Western traditions, is problematic largely because modern cosmology differs radically from biblical and traditional cosmologies. The spatial and absolute categories of traditional theologies, and especially Judeo-Christian-Islamic Scripture, are not only difficult but incoherent to the nontheistic foundations of modern thought. And at times, too, the philosophical foundations which have underlain and guided the formulations of those categories have been misused, misunderstood, or simply been wrong.

For many today, religious language is tied to the outdated worldviews of their ancient founders, wedded in a way that inhibits if not prohibits contemporary reexpression in light of contemporary understanding of the world. The use of these semantic artifacts easily becomes ingenious, distorting and blocking off the possibility of real meaning for such language today. "Consider," says Mark Johnston in *Saving God*, "making the common and unquestioned racism of the American Founding Fathers an essential feature of the intent behind the Constitution, and then finding, as a result, that the Voting Rights Act is unconstitutional."[4]

The cosmos, we have found, is really quite different than we supposed or even imagined. Present-day particle physics and particularly the Higgs field have presented us with an "other" even more mysterious in many ways than the various religious concepts of "god." This exploration does not undertake an in-depth discussion, much less an explanation of particle physics, Higgs boson, leptons, and such, having no claim to expertise; the explication of that field is left to others. But an understanding and continuing exploration

---

3. The word "language" will be, unless otherwise specified, used to denote not only the words used to describe the philosophical and theological concepts at play in this discussion but the concepts themselves. Although words themselves are often a poor vessel for conveying the constructs of the mind, words are all we really have aside from the emotive power of art in all its forms. But then, to discuss the meaning behind art's emotional "tug" requires a language.

4. Johnston, *Saving*, 40.

of the implications present of that world around us will necessarily be the jumping-off point for our quest.

In the same way some acquaintance with the philosophical and theological language and terms and history of intellectual turmoil around this exploration of mystery will be necessary. Our modern culture is in many ways becoming not only more anti-scientific but also more anti-intellectual preferring to substitute unconsidered opinion for rigorous thinking and engagement with ideas. This criticism is not a conservative yearning for a by-gone time nor a curmudgeonly rant against change and novelty in the modern age. Indeed, change—the change fostered by intellectual exploration and advancement—is precisely the point, and our conceptualities and language need to reflect those understandings.

The argument made here does not seek to anthropomorphize science or to use it to point to some supernatural guiding hand transcendent to it all, nor to advocate a reductionist version of a naturalism position. Far from it. For the truth of any reexamined vision to be relevant or considered at all, it needs to be submitted to the cross examination of the world for judgment. At the same time the very nontheistic, classical Western philosophical mindset which has driven science forward can also be obstructive to any meaningful discussion of the metaphysical. Negotiating between these two in that examination demonstrates how problematic to a twenty-first-century worldview such a message and the role of metaphysics, "God language," can be.

In any discussion, the words *meaningful, meaningless, intelligible,* and *appropriate* play a significant part. For purposes of clarity a distinction is made between meaning and meaningfulness.[5] Something, a system of thought or a belief, can be said to have *meaning* when it is expressed conceptually with internal coherence. However, this system may have no relation outside of itself to the actual reality in which we live. Thus Tolkien's Middle Earth may have a meaning which is understandable to us but which nevertheless does not disclose an authentic dimension of our experiences as selves.

This latter disclosure of authentic dimension to actual experience defines *meaningfulness.* Something is meaningful, then, in the sense of genuinely disclosing our authentic lived experience. The lack of this connection to authentic experience results in the meaninglessness, the total disrelation, of a given set of concepts to experience and to life.

---

5. The following distinctions are based on Tracy, *Blessed Rage for Order.*

Intelligibility, in a sense related to meaningfulness, is concerned with the understandability of a system to the concern of the present situation. In other words, it "makes sense" to our worldview.

Ultimately any formulation or explanation to be adequate for the task proposed must meet the further requirement of *appropriateness*. Something is appropriate to a formulation, for example "faith," when it re-presents the same understanding expressed in the data of that formulation's traditional discourse. The development of the formulation cannot lose touch with the symbolism being interpreted. Of course, that traditional discourse or witness is used with the knowledge of its historical conditionedness; but formulations, especially theological formulations, also need to account for the full range of the tradition's claims in order to be appropriate.

The purpose of these chapters is to explore how the language of spirituality might be found to have not only meaning but be meaningful in our modern context. Spirituality, the Spirit, can have a wide variety of meanings but at root it is a metaphysical concept for which the "divine" or "God" has been the common marker. Whatever the antecedent meanings and understandings of the term "God" are or have been, and they are plentiful, we need to begin with the question, "What does 'God' mean for us, if anything at all, now?" How are we to appropriate that language, that understanding, that symbol for our times? What significance, if any, can the symbols, rituals, texts, and events associated with "God" have for us as heirs, whether believers or not, to a historic tradition, a tradition that has shaped much of our world.

And this is precisely the point: the *historical* nature of this inherited understanding of the "Ground of Being," the "Author of Creation," the "Ruler of the Universe." "God" comes with "baggage." Emotional, linguistic, but most of all *historical*. As noted in the coming chapters, this means: which God, whose God? What of the nontheistic understandings of the Ultimate? This symbol designating the foundational underpinning of Reality comes with a variety of understandings, stories, and interpretations.

In our time of crisis of culture, of faith, of intellectual self-understanding, interpretations matter. Our ways of understanding and acting no longer work; even our experience is estranged from that of the past. Our inherited culture and tradition is not able to speak to us in a way that makes the experience which was foundational to that culture and tradition comprehensible to us. We need to discover new ways to express that experience, new ways to interpret as active participants in and not passive recipients of that to which this symbol points.

The question "Why?" leaps immediately to mind. Why should we be bothered with such a concept that no longer speaks to many in our day?

Especially those for whom such belief systems are antiquated gibberish from a more unenlightened time. And the question is just as readily asked, "Why do we need a new interpretation, a different understanding from the 'Faith of Our Fathers'?"

To the first audience, the relevance of formulations of "God language," if not spiritual language, is the same as the relevance of the understandings, categories, and formulations of Aristotle, of Adam Smith, of Karl Marx, of the Enlightenment humanists, and on. These ideas are foundational to many of our modern institutions and to the dialogues surrounding their efficacy for the human community. In the case of "God language," if the categories in which they are delineated no longer make intellectual sense but nevertheless operate to direct human activity then it is at least incumbent upon us to examine whether or not such language is at odds with the intended result. A very simplistic example would be relying solely upon belief and prayer as a remedy for diseases such as Ebola or smallpox to the exclusion of medical intervention.

As with any philosophical discussion, any topic, or even simplistic argumentative example, has a variety of onion-like layers of refinements, related issues, and relevant topics. Glossing over them here might seem to be an oversight or neglect of subjects of critical importance. However, they are set to the side for the express purpose of underlining the importance of the core message: the basic relevance of the interpretations themselves. If nothing else, such literacy allows for understanding and dialogue in order to address common issues with a mutual understanding.

For the audience of believers, the question of "Why?" is no less important. At a very practical level the relevance of the interpretation of "God language" is crucial to the future of outreach and mission, of "evangelism" to use a Christian term. This may seem like a "first-world problem" since fundamentalist- and literalist-based religious communities are growing in the third world. But as educational, scientific, and twenty-first-century vocational growth takes hold in these presently impoverished communities the same questions of relevance will increasingly come to the fore.

As that reexamination of the interpretation of "God language" takes place, David Tracy argues in *Plurality and Ambiguity*, the plurality of voices and understandings and the ambiguities present in each of those interpretations will surely make themselves felt.[6] In every moment, in everything we do, we are interpreting. "To understand at all is to interpret . . . a situation demanding some action and to interpret a correct strategy. . . . Interpretation

---

6. See Tracy, *Plurality and Ambiguity*.

is thus a question as unavoidable, finally, as understanding, deliberation, judgment, decision, and action."[7]

Tracy has a lengthy discussion of that plurality and ambiguity as it relates to both history and more specifically religious language, namely "God." I have used his discussion in encapsulated form as platform to examine the need for reformulating "God language." My argument and conclusions here are my own but the reader would be well served by reading this slim volume.

Interpretation, as a human activity, has both pluralistic and ambiguous aspects. Consider our understanding of historic events. History is not a straightforward list of factual data; even the "historical facts" themselves have a set of interpretations. History is fraught with ambiguity; to be an American is to live as part of both a two-centuries-old experiment with freedom that has inspired the world for generations, and also a national community that enslaved hundreds of thousands of people, that exterminated thousands of those native to this land.

How then do we even know what that history is? The understanding of that history, to realize the meaning of that history for us today, necessarily involves a complex chorus of voices, a plurality of viewpoints relating how that story has unfolded. To rightly understand that history requires taking each of those voices seriously, to examine critically each of those pieces (and their veracity certainly), so that a better understanding of the whole tapestry can be reached.

That is not to say such interpretation is ever complete, nor is it ever perfect. The shortcomings of our human condition all but guarantees that. Yet, for that story to be truly our story, for us to learn what it means for us today to be an American, that is, the relevance of that history for our actions moving into the future, such an enterprise is crucial. The results may be ambiguous, the plurality of understandings may leave rough edges over which we as a community may argue, but we ignore such interpretation at the peril of ourselves and our future.

What is true of history or a historic event is just as true of symbols and symbolic language of which "God language" is a prime example. By "symbolic language of which 'God language' is a prime example" I merely mean that the concept "God" is not contained within the word or words which are used to describe "God." If "God" is "infinite" or "ultimate" then this "Ultimate Reality" or the experience thereof, whatever the tradition, by definition cannot be exhaustively described by or within such finite containers. Thus such language is symbolic as representing what the believer or interpreter (believer or not) desires to express.

---

7. Tracy, *Plurality and Ambiguity*, 9.

"God" has both a history and a language, no matter the tradition. We as hearers and inheritors of the traditions of "God" and "God language" have no less a history and a language through which those words, symbols, and understandings have passed. That complexity of histories and languages we call tradition. Those traditions contain a number of "preunderstandings," sets of meanings and contextual landscapes that shape the import, connotations, and "sense" of the tradition. The further interpretation of tradition requires engagement with these preunderstandings, especially when the set of meanings and contextual landscapes are dissonant or foreign to contemporary understandings of reality.

This is what has happened to the symbol "God" and the language concerning "God." The underpinnings, the preunderstandings, are based upon a system of understanding reality that is no longer comprehensible to a modern age. Most of the time we use the language of "God" but have no real understanding of what we mean, of what reality there might (or might not) be behind that word. Not thinking about whether or not such a word or symbol makes sense or has any reality is easier than confronting the dissonance or fear that might be unleashed in a meaningful examination of our belief system.

But the "rules of the game" have broken down and a common agreement as to the game itself, let alone the rules, is problematic. The game here is the description of what constitutes "Ultimate Reality," "God" to use one past descriptor. The rules are our basic understanding of "how the world works" which the scientific examination of our universe has over the past five hundred years changed. A new paradigm informs our perceptions to such an extent that the concepts and imagery, the underpinnings which formed our traditional language about "God," have been marginalized as incapable of describing anything "real."

Chapter 2

Staunch believers in any of the three major monotheisms (Christianity, Islam, and Judaism) may take offense when I refer to their holy scriptures as stories. But many of those same believers would be quick to say that narratives about Zeus or Thor or Shiva—the Hindu god of destruction—are just stories. . . . Through the history of our species, sacred fiction has dominated human existence like nothing else. Religion is the ultimate expression of story's dominion over our minds.

—JONATHAN GOTTSCHALL[1]

Ask someone how they are or how their day is going and inevitably you will hear a story. Sometimes the tale is amusing and informative. Sometimes the narrative will drive the hearer to seek the nearest escape route, or at least a polite excuse to move on and avoid further remarks.

We humans are storytellers. The stories we tell help us to organize our world and our experiences, to understand both our world and ourselves. The narratives we tell shape us and shape our perception of the world. These stories can shape a narrative for ourselves that is congruent with the understanding of others. They can mirror commonly held scientific understandings. Or, they can be wildly incongruent, at odds with those around us, including what others understand to be normative scientific understandings.[2]

Earliest humans told stories about themselves, their family, their tribal unit, and their "people." These tales differentiated the tellers from others, the unknown or the known but alien and perhaps menacing. They told stories

1. Gottschall, *Storytelling Animal*, 118–19.

2. Of course, there are also stories that have fallen into a more or less commonly defined web of psychosis or mental illness. These narratives are anomalies to the self-integrating and worldview building sorts of stories we all have, whether or not we share a common "thread." These are not a part of this discussion.

to explain the changing of the seasons, the regular courses of a fiery ball of light by day and a cool luminous light in the night. Stories were created about the points of light in the sky, about the various creatures encountered and their origin and function within the world.

These stories covered all manner of questions that the human mind could conjure over the millennia, including the mysterious cycle of life and death that seemingly affected everything. The stories created and influenced behaviors and cultural attitudes, whether toward relations to other humans, the surrounding natural world, or even an "other world" where the mysteries of life and death dwelt.

We know these stories, the mythoi of peoples around the world. We have read them in folk tales and fairy tales, and in a wide variety of mythological stories about "the gods," "demi-gods," or other supernatural beings from that "other world" touching our own. The tales come from the Greeks and Romans, Native Americans, the Norse peoples, the various peoples of Africa, the Indian subcontinent, Japan, China, and so on.

We also know them in the biblical stories, of Adam and Eve, of Cain and Abel, of Noah and the flood, of Sodom and Gomorrah, of Elijah's fiery chariot, and on to various biblical testimonies.

These stories construct and shape our understanding of who we are and what the world is "really" like. Such stories of human experience have been amply described and analyzed by any number of authors religious and secular, including the masterful explications of Joseph Campbell. There is often a commonality to the underlying characters, archetypes, and structures of reality to which these narratives point. Yet, there is also often a fundamental contradiction of narratives in relation to each other which has been the basis for bitter conflict over the millennia.

When our own story is challenged we become anxious, uncomfortable, and very often angry. Counter-narratives which oppose the story we tell threaten the underpinnings of who we are and how we understand ourselves. We can see this in our own times, rich versus poor, "the haves" and "the have nots," a white cultural narrative versus a narrative held by people of color, East versus West, the cultural clash (perceived or real) between various religious and ethnic groups around the world. And on and on.

Stories matter. How that narrative is constructed, what it includes and more importantly what it leaves out, shapes not only our view of ourselves and our place in the world but the status of those around us, especially "the other," the weight given to their thoughts and feelings or even if they are worthy of being considered at all. Thus, the stories we hold have a tremendous importance not only to us but to every other living thing including our planet.

Up to this point only passing mention has been made of religion or religious narratives in the modern world, whether in various forms of Christianity, Judaism, Islam, Buddhism, Hinduism, or some nondenominational amalgam. These, too, are stories, "narratives" that shape how we understand ourselves and view the world as a whole.

For the Judeo-Christian tradition, and ignoring for the moment the various strands from conservative to liberal/reformed, the basic narratives informing believers are found in the Bible. The Bible is a rather broad term which incorporates both the Jewish textual canon, the Law, Prophets, History, and Poetics (termed the "Old Testament" by Christians) and for Christians the foregoing plus the "New Testament" comprising the Gospels regarding Jesus of Nazareth, early church "history" ("Acts of the Apostles"), various letters, and instructional documents. To that list could be added a number of apocryphal documents, exegetical interpretive works, and tomes of theological rumination.

For Jews and Christians these foundational documents tell the stories upon which a worldview and a self-identity are forged. History, and those documents themselves, is rife with lessons showcasing the result of questioning that narrative in ways large or small. From the "heretics" of the Reformation to the centuries-long clash of Protestants and Catholics to the trials of Galileo, the State of Tennessee v. John Thomas Scopes, the persecution of Jews through the millennia reaching a frenzy in the Holocaust of World War II, to the demonization of Islam in the wake of various Middle Eastern wars and a "War on Terrorism." The outcome is never pretty.

Whenever a counter-narrative is introduced, or a portion of the foundational narrative is questioned, fear and anxiety provoke an atavistic, angry response. Since the new information or narrative runs counter to existing belief about self and the world any dialog concerning this dissonance is often next to impossible. Thomas Kuhn in "The Structure of Scientific Revolutions" described this situation. Anomalies or failures arise or are pointed out in the current narrative or "paradigm" (the present belief system is challenged with new and conflicting information). Many who operate within that belief system (paradigm) dismiss the validity of such challenges or questions lest they suffer a loss of faith. To accept a new narrative would be to lose one's religious identity and all that means to self-identity.

Of course, looking at the variety of Jewish and Christian faith traditions there is quite a range in how that received tradition is interpreted. On one end of a sliding scale, there is the literal interpretation that ignores or denies anomalies in the narrative that science, contact with other faith interpretations, traditions, or even internal textual contradictions bring forth. On the other end, there is an interpretation that is more open to nuance, metaphor, and holds traditional narrative and scientific understanding in more or less tension.

Even in this latter group the significance of these anomalies though meaningful is still such that adjustments and tweaks of the overall paradigm are needed. This adjustment might come in the form of explicating metaphorical language (fiery chariots, the sun standing still) or in the form of specific theological language reformulations that acknowledge the new scientific paradigms within which we live.

Rather than tinkering "at the edges," however, the time has come for a new narrative, a new paradigm, that seeks an understanding of "the mystery" for our age. The current narrative contains a disconnect, a fundamental contradiction between the received ancient story and present lived perception of life in the modern age.

From an intellectual perspective, the old religious paradigm and the language used to describe those religious understandings are stretched to the breaking point in relation to a scientific understanding of the cosmos, the universe around and within us. These narratives, or language traditions, are based upon two-thousand-year-old narratives formed with a cosmological structural understanding radically different from our own. Our view of the world and our place in it has changed remarkably over the millennia so that such religious and theological language is no longer intelligible to a scientifically literate population.

That such an archaic worldview fails to connect with the sensibilities of a modern world is hardly surprising and has resulted in the irrelevancy of such religious communication for many people. As has been noted by various mainstream denominations within the United States and England, active participation in religious communities or life has been falling off for some time.[3]

Whether the world's population as a whole finds such language irrelevant and archaic will not be argued here. A 2010 Pew Research Center demographic study estimates some 84 percent of the world's population self-identifies as religiously affiliated.[4] However, what is considered religious affiliation ranges from traditional religious groups to folk/traditional/other religions to religiously unaffiliated but believing in "God or higher power." Indeed, this latter group (which includes atheists and agnostics along with those with some belief system) is the third-largest

3. D'Vera Cohn and Andrea Caumont, "10 Demographic Trends Shaping the U.S. and the World in 2016," *Pew Research Center*, March 31, 2016, http://www.pewresearch.org/fact-tank/2016/03/31/10-demographic-trends-that-are-shaping-the-u-s-and-the-world/.

4. "The Global Religious Landscape," *Pew Research Center: Religion and Public Life*, December 18 2012, http://www.pewforum.org/2012/12/18/global-religious-landscape-exec/.

world grouping, behind Christians and Muslims and about the size of the self-identified Catholic group.

At first blush, the disconnect between religious language and conceptualization might seem just to be a "first-world problem." But this study mixes such differing spiritual understandings and traditions that the self-identity as religious is not necessarily indicative of a lack of scientific dissonance with religious concepts. Nor does the prevalence of falling religious affiliation in the West indicate a more educated, scientifically literate population. Correlations between secularization/education and religious non-affiliation seem rather weak at best and no study at present can make a good argument for such an outcome.[5]

Regardless of present religiosity trends among the world's population, the tension between scientific understanding and religious (specifically Judeo-Christian-Islamic) language and concepts is at a critical point with the failure of the religious paradigm to take into account the observed scientific data.

Why is this a problem? Because beliefs matter. As stated previously, beliefs, or more specifically faith narratives, shape how we see ourselves and the world around us. An ethnocentric belief system allows the extermination of those outside. A belief system with a narrative that denies the centuries of scientific exploration and understanding of our world marginalizes the natural world to an imperial humanity and rejects the scientific consensus around the jeopardy global climate change poses to our planet. A belief system that values male over female, anthropomorphizing a deity as a dominant male, denigrates over half the world's population and supports their oppression. A belief system that fatalistically rejects human agency to await the intervention of a supernatural entity risks death over life in the pursuit of faithfulness, and not only for the "faithful."

The current religious paradigm, even with dissenters at the margins, has created a population inimical to each other and the planet upon which we live.

One might argue that this is the result of incorrect or false understanding of doctrine. And in some respects this may be correct. But the argument might be better framed over a belief that at best should be radically re-understood, if not jettisoned.

This crisis calls for boldness, a revolution of risk-taking to explore alternatives so we can formulate or reformulate our religious language and

---

5. "3. Educational Attainment among the Religiously Unaffiliated," *Pew Research Center: Religion & Public Life*, December 13, 2016, http://www.pewforum.org/2016/12/13/educational-attainment-among-the-religiously-unaffiliated/#unaffiliated-sidebar.

concepts. At root, the paradigmatic anthropomorphizing of spiritual concepts is the fundamental issue.

And yet.

And yet, we humans are storytellers. Stories are the way we come to understand ourselves and our place in the cosmos. The individual within and among the "we humans" arises from that communal humanity; who we are, what we are is understood within the web of relationships from which we arise. The stories we tell about our ancestors, about the journeys of their lives and ours, give definition to the self-understanding of both the individual and the group. Oftentimes these stories are meant to exclude rather than widen the scope of our common humanity. Counter-narratives are offered but their altruism is trumped by tribal protectionism.

We need new stories, new narratives, shaped by a new vision of who and what we are, and that Mystery which lies around and beyond us. Elsewhere, in other chapters, I argue for a new and different epistemology, the way we know what we know. Epistemology is, essentially, the explication of the stories we tell—whether couched as theology, philosophy, or biblical worldviews. Getting a handle on these ways of understanding are helpful to the creation of new narratives through new awareness and insight into the world. But modes of thought are not what drive us humans as storytellers. Modes of thought, though necessary to finding our way to new stories, are not enough to show us how to get on with life. Stories are the instruction manuals, like Aesop's Fables, that help make the operations of life understandable, or at least create a bit of organization within the messy and chaotic thing called Life.

Our current theological situation forces us to reconsider our assumptions, presuppositions, and methodologies in speaking of the divine. None of them is directly helpful to us in the dilemma that confronts us. We need to begin with ordinary secular experience which defines itself as devoid of transcendence, taking into account the contemporary awareness of passage, contingency, relativity, and perhaps most important, the modern assertion of freedom and autonomy.

However, to speak of "God" we need to be able to move beyond the immediate, which is the secular limit. It is necessary to search for glimmers of the transcendent in ordinary experience before we attempt to speak of "God" acting in general historical experience. In order to do this we need to show that in secular life and discourse there is an ultimate dimension, though unrealized or denied, and that therefore such an enterprise has meaning. We will need to ask realistically and honestly what the ground for theological action is to be, what the issues are, and be bold and independent enough to formulate new answers.

Chapter 3

The first thing to understand is that "God," if it is a name at all, is not an ordinary proper name. . . . If "God" were an ordinary proper name, then the various monotheisms might succeed in referring to, addressing, and worshipping the same God, *despite* their very different and inconsistent collective beliefs about his nature and intentions.

—MARK JOHNSTON[1]

G od has been in the news lately.
A lot.

And not necessarily in a good way. "God" is alternately praised as the underpinning of righteous belief and action (in many and various religious forms), and blamed for all the sectarian and bigoted actions, large and small, that afflict the world. Hope in God's justice and faith in the promise of God's ultimate victory over the vicissitudes of a finite world are a source of comfort and a spur to action. But the fruit of that very hope and faith often engenders actions that are morally reprehensible.

The argument ensues: Whose "God" is the correctly understood one? What is the correct way to understand "God," to relate to faith traditions of "God"? "God" or "No God"; "God" being a meaningless holdover from superstitious bygone times. Science versus faith and religion (with a variety of nuanced and parsed understandings of this matchup). On and on.

Not much gets settled because each has their own settled landscape, thank you very much, you godless heathen/immoral/superstitious bigot.

Even the word "God" becomes a point of contention. In spite of the fact that "god" is merely a linguistic marker specific to one language group which was used in the sense of "that which is invoked" or a spirit immanent

1. Johnston, *Saving*, 4–5.

(in a burial mound?). "God" is, at bottom, a word, freighted with all sorts of cultural baggage over millennia to be sure, but just a word.

What do we mean by "God" or a nontheistic no god of Buddhism?

Before journeying into the realms philosophical, theological, and historical in the search for a metaphysical language informed by the new paradigm within which we live, what is meant by the term "God" ought to be spelled out. "God" gets quite a workout and, capitalized or not, refers to a multitude of things, attitudes, feelings, and situations (some not at all religious).

But the word "God," by which most often in Western culture and specifically in the United States is named the "Supreme Deity," is not a name nor is the word itself used in any Bible, whether Jewish, Christian, or Islamic (nor those groups closely related). "God" comes from the Old English by way of the Dutch "god" or Germanic "Gott." Further attempting to trace the origins of the word (and related Odin, Wodan, etc.) into proto-Germanic and proto-Indo-European language groups swiftly becomes a trip down the rabbit hole of linguistic conjecture and argument.

"God" is used in reference to and translation of words in Hebrew and Greek biblical texts, words referring to the Supreme Deity, and mostly taken from Greek translations of those biblical texts. In Greek *theos* (θεός) and Latin *deus*. The proto-Germanic word itself finds first reference in the sixth-century Codex Argentus, a manuscript which contains a fourth-century translation of the Bible into Gothic language. The Greek and Latin and thus the Germanic/English "God" is most often a translation of *Elohim* אלהים, itself a plural (which theological import will be set aside for the moment).

Even given this, "God" has become the "go to" in naming the Deity, Creator, and so on. However, referencing the term "God" for the "Supreme One," whether by any of the monotheistic religions or even atheists, lacks any clarity as to what is meant.

Other languages and cultures have their own words that are used to point to that which stands beyond the mortal, finite: *YHWH* (Yahweh) יהוה, *Adonai, Elohim* אלהים, *Deus, Theos, Brahman, Wodan, Elah, Shén, Allah, Allahu, Hu, Bahá, Bhagavan, Ngai*, and on and on. Plus there are faith traditions that reject a singular creator deity in the sense of the monotheistic and polytheistic religions. "God" as a concept of "godliness," not as a word, becomes more a state of perfect knowledge, bliss, and peace—a liberation from the cares of finitude.

Beyond such sectarian and cultural clashes in the appropriation of "God" as a term, language about God and God's activity in the world has become unreal for much of our contemporary, pluralistic society. To be sure, such language may have meaning within certain spiritual or existential contexts or in specifically religious settings, whether or not being meaningful to a larger societal audience. But God language, discourse about God's activity in ordinary experience, is problematic today. That God language and our general experience of the world are discontinuous has increasingly been the case since the Renaissance and presently the problematic nature of theistic language has a cultural context. In this context any ultimate structures of coherence, order, and value in life are denied, or at least ignored, and thus religious language is irrelevant and meaningless.

Laity and clergy alike share doubt as to the reality of God, or at least they have difficulty in defining God's activity in this empirical, scientific world. Recognition of this situation implies a radical reappraisal of the church as "faithful hearer" seeking to communicate to a distinct and "doubting" world. The line has become blurred and that doubt goes right to the core of religious affirmation in questioning the reality of God. The question is no longer "how to speak of God," but whether such language is even possible.

The cause for this shaking of the foundations is the "secular spirit," the mood, the fundamental self-understanding of reality and our being in the world which is dominant in our minds.[2] Our "coming of age" as a technological, urbanized society away from the world of nature and of an eternal, static order describes this movement. Our social locus is understood to be that of a changing, relative order of human arrangements, not divinely established facets of a natural order but rather creations of history, geography, and human forces. The cosmos in which we live takes on the contingent, relative character we find in our lives. And because we are radically empirical in our assessment of that reality which we experience as flux and passage, change and process, our knowledge encompasses only those contingent, finite factors around us that we can directly experience and verify.

At the heart of this secular spirit is the notion that human experience is "devoid of relation beyond itself to any ground or order."[3] This mood expresses the total secularity of all existence, that a relation to a divine, that is supernatural, ground is impossible, irrelevant, and destructive to humanity. Any language concerning a divine dimension to reality which is thus beyond the knowable finite is meaningless because there is not a referent in modern experience. Four general characteristics of this secular mood can be discerned which account for the lack of any transcendent or ultimate dimension in modern life and which thus render contemporary theological language problematic.[4]

2. Gilkey, *Naming*, 34–39; Armstrong, *Case for God*, is a more recent publication with a very detailed explication of the clash of "God language" and the modern secular spirit, esp. chs. 9–12.

3. Gilkey, *Naming*, 188.

4. See Gilkey, *Naming*, 40–70, for an extended discussion. Gilkey's analysis of the

Contingency is an essential part of the understanding that reality exhibits no ultimate order. Further radicalized from its seventeenth-century roots, contingency in reality is the sense that all that exists is the result of random events, accidents. Though a proximate order may be perceived, enough to allow statistical prediction, no rational, necessary, or purposive order stands behind these events. The world given, then, is ultimately arbitrary and all knowledge and understanding are limited to the immediate, which is all that can be known.

Resulting from our historical consciousness developed in the late eighteenth century, a sense of interrelatedness or relativity defines our age. All reality is in flux and is determined by its history, shaped by the environment in which it exists and ultimately ceases to exist. Nothing is changeless, unrelated or self-sufficient, standing over the causal nexus of the world. This characteristic of a system of social relations implies change, process, and context. Everything is a changing result of the interactions of one thing with another, set in its own context of becoming. This causal network further implies that history's structure, events, and creations by humans are relative to their time and place. Therefore nothing we think or create is absolute, eternal, or transcendent to the flux of the world. Finally, a relativistic understanding assumes that explanations as to causes and factors are confined to the interacting nexus of relative causes and factors with nothing outside entering and acting. Assertions about reality, then, are confined to the finite range of factors we are given as we also saw with the category of contingency.

A close corollary of interrelatedness is the secular sense of temporality, the sense that all is becoming and so mortal, denying any dependence on that which is not transient or in passage. The sense of temporality is total; all is mortal, becoming, changing, perishing. This is the range of experience. Together with relativity, temporality has pushed us to examine the patterns of development and process that we find in life. Meaning for us now comes from such patterns and not from some eternal, changeless order. Time and history have become extremely important for us as the locus for human meaning. This has also helped to center us on the immediate, the temporal process as the stage of action, where hope lies.

Autonomy is a corollary of the others. Humanity is free to know its own truths and to give structure to the arbitrary, random events of experienced reality. This value of freedom is essential to modern self-understanding and hope. Contingency, relativity, and temporality acted to destroy all

---

cultural background of this secular spirit is used because of the concern evidenced in his works about the coherence of contemporary theological language and his understanding of the ferment over its unintelligibility. Again, Armstrong's more contemporary work details the historic and intellectual roots of this dilemma.

"gods" so that autonomy could open the present and future to creativity and rise above the historical nexus (though remaining in tension with it also). Any new theological formulation needs to take account of this anthropocentric assumption that external authority will ultimately crush our humanity and creativity.

These elements of the secular spirit have had very serious implications for theology. Contingency and temporality no longer point beyond themselves to an eternal, sacred realm as they once did in traditional theology. The insistence on remaining with the arbitrary given has made metaphysical or speculative statements irrelevant if not impossible, and leaves no room for a transnatural "God." Relativity has also had an influence on religion. Not only has a transcendent "God" become a dubious possibility (if that), but the relativism of history has made impossible any sacral evidence of "God's presence," since in the flux of history the ultimate events of revelation become drops in the sea of time. That the incarnation could be the center of history is not tenable. Neither is a permanent or ultimate authority to be found in history, least of all in historically produced human documents. Relativity has destroyed any basis for authority in religious belief.

These elements of contemporary mindset have signaled the end of belief in an eternal, unchanging, self-sufficient God (though this might not be apparent within a nonreflective faith or belief system). Eternity no longer holds meaning for transient humanity. Nor can anything remain untouched or self-sufficient in an interrelated process of becoming.[5] Traditional symbols of Christian hope and theology—everlasting life, eternal judgment, eternal salvation—have been emptied of meaning as eternity itself has become meaningless.

The final blow comes from human autonomy. If "God" was not nudged out by now, the challenge to any external authority, to "God's" right to even exist, would finish the job. "God," more than all other social authorities commanding obedience, faith, and submission is the final challenge to autonomous human creativity.[6] "God" destroys humanity's control over its own destiny in the infinite possibilities before it by posing as the power over a weak, submissive, and empty creature. Humanity would therefore be denied the ability to create its own values and meanings, to be self-creative in a contingent, changing world.

---

5. There is a huge body of literature examining the particular (peculiar?) American mythos of "self-sufficiency" as illusory and based upon political power dynamics. This context will not be examined in this work as it is tangential to the main point. There is a tension between interrelatedness and autonomy in many philosophic traditions. This autonomy is, I also believe, ultimately illusory in the dualistic context of object-subject.

6. Gilkey, *Naming*, 61.

The spirit of secularity sets the background, then, for the theological ferment today and the baffling question of how to speak of "God" in this mood, if that is even possible. We have to come to terms explicitly with the modern world. If we are to be modern in life then our faith ought to reflect this modern life, if our faith is to have any meaning and vitality for us. The mood of secularity expressed in the church by the lack of relation between religious and social dimensions of life denies the church's reason for existence and necessitates inquiry into how it will creatively respond theologically to the world come of age.

Before turning to the, mainly Western, religious/theological responses to this dilemma, the stage, so to speak, upon which the action plays out should be examined.

Chapter 4

Why does the universe go to all the bother of existing?

—STEPHEN HAWKING[1]

Why is there something instead of nothing? How did it all start? Why should the universe exist? Why do I exist? What can I really know for sure? How can I know it?

For ages such questions have plagued philosophers, theologians, scientists, thinkers, and pretty much anyone with a self-aware curiosity. Any answers, let alone the questions themselves, are, however, caught up in the conceptualities, the "word pictures," of the mind and the language used to express them. Indeed from earliest times humans have contemplated these mysteries; but the horizon of those thoughts has changed quite a bit.

The reader can be forgiven, at this point, for wondering what the exploration of "something" versus "nothing/nothingness" has to do with the topic at hand, namely the positive affirmation of a spiritual dimension to our life and the search for language which can adequately describe that spirituality in a meaningful way for our age. The excursion into "something" and "nothing" traverses territory that both science and theology/philosophy have sought to describe, often in ways not too dissimilar. The question of "something" and "nothing" also delineates a difference in outlook within scientific, philosophical, and theological communities.

Premodern cultures created numerous stories, what we term "myths" today, to give some order and explanation as to how the universe came into being and continues to operate. For the most part, though, the tales were not about something versus nothing. The existence of the world was taken as accepted. "Nothingness" as an explicit state was not a concept;

1. Hawking, *Brief History*, 174.

not until the Enlightenment would "nothingness" become "something." To understand why this is important to the task of this book, a closer look at "nothing" is warranted.

The concept of "nothing" is today represented in mathematics by "zero." This statement may be a bit of an oversimplification of the matter but will serve the purpose. That concept, however, is not something that the Western civilizations possessed in their early stages. For the Greeks and the Romans "nothing" could not be a "something." The use of "zero" as a placeholder in mathematics was something imported from the Eastern civilizations. Its utility is immediately apparent to anyone who has multiplied Roman numerals.

"Zero," no-thing represented, was a Hindu concept. Neither Hindu nor Buddhist cultures had the problem with "no-thing" (the sense of "emptiness") represented symbolically that the West had. This notation came to the West through Arabic scholars and traders in the Middle Ages. In particular, trade between East and West, monetary exchange and accounting, were primary factors in the acceptance of this new "nothing" placeholder.

However, prior to this time in the "ancient" days of the West and Western religions (and here I am including Christianity, Judaism, and Islam along with the various Greek/Roman and other Euro-Asian and American religious conceptions), conceptualities of how things came to be did not include "nothing" as we presently understand the term. That concept of "nothing" versus "something" still awaited arrival from the East.

These premodern creation stories related how a divine being pulled our present world from chaos, from a disorderly soup of earth and water (Hebrew, Babylonian), from fire and ice (Norse), from dark filled with water and wind (Apache), a rather messy, chaotic, and ambiguous "void" from which the creative elements such as Gaia Earth arose (Greek). The point here is that there was something, perhaps ambiguous and unclear, from which the world arose once "order" was imposed.

The idea of a world being created from nothing starts to take shape in the second century CE when the Christian church in opposition to perceived conceptual limitations to God, deemed heresies, expressed *creatio ex nihilo*, "creation out of nothing." In this view God's Word, *Logos*, alone called forth creation without preexisting elements, beings, or conditions. Later Jewish (Maimonides) and Islamic (Al-Ghazali) thinkers incorporated this conception into their theological systems.

"Out of nothing" still did not imply "nothing," however. It may sound like splitting hairs, but *ex nihilo* meant only that God did not need "anything" with which to create the world. "Nothingness" as juxtaposed to that which is, that exists, still wasn't a category. But, the question seemed to have been raised.

In the seventeenth century, René Descartes, breaking with hundreds of years of philosophical tradition, posited a new dynamic to knowing, and thus understanding the world. His new approach to the philosophical question of "knowing" was in a way just as, if not more, important than the revolutions of the eighteenth century, the Industrial Age, or the Information Age. The Cartesian method became the basis of modern science which opened up the intellectual and material expansions that followed.

Beginning with doubt, Descartes dispensed with all "knowledge" save that he "existed," something he could not doubt. The process of self-aware thought led him to conclude that, if nothing else, he—Descartes—existed. From this starting point Descartes rebuilt an understanding of the world with the categories of matter, the material (*res extensa*), and the mind (*res cognita*). He created a new, mechanistic method for examining phenomena, measuring and cataloguing the operation of the world. Much of our scientific method is still based upon these Cartesian principles—asserting nothing on faith or authority but only seeking knowledge through questioning assumptions and seeking provable observations.

In a sense Descartes, by his assertions, was also laying a foundation for the ascent of "self," declaring the empowerment of the individual, the individual mind, over sovereign and church. This declaration of independence of thought was also foundational to the Enlightenment and the modern age.

From a present-day perspective Descartes's dualistic view of mind and matter (a problematic conceptuality which will be explored in a later chapter) seems to have been overturned by modern neuroscience and even philosophic thinking. Descartes concluded that mind and matter exist in different categories, that mind and thought existed on a plane different from the physical world. Neither mind nor matter could be understood in terms of the other. With modern neuroscience has come an appreciation of the connection between the mind, and its various chemical and electrical processes, and the body.

For the present purpose, however, if, as Descartes posited, I can exist, should it not be equally and logically possible that I can not exist? This, too, cannot be doubted even if the process of self-awareness cannot, by definition, experience the lack of existence. This is of course based upon a conception of individualistic self-awareness as opposed to a universal unity of mind or consciousness which will also be a later topic of consideration.

The potential existence and nonexistence of self seems to be fairly obvious. We recognize that there was a time when we were not and there will be a time when, again, we will not be. This would appear to be the course of history and human events. But what of the universe? Why does it exist? Could it not exist?

In 1714 in another Enlightenment contribution to the premises upon which the scientific enterprise is based, Gottfried Leibnitz proposed, in "Principles of Nature and Grace, Based on Reason," a principle of sufficient reason, which stated that every fact must have a reason why it is so and not some other way. Here it is that Leibnitz raised the question, "Why is there something rather than nothing?"

Leibnitz reasoned that the existence of the universe necessitated a First Cause, a reason why it existed. That First Cause, Leibnitz posited in a nod to religious orthodoxy, is God. God created the universe freely and out of infinite goodness. But if God created the universe and everything must have a reason why it is so: "Why is God?" "What created God, the 'First Cause'?"

At this point Leibnitz stated that the reason for God's existence was, well, God. God, Leibnitz posited, was necessary, noncontingent, in relation to a contingent universe. Leibnitz, here, was arguing in a not dissimilar vein to Descartes even though Leibnitz found Descartes's formulations faulty, "not sufficient." Descartes saw God as a being who possesses all perfections and, existence being a perfection, thus God exists. Leibnitz thought this was not complete enough and that existence itself ought to be proved by argument to be a perfection, that necessary existence belongs to the essence of God.

Leibnitz argued, in short, that: God is a being having all perfections, a perfection is a simple and absolute property, existence is a perfection, if existence is part of the essence of a thing then that thing is a necessary being, if it is possible for a necessary being to exist then a necessary being does exist, it is possible for a being to have all perfections, therefore—a necessary being (God) does exist.[2]

This might seem a bit beside the point as both Descartes and Leibnitz end up at the same result. However, it is worth noting that this is, again, a matter of language, of mental "word pictures" expressed through a commitment to an orderly usage both of words and concepts to arrive at a conclusion which is comprehensible and reasoned, both traits incidentally also important to scientific exploration.

Of course these circular arguments did not satisfy anyone save those already committed to a theistic understanding of the world. Later in the eighteenth century both David Hume and Immanuel Kant argued against such a necessary existence as intellectually dishonest. They argued, separately, basically that no pure logic necessitated such existence since, as

---

2. For a synopsis of Leibnitz's modal argument, see Look, "Gottfried Wilhelm Leibniz."

Hume stated, if we can conceive of something existing we can also conceive such a thing not existing. "There is no being, therefore, whose nonexistence implies a contradiction."[3] Which, Hume further reasoned, would include "God."

And yet neither Hume nor Kant would address "Why is there something instead of nothing?" For Hume, such a question asked about something which is outside of human experience and thus illusory. Kant argued that extending conceptualities with which we understand our world in space and time to a reality without such structure would be illogical and any rumination erroneous. Thus was the can kicked down the road.

The following century and a half did not advance the question much further. The resolution to the mystery of existence was deemed foolish, impossible, and with Hegel a dialectical vanishing of being into nothing and the vanishing of nothing into being. The tension there being held in "becoming." All of which Kierkegaard dismissed. Later, into the early twentieth century the matter was still dismissed as illusory; nothingness was self-contradictory, a pseudo-question.

Even Wittgenstein, who found the existence of the world to be a marvel, saw the question of "why is there something rather than nothing" as senseless.[4] Crucially here, though, Wittgenstein does not dismiss the question, nor the importance of seeking an answer. From his perspective, this question as with ethical and religious conceptualities lay beyond the language of science and reason per se, and were problems to be addressed within another category of thought and language, though with just as much reality in its own right. Still, even his insights did not provide criteria for the distinction between knowledge and belief.

The answer by the middle of the twentieth century seemed to be, as Bertrand Russell put it, "The universe is there, and that's all there is to it."[5]

The scientific consensus agreed. From Copernicus to Einstein an assumption of an eternal and static universe was the operating premise. However, with Einstein's theory of general relativity the question took on new life, so to speak. Einstein's equations indicated that the universe was either expanding or contracting prompting Einstein to add a cosmological (gravitational) constant to his equation to preserve the eternal and unchanging nature of the universe.

3. Hume, *Dialogues*, 163.

4. Wittgenstein, *Tractatus Logico-Philosophicus*, 6.5.

5. Bertrand Russell and Frederick Copleston, "Debate on the Existence of God" (1948), in Hick, *Existence of God*, 175.

In 1927 Georges Lemaître, a Belgian Catholic priest, published solutions to Einstein's equation that indicated the universe was actually expanding. This discovery was independently corroborated by Alexander Friedmann in 1922. At first Einstein dismissed such solutions, but Edwin Hubble's 1929 report on the red shift of celestial objects (which further turned out to be distant galaxies like our own and not parts of our own galaxy) indicated that indeed the universe was expanding.

Lemaître argued that if objects were receding at present then at some distant past point such objects must have been closer. He went further in proposing a time when everything was in an extremely compressed state from which in an explosive beginning the universe erupted. This latter proposal proved too much for the scientific community at the time which rejected the concept of a "big bang" (so named by Fred Hoyle in a 1949 BBC interview). Not until Bell Lab's inadvertent 1965 discovery of cosmic microwave background radiation (CMB or CMBR), leftover electromagnetic radiation from the initial conditions of the "big bang" and predicted by the theory, was the notion taken seriously. Cosmic microwave radiation is now a part of the standard theoretical model describing the genesis and expansion of the universe.

Of course, some in the religious community were quick to jump on this new "point of creation." A finite universe with a historical starting point seemed to bolster, at least in some way, various creation stories and the ability to posit an infinite Being controlling the process, or at the least setting it in motion. But, in a very real sense, the existence of a creator or not was beside the point. For millennia humans viewed the cosmos as eternal, imperishable, unchanging in juxtaposition to our own all too precarious and perishable existence. Now, it seemed, the universe itself shared in that precarious, perishable status, albeit with a longer shelf life.

There was a "time," a nothingness, when the universe did not exist and an ultimate end again in nothingness. At least these seemed to be the operating categories based upon past, historical philosophic reasoning.

The question of "Why is there something instead of nothing" seemed inescapable now, along with at least the corollary, "How did something (the universe) come into existence?" And again there seemed to be an opening for theological positing while, from a scientific perspective, the question posed a number of challenges for inquiry and a multiplying range of possibilities as our understanding of the operation of that universe grew. Among the possibilities presented for "How" from the perspective of quantum theory and rejecting causation itself is that the universe spontaneously came into existence from nothingness, no First or Prior Cause needed.

"Nothing" really exposes the tensions between the scientific and theo-logical/philosophical communities (and among the respective communities themselves) as the question of how "nothing" became "something." Even within each of these communities there are opposition sides believing either that "something" can come from "nothing" or that such a belief is utter nonsense.[6]

Starting from the symbol for nothing imported into Western mathe-matics, "zero," a whole range of conceptualities have been created to provide an answer as to whether or not there actually is "nothing" and can "something" be generated from "nothing." Mathematically, "zero" itself is stable, unchanging. Added to itself zero still yields zero; multiplied, subtracted, or divided—still zero. To move beyond zero, "something" must be added to "nothing" as "nothing" cannot produce "something."[7]

It must be added here to clarify that by "nothing" is really meant "noth-ingness"; the lack of anything, nonbeing. The ontological status of "nothing-ness" has been debated but as a concept "nothingness" expresses a state in which not a thing exists. The debate of course for scientists, philosophers, and theologians is whether or not such a state of "nothingness," the absence of anything, can actually exist.

From a scientific viewpoint, any point "preceding" the big bang and the subsequent inflationary period of the universe, could not be described since space-time was nonexistent by definition. Philosophically various thinkers have attempted the thought experiment of imagining "nothingness" only to conclude that, if nothing else, the contemplating self still remained, thus rendering "nothingness" impossible. The onset of the universe, the point at which the big bang occurred, is a temporal boundary. There is no "be-fore," no anticipation, no coming into being as it were. That singularity from which the universe unfolded, and still unfolds, into complexity contained all the mass and energy existing today along with the infinitude of time.

Even considering the conditions of the "bang" itself, as the work of Alan Guth and others have proposed, that of an enormously energetic Higgs field, an "inflaton" field, which was driven to quickly burst outward, we are left with the question "From what/where did such a field arise?"[8]

---

6. For a remarkable and extended delineation of the "nothing" debate, the reader is referred to Holt, *Why Does the World Exist*.

7. I am, of course, ignoring a vast mathematical landscape on this subject, particu-larly set theory which posits an "empty set"—a something containing nothing—that it-self generates a universal web of somethings. The arguments pro and con seem fraught enough to leave the reader to explore this matter further.

8. For a comprehensive discussion of inflationary cosmology, see Greene, *Fabric of the Cosmos*.

From a placeholder for calculation, "zero"—"no thing" has become a conceptual category truly without a meaningful referent, "nothingness." Such a category, debated in the West from the time of Plato, has played much mischief in our ability to find language and concepts to express metaphysically what is meant by the "divine," the "spirit," "God" in that these concepts have become tied to an absolute and eternal conceptuality, timeless and noncontingent in quality in the attempt to preserve the "divine" from contingency and allow the "divine" to call the cosmos forth, *ex nihilo*, as Unmoved First Cause.

"Zero," however, as in "zero degree" or "total absence" (as in the sense of the "nothingness" expressed previously) in that argument really is meaningless. That concept seeks to describe a timeless, spaceless reality of nowhere and nowhen; but meaning vanishes in the vague and really unintelligible. Tying the concept of the "divine," of "God," to such abstract infiniteness only ties "God" to empty abstraction, really a negative idea and a negative word.

More helpful from a philosophical perspective, moving forward, "zero" or "total absence" is better understood to be implicitly known only if there is a least quantum or finite minimum taken as referent.[9] For example according to the Planck's constant there is a finite absolute minimum of light, one photon; less than that is no light. A more pedestrian example: We can observe "zero" of elephants because there is a finite minimum of what is described by the word "elephant." In such cases "zero" can be understood to be an abstraction, an "inactuality"; infinite perhaps but only in a negative sense.

In the end such terms as infinite, timeless and their kin as defining descriptors of the "divine" or of "God" not only empties those terms of meaning, as an "inactuality," but also flies in the face of millennia of relational language used when describing "God" and the "world" from Job to Plato to many other traditions. Removing "God" from the contingent and time-full also removes "God" from the relational, which has been the genesis of countless theological gymnastics and conceptual constructions to redress.

Complicating matters is the question of just what our universe is. Our universe seems to exist in temporal finitude. Or, is our universe simply a "bubble" in a more vast and eternally expanding multiverse, as some cosmologists conjecture? All of which still leads back to the question of why *this* universe, with these particular rules, or really any universe at all?

With such a "universe" of pathways to follow in our search for some "ultimate" understanding of our universe and our place in it, how can we proceed? How can we fashion a language, what "word pictures" might be conceptualized, to help us make sense of the "spiritual" and the place, if any,

---

9. Hartshorne, *Zero Fallacy*, 166.

that the word "Spirit" may hold? Is there, can there be, a necessary ontological ground for a contingently existing cosmos and we who reside therein?

The search for "ultimate" meaning, whether scientific, philosophical, or theological, in a timeless or transcendent "realm" is a distraction and beside the point. For the modern ethos, such categories are meaningless as contingency, process, becoming, the autonomy of humankind (as opposed to a controlling transcendent being) have all increasingly shaped our understanding of the world in which we live over the past three hundred and more years. The progression from a timeless divine being to a timeless nature (with a belief in the ultimacy of Progress) to this modern context necessitates a new conceptual framework and descriptive language if we wish to affirm any place for the "spiritual."

The discovery of the universe is also a self-discovery with implications both scientific and intellectual (philosophical and theological). That exploration yields a sense of our place in the cosmos. That discovery reveals the perishableness of nature. As humans, especially against this backdrop, we desire order and stability, even as our cosmological viewpoint has shifted from myth to a scientific statement of the physical. In either case there is still a worldview being expressed whether religious or philosophical. This holds true even for scientific inquiry as has been noted above in Einstein's reaction to the findings of Lemaître and Hubble, and yet again his difficulty accepting the implications of quantum mechanics.

Of course, it will be argued, attitudes and viewpoints changed as the data, the facts, gathered through scientific inquiry were amassed and examined. However, the change in attitudes and viewpoints is also an indication of a shift in paradigms, of the structural basis for the inquiries, the understanding of what narrative the data holds, and even what data are sought. Neither scientific nor philosophical/theological thought and language are immune to these shifts and changes.

Every culture has a unique view of the cosmos whether that culture is ancient storytellers or modern cosmologists. Both are channeling the mystery, the awe, of this universe and also the fear and terror of uncertainty and endpoint. Even with our modern scientific and mathematical underpinnings and our confidence and reliance on "immutable" physical laws there is a touch of mysticism. In astronomy, for instance, most of our information is indirect, second-hand; we observe radiation arriving on earth filtered through unknown media (not only dark matter) that can and does distort, disrupt, and change the message received. Our data, then, is incomplete—we still struggle with what dark matter and dark energy, the invisible might be.

On the other hand, even if speculative our observations still give a consistent view of how the universe operates, to the best of our ability to measure. We know from experience that those observations will change as we refine our abilities. In this light, there is a need for humility (whether scientific or theological) in the face of changing views and understandings of the cosmos.

"Why is there something instead of nothing?" Perhaps one day we may come to a scientific understanding. For now, posing that question is indicative of the astonishment felt in our sheer existence, the awe of the mystery of being.

The purpose in these chapters is not, though, to argue as to "why" there is something instead of nothing. There is something and to the acceptance of that something, to the search for meaning (if any) inherent in that something, is the task at hand. To ask the "why" question is, at least in one sense, fruitless as neither religion nor science can readily give a satisfactory answer.

For science even finding that origin point of the universe—the big bang—is still "something." Unless there is a way to step beyond that point, the nature of objective inquiry will always necessitate an "object." How, otherwise, do you measure "no thing"? Perhaps one day there will be an answer but it is not today.

From a religious viewpoint the argument that God willed or created the "something" moves God into the category of "no thing" and a negative existence, unless the category "God" is argued as a special case. One either accepts that proposition or not. Ultimately that argument does not create a cohesive answer about the divine/spiritual and the world. Perhaps our consideration is better focused on what might be considered the spiritual dimension of the "something," our universe—the "Ground of Being" if you will—and how to describe our relation to it.

As this exploration proceeds a relationship with a scientific understanding of the world is not to be rejected. The search for meaning ought not contradict scientific inquiry just as both theological/philosophical and scientific inquiry should stand ready to adjust or change in relation new discoveries of the world in which we live. Indeed, perhaps, the two might enhance each other.

Chapter 5

It is as essential to surmount a consciousness of an unreal freedom and to recognise a dependence not perceived by our senses.

—Leo Tolstoy[1]

The overarching lesson that has emerged from scientific inquiry over the last century is that human experience is often a misleading guide to the true nature of reality. Lying just beneath the surface of the everyday is a world we'd hardly recognize. . . . By deepening our understanding of the true nature of physical reality, we profoundly reconfigure our sense of ourselves and our experience of the universe.

—Brian Greene[2]

Whatever else he had in mind in this line from the epilogue to *War and Peace*, Tolstoy points to a greater truth: that what we "sense," what we perceive as happening or is real, may not in fact be what is actually going on. This applies in equal measure to our understanding both of science and of philosophy or theology.

For theologian Langdon Gilkey, and from the perspective of religious or theological discourse, this ferment underlies the very question of the reality of "God," both without and within religious communities.

> Any current theology . . . that does not recognize and seek reflectively to deal with this presence of secularity, of doubt, of skepticism, and so of a sense of the meaninglessness of religious language inside the Church as well as outside, and so inside the

1. Tolstoy, *War and Peace*, 1386.
2. Greene, *Fabric*, 5.

theologian and believer, is so far irrelevant. . . . Not only is the situation radical because the community of Christians itself is experiencing this upheaval; even more is it radical because it is the most fundamental of all our Judeo-Christian religious affirmations that is under searching and critical scrutiny by all, and forthrightly rejected by many. For it is the reality of what our tradition has called "God" that is now the subject of theological debate, and the question of God is, of course, the most fundamental of all theological questions.[3]

Tolstoy posits the need for a necessary change in our perception; Gilkey asks how, or if this is indeed possible, that "God" language can be meaningful in our modern context. So, what of that context?

Our entire existence plays out over a period of time, in a particular space or spaces. We are born; we live; and then we die over a temporal interval as a physical entity taking up and moving through space. But the fact of the matter is: we do not really know what either space or time is. Thus, how are we to understand the "reality" of this entity, our self, in its ever changing spatial and temporal location?

That may sound a bit weird but a moment's reflection can bring us up short. Are time and space actual, physical things? Or, merely useful conceptions, a way of making sense of our individual perceptions of the world around us? If they are actual things, what are their properties? Are they intrinsic to the cosmos? Are they fundamental? Or, are they made of other constituent parts?

We might be tempted to say, "Well, space and time, that's just reality!" But, then, what is "reality"? What do we mean by that word or concept? Philosophers have noted for hundreds of years that as we ponder space and time, the events around us, we truly only have access to our own perceptions and thoughts concerning them.

The sense of "now" is highly specific to where a person is and what they are doing. Even as we live "in the moment," "now," everything we experience comes from the past. Every image we see, which is light coming off whatever is illuminated before us is several nanoseconds (those objects near to us) to billions of years (objects in the distant universe) in the past. Every sound we hear is a wave generated in the past only to reach our eardrums and thence the brain's processing center. Every sense we have ultimately travels a path through the world, through our neural system to present an experience which has already passed.

How can we be certain that those thoughts and perceptions are actually reflective of an external world? Moreover, how does the paradigm or

3. Gilkey, *Naming*, 10.

conceptual framework through which we view or experience the world affect, distort, shape what it is we think we experience? Is that a "real" or just a truncated and stultified experience? Are differing viewpoints or perceptions equally valid encounters with reality? Is reality changed by these differing viewpoints or just our personal experiences and interpretations?

We perceive ourselves, and the world around us, as solid objects which on a macro level we and they are. But in reality we are made up of molecules and atoms, particles with more "empty space" between and among than actual physicality. These themselves exist as vibrations in pervasive fields that comprise our universe. So, what is the reality of our existence?

We perceive the sun and moon as rising and falling through the sky, going around us, when in reality the sun, moon, earth are all parts of a larger orbital system which itself is part of a larger collection of systems in a rapidly expanding cosmos. Our earth and the system within which it exists is speeding through time and space, not statically standing in one place. What is the reality of our existence?

Our bodies are made up of countless cells (themselves made up of innumerable particles) which live, generate new cells, die and slough off. We are, in fact, an ever-changing, new set of cells constantly throughout our lifetimes. Who, then, are we? If we are a new suit of cells at age forty, different from age ten, are we the same person? Or many persons throughout a lifetime? What is the thread, if one there is, that ties a personality together if all physical cells are continually dying and renewing? What creates the persistence of personality, if any, over time? How is consciousness carried forward? Who are we really?

Our perceptions color or define "reality"; what we think defines what we see. Are differing viewpoints equally valid encounters with reality? Is reality changed by these differing viewpoints or just our personal experiences and interpretations? In science a Newtonian or quantum perspective defines the perception of reality. In much the same way, each religion or religious conceptuality defines how reality is perceived.

How do we find what is real? Or, perhaps, how do we interpret what we perceive as real?

All that said, observation is all we have. Our scientific knowledge is based upon shared observations using shared understandings, such as a mathematical framework, to arrive at theories which can be tested using those frameworks. Limited in some ways by the rigorous standards of the shared frameworks and shared understandings, neither unrestrained imagination nor unrelenting skepticism can be allowed. We know there is always "more to the story" and that the present framework of understanding can also fall to a better, simpler version which preserves the observed data.

In order to perceive the world around us we require and construct a mental model into which we are able to "fit" its various elements; a model that agrees with and can be agreed upon with others. This mental model becomes the paradigm, the lens, through which we interpret the world and becomes our basis for rationalizing the phenomena we experience. Once such a model is in place any attempt to dislodge or overturn it is felt as an existential threat. Which goes a long way toward understanding the long struggle of science, tradition, and religion in our past.

But which model is to be chosen? How are challenges to that model to be understood? What criteria are accepted as affirming or, alternately, able to modify the model?

These questions pose an acute challenge for us, even more perhaps than our ancestors. Within a single lifetime we have spanned the globe with communications, left the soil of our planet and trod on another world, peered far into space and time, split the atom, cloned new life. We have learned more about our "cosmos," about human life, about the nature of quantum reality than previous generations could possibly have dreamed. Those discoveries have challenged old mental models and created new ones, not only scientifically but philosophically. The old models, especially the philosophical and theological, have often rebelled or outright rejected this new information, or ignored the import of such information for the intellectual and emotional underpinnings of those "traditional" philosophical and especially theological concepts.

Langdon Gilkey, in the above referenced *Naming the Whirlwind*, points to an article by Thomas O'Dea,[4] which though written in 1967 has a contemporary ring as a chronicle of the crisis of religious consciousness. O'Dea traces the human evolution from mythic understanding of the world by our prehistoric ancestors through the demythologizing substitution of a transcendent deity to create meaning against meaninglessness, to give humanity a place within the world. And yet, as O'Dea points out, neither Hebraic religious nor Hellenistic rational formulations could withstand the evident indifference to meaning that the world, nature, seems to have. In Ecclesiastes and again in the book of Job are found the struggle to find a balance or even a bulwark against such nihilism.

With the broadening of human control of the world around us, and with the ever-advancing conceptual understanding and ordering of the processes which make up our world, social existence has enlarged the area of experience and thus crowded out the sacred's purview.

---

4. O'Dea, "Crisis," 116–34.

Faith and doubt, both concurrent and yet incompatible, play the central role in our present crisis as they have throughout human history. From the prophets through the early Christian church and its testament and writings, doubt became ever present but ever subsumed under the rubric of faith that yet "God is God." Melding the rationalist understanding of Greek thought to the transcendent vision of a God present through mighty works evident to the "eyes of faith" Christianity was able to stave off, for a time, the crisis of doubt.

But those elements of crisis were never far away.

> First to be doubted was . . . the proposition that God had performed works that truth might be made manifest to man. [The] proposition that nature was rational and that rational man was, therefore, at home in the world stood up longer. Religious doubt in early modern times did not, by and large, transgress the cosmological and human limits of earlier Christian views. Progress replaced Providence; perfectibility through grace gave way to perfectibility through effort. The city of man belonged in the world of nature. History was no longer a religious drama but a natural process.[5]

The overtly religious thinkers (and this can be thinly slicing a definition especially with regard to seventeenth- and eighteenth-century figures) were not alone in the angst that increasingly rationalized, scientific inquiry was creating. For those thinkers and philosophers who championed science, whether in revolt against other-world religion or not, the threat of meaninglessness, of nothingness was still potent. From Descartes to Kierkegaard each attempted to create their own "peace" with the conflicting views of a secularized and rational world, on the one hand, and a world created and sustained by that other-worldly God.

Emblematic, perhaps, of this struggle was Pascal, who

> had faced, as a Christian, the implications of man's aloneness in the new world that science and philosophy were making known. He saw a silent universe that did not answer man's cry or longing, but remained alien and indifferent to his aspirations. Before the incomprehensible immensity of that world Pascal was frightened. He came to see man's aspirations rooted in reasons beyond reason and made his wager on a hidden God who was still the God of Christianity. Yet he retained the classic pride in

---

5. O'Dea, "Crisis," 127.

man's capacities as a thinking reed superior thereby to a universe that might at any moment crush him.[6]

The scientific pursuit has removed the mystical from any status in investigation, focusing on what can be observed, tested, and categorized. This is not to denigrate science but only to point to a methodological and epistemological orientation of rational investigation. But this orientation has thereby removed the world in which we live from the interactivity of the divine, whatever spiritual form that may have taken in human history.

Indeed, the history of humankind and its accomplishments, removed from this connectivity of divine interaction, is a story of relativity, of chance formations based upon various and competing interests, power, and ideologies. All of which can and will be swept away in the course of that history. Even individual identity has become problematic as formed through contingent circumstances and set against a void without ontological meaning save that given by such a creature.

Against such a backdrop how can modern humanity assert a resonance with the spiritual, with the divine? Indeed should such an assertion be made; is there a basis for the reality of such a resonance?

Nietzsche saw only a nihilistic landscape where "God is dead. . . . And we have killed him." That symbol, that resonance lacked any substance meaningful to humanity. Kierkegaard felt this alienation, too, and found himself much like Pascal before him making a "leap of faith," trusting as Pascal to a reason beyond reason in a God whose face was hidden from us.

Today where previously the criticism in the late nineteenth and early twentieth centuries concerned the more fundamentalist notions of traditional Christian doctrine and dogma, the modern upheaval also includes liberal or sophisticated religion, really all forms of spirituality, as problematic. The early to mid-twentieth-century theologians such as Barth, Brunner, Tillich, Bultmann, both Niebuhrs, wrestled with the construction of a theology relevant to the modern ethos. But they operated with the assumptions, no longer present to much of our world, of the efficacy of divine revelation to faith and direct experience and of the universal meaningfulness of reflective theological language to give a more full explanation of human inquiry and effort.

Those assumptions no longer hold true for large sections of the world's population, especially in the West. In overthrowing a supernatural religion, banishing a tyrannical "God," the Enlightenment thinkers sought to free humanity and make way for a humane and rationally based "city of man." But that same revolution that produced the great scientific advances also left

6. O'Dea, "Crisis," 127.

a void of meaninglessness or at least an inability to give voice to the needs and aspirations of modern humanity for value and worldview which can form the basis for humanizing the condition of all the peoples of the world.

Contemporary and relevant religious language, let alone a resultant authentic faith expression, is impossible to communicate without a sufficient common language or conceptual basis. Religion and religious language, the language of the "Spirit," is the basis for aspiration. For what is "spirit," or even "transcendence," but aspirational? Pointing to that which lies beyond, a goal (whether achievable or an unattainable but guiding "light"). The inability of modern culture to articulate or even accept such a language, to point authentically to "spirit" or "transcendence" in a meaningful way, creates a stultified measure of what it means to be human, of what community ultimately means, of any coherent and viable vision for a humane world. Those people who adhere to religion today tend to do so uncritically accepting past practice. But the established tradition falters without a common basis of understanding to which faith can point. This is precisely the occasion today and perhaps explains at least in part the falling participation in organized religion and yet the avowal of personal religiosity of the West.

The questions are posed in our contemporary, historical situation and can be ignored no longer by the theological enterprise, whether liberal or conservative: "What do we mean by 'God'?" Is the concept at all intelligible today? Is it solely dependent upon ancient methods of thought, of mythology? Or, can the concept find a resonance within our present-day context?

If such an enterprise is possible then the implications from human experience—communal, interactive, scientific—need to be included within any formulation as much as "feedback" from a "spiritual" perspective. Finding the words, the conceptualities, to communicate the human exploration and experience of our cosmos is, then, the task.

To *language*, the tool with which we communicate, whether to indicate some immediate need or desire ("I'm thirsty," "Look out! A bear!"), or to share symbolic concepts, values, feelings, or other information we must turn to create a sufficient common conceptual basis. Language by nature is a communal enterprise; we use language for mutual exchange in an outward manner of what takes place inwardly as we experience the world. In this exchange and in the formulation of the symbols of this conceptual exchange (language) there is a sort of feedback loop. Language "feeds back" the symbols and concepts, words, used in communication so that our interior "conversation" is influenced by the exterior symbols, concepts, and patterns used.

To clarify, the term "language" does not refer necessarily to a particular linguistic construction: English, French, Arabic, Mandarin, Tagalog,

Algonquin, or any of the multitude of human linguistic forms. "Language" here refers to the conceptual framework to which particular linguistic constructions point, their meaning posited within those constructs, and the web of conceptual relations that follow, for the world is shaped by images.

To be clear, I seek to avoid a viewpoint that posits language shaping thought; if you can't express it linguistically you can't think or imagine it.[7] That the mind takes precedence over language or linguistic forms is fairly obvious in that you can think of a concept that you don't have a word for. At the same time language might influence the direction of one's conceptualities. Many languages only have linguistics for numbers less than seven, anything higher being a nondescriptive "many." Thus, precision can be lacking, and complexity, though perhaps imagined, is difficult to express.

Languages, linguistic technologies, can make the expression of certain thoughts and the communication of those thoughts more efficient, easier, or clearer. Though language does not prevent thought, language can hinder precision and clarity. Also important to realize, as will be discussed in more detail later, even the mind may have difficulty conceiving of certain things, such as the actual nature of our existence. This is especially true of quantum mechanics where imagination, let alone language, pales in the ability to adequately describe its nature apart from the abstractions of mathematics.

Language is an important tool, closely guarded by not only our interior "monitor" but by the community at large that uses the language. Language creates a standard of communal understanding, an agreed upon stable base with which to describe our world and the events that take place around us. Thus misunderstandings in language, or miscommunication of meaning, create disequilibrium and confusion. The inability to speak clearly, in plain language understandable by anyone, is as problematic for religious language as it is for scientific explanation.

This is also why new words, new ideas and concepts, find difficulty working themselves into our linguistic structures and are often violently opposed as upsetting the status quo. Sometimes, in the case of minor additions that engender no real threat to communal understandings, that opposition is short lived and the new addition is incorporated. But many times the consequences are severe when the words or concepts go to the foundations of the communal understanding.

---

7. Called "Whorfianism," more broadly, the "Sapir-Whorf Hypothesis," which has a strong and a weak form. Though still a debated topic in linguistics, "Whorfianism," especially in its strong form, is debunked. For an interesting discussion, see Greene, *You Are What You Speak*.

Language forms the basis since prehistoric times for the communication of ideas and the thought process. Over time we have built a repertoire of words and concepts based upon those words that are a toolbox for more or less unambiguous communication. These concepts have been crafted over time, for most of us without much critical analysis, until we think we know more or less what the words and thus concepts mean.

But words, and thus language, are often not as clear as we might think. Take for example the word "piece." We can have a "piece" of wood or a "piece" of pie but not a "piece" of water. "Piece" has a limited, ambiguous meaning. More problematic for words and concepts are the words "red" and "green." When used by someone who is colorblind, what is the actual applicability? Their range of meaning must be different than that of people who are not colorblind.[8]

Words have an intrinsic uncertainty. Recognition of this led to the creation of dictionaries which "define," give "definition," that is "set boundaries" for where and how a word is used and its meaning in such cases. But the definitions themselves depend upon other words and concepts to create the very boundaries necessitated by such ambiguity. Some words and concepts are thus necessarily used "as is" without such analysis to avoid total indeterminacy.

Both in scientific exploration and explanation and in religious, spiritual, or theological expression clarity not only in what is being referred to but also in the greater context and meaning of those words are crucial. For they create an image as much as they attempt to express, in concrete terms, an image to which and in which the "mind's eye" sees the world.

Religious or spiritual language and images are not alone in the problematical nature of the clarity of words and images. Scientific conceptualities, too, have been subject to necessary reconstitutions as paradigmatic shifts in understanding experiential data have rendered old ideas empty or unable to adequately describe the cosmos within which we find ourselves.

This will have an important implication for the explorations that follow. But it is the problematic nature of theological, spiritual words and images that is the focus of this work, the reformulation of which plays out against those ever-correcting scientific understandings.

In addressing the reformation of spiritual conceptualities, the fact of the matter is that we live in a pluralistic world, with a variety of religious orientations, traditions of spiritual conceptualities and imagery. Christianity, Judaism, and Islam face these issues with these reactions in greater or

8. For an extended discussion of language and its relation to reality and modern physics, see Heisenberg, *Physics and Philosophy*, 167–86.

lesser degrees. Interestingly, Buddhism finds itself troubled with these is-sues to a lesser, or perhaps a different extent. As will be explored later, an infusion of Eastern/Buddhist[9] conceptuality might provide some direction in rethinking the relation of religion and spirituality with the modern scientific worldview.[10]

9. Within these two words lies a richly diverse and complex world of religion and philosophy of which scant, if any, Westerners are aware. Although this work does not seek to bring forth a rigorous or thorough examination of this range of thought, various concepts and insights will be useful, later, in the new construction and understanding being sought.

10. Theologian Charles Hartshorne, as well as diverse scientists such as Werner Heisenberg, Edwin Schrödinger, and Matthieu Ricard and Trinh Xuan Thuan make much the same case as will be referenced in this work.

Chapter 6

Science tries to give its concepts an objective meaning. But religious language must avoid this very cleavage of the world into its objective and its subjective sides; for who would dare claim the objective side to be more real than the subjective? Thus we ought not to intermingle the two languages; we should think more subtly than we have hitherto been accustomed to do.

—WERNER HEISENBERG[1]

The conundrums inherent in the images of reality which our mind holds and their relationship to the language formulated to express them are not new to our age. The ancient Greeks recognized the problematic nature of language. The whole of Socrates's life was taken up with the content and meaning of words and concepts. Aristotle, too, used logic to formulate methods of analyzing and validating the thoughts in argumentation to clarify meanings and conclusions.

Language influences thought and perception as it forms "word pictures" that may approximate, or try to, what is seen or conceptualized, not the other way around. In communicating our perception and thought we seek to share our experience, to concretize what cannot, perhaps, be made concrete. And so language forms, changes, and influences the direction of what and how we perceive and think about something, even when there is a part of us that knows that the description is incomplete somehow, incorrect or lacking. Language creates a point of view and until a new set of linguistic characters are created to challenge the old thought the paradigm of the previous viewpoint will hold sway.

In other words, the problem is not that language limits our conceptuality from the beginning but that often language is inadequate to the task of

1. Heisenberg, *Across the Frontiers*, 226.

"concretizing" the mind's apprehension, oftentimes to the point of distorting meaning in ways that skew further communication of that concept away from a fuller meaning. Such is the case with the anthropomorphism that colors most religious language, especially in the Judeo-Christian-Islamic traditions.

The quest for new terms, those new words and concepts—new wineskins for new wine—creates a crisis of consciousness as well as of language. For, as the paradigm for understanding shifts, whether in science or religion, traditional understandings, those maps and charts which have provided guidance over the ages, fall away and we are "in uncharted territory." A sense of disequilibrium is thus occasioned by a loss of what was solid under foot while we struggle to find a new grounding, a new pathway.

At the root of this human quest for understanding is the equally human desire to create order and stability, to seek out orderly patterns, even where none may exist.[2] Just as great an impulse is the pursuit of unity, of a unifying dynamic to our understanding whether in science or religion. The questing for oneness, an intuitive realization though often without the words or conceptual framework to express it, is not vain or spurious. From a scientific perspective, all science is a reduction of multiplicities to an identity, a "oneness" that captures the essence of a variety of similar recurring phenomena. There is a similar impetus in the search for spiritual unity, of a "one-ness" in the conceptual metaphysical underpinnings of reality.

There are two ways of looking at the world, two limiting conceptions, in the history of human thought, equally valid but in their respective extremities mutually exclusive in their particular exploration and explanation. Even though no genuine reality corresponds to them, they have helped to shape understandings of our world. On the one hand is the idea of an objective world which operates independent of any kind of observing subject. Modern science is guided by this image. On the other hand is the idea of a subject, mystically experiencing the unity of the world and no longer confronted by an object or by any objective world. This image guides the mysticism of the metaphysics, whether Christian, Judaic, Islamic, but especially in the Asian mysticism traditions, Hinduism and Buddhism. Maintaining the middle, between these two limiting conceptions, creates a tension that prevents one or the other pole from predominating and curtailing useful exploration and explication.

The disregard of the tension between these two poles has led both to bad science and religion and to the rejection of the efficacy of one pole by

2. For an extended discussion of this pattern seeking behavior, see Schermer, *How We Believe.*

the other. Given their opposition attempting to create a unity, a blending of these languages, would do a disservice to both. We should not allow religious thinking to cast doubt on tested scientific results. Nor should "the ethical demands stemming from the heart of religious thinking . . . be weakened by all too rational arguments from the field of science."[3]

In this way we may start to understand what Heisenberg means in saying that there are two different kinds of language for two different kinds of truth. And yet, might not this dualistic understanding be easily stretched too far? Perhaps the perspective from which a viewpoint comes limits the conceptual perception and linguistic construction.

We need also to acknowledge that the Reality to which either language points is neither uncomplicatedly straightforward nor apprehended solely by unmediated sensory experience. The metaphysical, the divine, cannot be divorced from the phenomenological world but neither is it encompassed or exhausted by it.

In empirical science, such as astronomy or chemistry as examples, the unaided eye can only go so far without the aid of instruments to enhance vision so that much more is seen. Nothing in everyday experience gives reason to think that water is made up of hydrogen and oxygen, molecules imperceptible to human sight. But when treated to certain conditions and with perceptual aids we find it is thus.

So too with the metaphysical. Natural science is empirical but not confined to human experience in unmodified form. Why should the theological/spiritual enterprise be obliged to such a handicap? To apprehend the divine perhaps we need to step beyond the mere human to change and expand our knowledge, to what the Buddhists term "mindfulness" or to an appreciation of the full meaning of Rumi's poetic "The astrolabe of God's mysteries is Love."[4] This insight is captured, too, in the spiritual understandings passed along in various traditions that the divine Reality is not directly apprehended except by "the pure in heart," "the poor in spirit." Why should this be so (if such Reality there be)? We do not know, but there are thousands of years of human experience, stepping beyond the merely experiential, that say so. The question to be taken up in these narratives is: to What does such apprehension point (if anything at all)?

Even before a rudimentary type of "scientific" exploration could begin, in the attempt to make sense of this world humans constructed a variety of beliefs and customs to give meaning and value to life as juxtaposed against

3. Heisenberg, *Across the Frontiers*, 227.

4. Rumi, a thirteenth-century Islamic poet, scholar, and jurist, was also a Sufi mystic. His *Jalálu'd-dín Rúmí* (The Persian Mystics) was translated in the early twentieth century by Fredrick Hadland Davis.

the suffering and pain which seems woven into existence. If humans had come to a singular set of understandings and beliefs about the cosmos, our world, which updated itself as our own awareness and understanding of the universe changed, a volume regarding such evolution would be only of academic interest if any at all. But the cultural and religious differences that have arisen from the variety of human self-understandings have led not only to religious conflict but to a modern divide between secular and religious consciousness.

Thus it is that we have come to understand that language shapes thought. How we think about something and the words that we use for that description or conception give form to further thinking, talking, acting, writing, storytelling, and even how we evaluate the narratives we thereby construct. When there is a paradigmatic shift, as has been the case in the Enlightenment understanding of Newtonian physics and more recently in the wake of the insights of Einstein and then quantum physics, new forms are required to express radically different understandings. And yet, to paraphrase a biblical line, culturally we try to pour "new wine into old wineskins."[5] Is it any wonder the wineskins of our old conceptions are stretched to the limit and burst with the new wine of modern insight? This tension underlies, for the most part, the great divide and the ferocious antagonism between religion, especially the conservative and fundamentalist viewpoints, and modern science.

One central facet of the collision of the secular and the religious, and perhaps even at least one source of the tensions between religious faiths, that can be drawn from this is that twenty-first-century people still hold to basic conceptions of the world, knowingly or not, that are no longer serviceable, no longer tenable. Over time, without noticing, many concepts which had meaning in the context of an earlier time have come to mean something entirely different (or lack a specific meaning) or been rejected as meaningless.

We understand the world in an entirely different way than did our forbearers, even less than a century past. To speak of "spirit" or "demon" or "god" is, for many, to reference something archaic or nonsensical. More specifically, "spirit" in phrases such as "team spirit," "get in the spirit," "a kindred spirit" has no specific, and certainly no personal, reference point for meaning at all. Even though religious language may use many such terms, that to which they point no longer have a content within a modern or postmodern cultural world.

Consider another metaphor commonly used: "the ends of the earth." The phrase originated in a time when people literally believed that the earth

5. Matt 9:14–17; Mark 2:18–22; and Luke 5:33–39.

ended in a meeting of water and sky. One could go no further as there lay the terminator of heaven and earth. For the most part, this metaphor has evolved to mean the farthest reaches, the remotest places. Today no one believes "ends of the earth" literally.

Yet such language and specific archaic concepts continue to be referenced, to be used to call forth the mystery and wonder which lie at the heart of existence. Is it any wonder that religious and theological language has lost meaning for many? And those for whom such language is still operant, has not the content or meaning changed in various attempts to make them "work" in our time?

Not very many humans are articulate or conversant about such matters at any one time and so such ideas are left to artists, philosophers, inventors, scientists, and teachers of a particular era. Those concepts are woven into the culture through art, technology, writing as understandings of what it means to be human, what is the cosmos and our place within it. When the context for those understandings and meanings changes, unless the understandings and meanings themselves evolve in a relevant way they become empty vessels, holding no meaning or worse a meaning antithetical to their original intent.

The central argument in these chapters is that the change in our understanding of how the world operates entails a change not only in our consciousness but in the language we use to describe that world. In seeking a place from which an understanding of spirit, spirituality, and religious imagination can be formulated for our time we need to acknowledge the relevance of modern scientific understanding and undertake a radical reorientation of faith language so that the content of those statements may have a relevance to our world and the problems we all face.

For millennia humanity understood their position in the cosmos as a stationary point about which all else revolved. Only a few hundred years separate us from the beginning awareness that, perhaps, this planet earth and those other "wanderers of the sky"[6] orbit a central star, our sun. And even fewer years, the late nineteenth century and early twentieth, separate an understanding that our solar system is a minute part of a larger galaxy which in turn is only one among billions of other such collections of star systems.

Our conscious understanding of this truth has still not caught up with our emotional attachment to the archaic religious interpretations of our central place within the universe as a stationary point. Although they may

6. The word "planet" comes from Middle English by way of Old French planete, which in turn derives from late Latin planeta or planetes, and originally from Greek planētēs, "wanderer, planet," from planan, "wander."

verbally acknowledge that we circle a star within a system which itself is moving through space as part of a larger collection of stellar material that hurtles through a vast void, for most people the fact that they exist as a small part of an inconceivably enormous moving system plays no part in their understanding of themselves or the cosmos within which they exist.

However, viewpoints like the language that shapes them have consequences.

The evolving technology that brings everything from a global communications network to space flight and more would not be possible within a stationary planet point of view. The laws of physics that help mold all we understand today are only possible because a revolution in thinking, a change of viewpoint, shifted from a stationary earth model to seeing the universe as a moving system.

Even the very scientific systems that grew early out of that paradigm shift have themselves been found to be lacking. Einstein's theories of relativity showed the imprecision of the early physics models. And then quantum mechanics indicated a complexity to our undergirding reality that most scientists find difficult to understand. And yet, working within that very complexity has led to the technologies that produce computers, cellular phones, and other modern digital devices.

Viewpoints have consequences.

Humankind necessarily had to let go of a static, stationary earth and recognize our place within a moving system, a revolution in awareness, in order to discover the rules and relationships that govern our cosmos and thus enable technological advancement. One can argue the merits of various pieces of modern technology (and many have, but my purpose here is not to examine those positive and negative aspects), but the shift in viewpoint necessary to all that followed is clear.

Viewpoints and the language of those viewpoints have consequences.

As a result there is for the human experience an "ever-present and essential demand for a credible system of symbols giving structure, meaning, and direction all of experience: to nature, history, society, and the self."[7] Whether the source of those symbols be traditional religious systems, or scientific/technological culture, or a conversation which navigates both to a new understanding is the task confronting us today. To chart the latter course it is imperative that critical reflective interpretation of both science and profound religion inform the self-understanding and awareness of scientists as well as those engaged in metaphysical/theological discourse.

7. Gilkey, *Blue Twilight*, 39.

One without the other inevitably will lead to totalitarianism, religious or cultural.[8]

Following chapters examine the role that particular and historical conceptual themes play in our use of language to describe our world and our experiences and how those themes have become dissonant. As the language and concepts that form the basis for our modern understanding of "the world," ever evolving as it does, confronts those archaic word and thought patterns, the disconnect can be profound. The result can be a schizophrenic retreat into "old-time religion" psychically walled off from everyday modern existence, strikingly evident in the Fundamentalist movements of the early twentieth century. Or trying to find eddies and spaces into which religious and spiritual concepts can fit, the "God of the gaps" of the twentieth-century theological debates.

Other chapters will examine the scientific context to our modern understanding of self and world. These will not be scientific treatises on physics, astronomy, physical science, and the like, but rudimentary explorations of how the framework of such understandings might serve our ultimate task, situating ourselves, who and what we are, finding "our place" in the cosmos.

8. Here, the reader is directed to Gilkey's discussion, in *Blue Twilight*, of the dangers of "demonic religion" that absolutism in either religion or science/technology can produce.

Chapter 7

Although I am now convinced that scientific truth is unassailable in its own field, I have never found it possible to dismiss the content of religious thinking as simply part of an outmoded phase in the consciousness of mankind, a part we shall have to give up from now on. Thus in the course of my life I have repeatedly been compelled to ponder on the relationship of these two regions of thought, for I have never been able to doubt the reality of that to which they point.

—Werner Heisenberg[1]

Whether . . . we look outside ourselves at intellectual movements in our cultural environment or inside at current changes in our feelings, attitudes, and convictions, we find religious concepts and certainties in upheaval, criticized not only by those outside the religious establishment, but even more by those within.

—Langdon Gilkey[2]

Whether in the experimental pursuit of scientific knowledge or the struggle to construct grand theological structures, concentration on the minutia of the correctness or aptness of concepts in premises, deductions, conclusions, and so on we "miss the forest for the trees." Other structures and associations, in this case of language, are missed. Ambiguity, secondary meanings, arising from half-conscious connections within the flow of words—the poet's muse—are lost.

1. Heisenberg, *Across the Frontiers*, 213.
2. Gilkey, *Naming*, 3.

The beginning of modern science is often seen as a clash between the truth of religious revelation (that is, the Bible and the "church fathers," the dominant thought of the Western Middle Ages) and the reality of experienced sensory data which when carefully checked by another could be doubted. But this argument neglects differing understandings of "immediate" experience from antiquity, that of Aristarchus, Aristotle, Plato, and the Pythagoreans onward, as to whether explanations and theories and favored opinions were being drawn from the facts or the facts were distorted, consciously or not, to fit.

Consider planetary motion.

Immediate experience teaches that the earth is at rest and that the sun goes around it.[3] "Rest" here has the general meaning that the earth is at rest and that every other body which is also at rest no longer moves relative to the earth. In this sense Ptolemy was correct and Copernicus wrong, in the sun moving about the earth at rest. But we can also reflect that "motion" implies a statement about the relation between two bodies and that reversing the relationship, making the sun the center of the planetary system, thereby obtains a simpler, more unified picture of the solar system.

In this sense, Copernicus applied Occam's Razor to create a "simplicity of natural laws," which really has nothing to do with immediate experience per se (immediate experience as we saw in the last chapter not being the most adequate of guides). The same with Galileo and falling objects. Immediate experience would teach that lighter objects fall slower than heavy objects; but Galileo's mathematical formulae for objects in a vacuum state otherwise. At the time testing in a vacuum was impossible to observe. The place of immediate experience was taken by idealized experience, "which claims to be recognized as the correct idealization by virtue of the fact that it allows mathematical structures to become visible in the phenomenon."[4]

Conformity to mathematical law then became the basis for the persuasive power of science. At the time these mathematical formulae were seen to be, as Kepler expressed, a visible expression of divine will, a recognition of the beauty of God's works and thus not a turn away from religion. Even when new discoveries contradicted church teaching the significance appeared slight to the extent that the immediacy of God's workings in nature was still an acceptable conception.

3. In spite of very early, especially religious, texts indicating the sun crossing the dome of the sky and other similar constructs of the movement of "heavenly bodies," the Greeks knew early on that the earth was round, whether attributed to the Pythagorean school in the fifth century BC or later with Eratosthenes or Archimedes. The practical effect of this understanding has taken millennia to find the notice of religious thought.

4. Heisenberg, *Across*, 215.

"God" in this instance can be understood in terms of the distant, "ordering," Creator, not the "God" of relation, in biblical terms of "help in time of trouble," "salvation," "forgiveness." With this separation the fragmentation of the term "God" was begun and the interconnected unity of the whole is lost. At the same time this process also became the basis for the fruitfulness of natural science.

This basis also became absolute principle: observed details are the parameters of discussion; any larger connection of the whole was "off the table." The elevation of idealized rather than immediate experience of observed details also, then, began the pursuit of experimentation and measurement under an approximation of ideal conditions. Under such conditions agreement can always be reached about the results of experiment.

Basing such conclusions derived from measurement under idealized conditions lead to confidence in a causal succession of events, understood to be objective and independent of the observer, which became the basis of modern natural science. Only in the present era of quantum physics has the limitation of this procedure become apparent. Yet there is a seeming unassailability to this criterion of truth, that the repeatability of experimentation makes agreement about the behavior of nature possible.

This tendency, however, also places a higher emphasis on the quantitative: precise conditions, accuracy in measurement, precise and unambiguous terminology, and mathematical presentation of the idealized phenomena—namely "exact science." In that term lies reliability, exactitude, and unassailability but also the inability to do justice to "the infinite wealth of qualitatively distinct experiences."[5] The necessity of those conditions of precision and reliability are demonstrated in ventures from space flight to lunar landings to the recent landings of reusable rocket boosters.

But worthwhile as these achievements are, they are still confined to a concentration on specific portions of reality and leave aside value questions in an ambivalent silence. Where modern science in the form of medicine prevails material suffering has been alleviated; likewise modern scientific applications in transportation and communication have made life easier. At the same time the application of scientific knowledge has also impaired and threatens our environment, from ozone depleting chemicals to greenhouse gas emissions to pollution of air, water, and soil, not to mention toxic by-products that are injurious to life.

The past sixty years have seen a growing shift from an emphasis solely on material welfare to explore other dimensions of existence which have been neglected. This has often led to a rejection not only of modern science

5. Heisenberg, *Across*, 217.

and its applications but also traditional modes of spirituality or at least a longing for existential meaning without an intellectual or conceptual framework resulting often in an individualistic, Romanticist ideation.

If we are not to go wholly astray in either pole, we need to find a vision directed upon the whole reality of what it is to be a human being and not just on a segmented portion of Life. Human mental and spiritual facilities arise only within the context of human, social community. The ability to reach beyond what we can directly sense, to recognize the web of interrelations that constitute our reality—to "see" not only outwardly but toward our inmost self—are a part of what we learn from the experience of being in community. Within this spiritual pattern, this communal ethos, Heisenberg argues:

> Man acquires the points of view whereby he can also shape his own conduct wherever it involves more than a mere reaction to external situations; it is here that the question about values is first decided. Not only ethics, however, but the whole cultural life of the community is governed by this spiritual pattern, Only within its sphere does the close connection first become visible between the good, the beautiful and the true, and here only does it first become possible to speak of life having a meaning for the individual. This spiritual pattern we call the religion of the community. The word "religion" is thereby endowed with a rather more general meaning than is customary. It is intended to cover the spiritual content of many cultures and different periods, even in places where the very idea of "God" is absent.[6]

Whether one measures up to the guiding ideals of that spiritual pattern, for example Christianity (and there is no doubt that human failing abounds), those guiding ideals still point toward a hope of improvement at least. Where there are no guiding ideals to point the way, the scale of values also disappears and with it the meaning of our deeds and suffering, and in the end only despair and negation remain.

"Religion," in the meaning expressed above by Heisenberg, is therefore the foundation of ethics, and "ethics the presupposition of life." For every day we must meet decisions and must know or at least have an idea of the values whereby we govern our conduct.

Guiding values/ideals arise out of the human community, from the modes of thought that transcend a discrete experiential model for a model that incorporates all of experience, that embraces all of life. These guiding values that encompass all experience are distinguished from strictly

---

6. Heisenberg, *Across*, 218.

normative, experienceable patterns of human community. That is, normative ethical behavior can be formulated and derived from a world outlook, but religion proper speaks to guiding values or principles toward which we strive but which we can only approximate. These ideals do not spring from "inspection of the immediately visible world but from the region of structures lying behind it," Plato's world of Ideas, the Bible's "God is Spirit."[7]

That religious truth and scientific truth have come into conflict since the seventeenth century should not be a surprise given the differing foci of each. Starting, arbitrarily, with Galileo's first encounter with the Roman Inquisition in 1616 over the Copernican theory of the planetary system (and setting aside the human shortcomings displayed on both sides), each side in the conflict believed themselves in the right and that major values were in peril. From Galileo's perspective, observation had shown that Copernicus's theory provided a much simpler and thus correct understanding of the planetary phenomena. Galileo was not, however, seeking to dismiss a divine order only to understand it more fully.

The Christian church, on the other hand, sought to conserve the centuries-old worldview unless a compelling need was offered. Neither Galileo nor Copernicus could offer such and in fact the Copernican proposition that the sun is at the celestial center (and immovable) is, as we now know, also wrong. The definitions of "rest" and "motion" in that sense have no absolute meaning and actually refer to a relationship between two bodies.

The fundamental conflict between a spiritual pattern of a community and science seemed, to Heisenberg, to hinge on the spiritual pattern being a static thing by nature and science being a dynamic and changing affair. That the spiritual pattern is of necessity static is not necessarily certain though, as Heisenberg states, "Complete uncertainty about all standards would be intolerable in the long run."[8] But science taken as a standard for a world outlook would of necessity be focused upon science past that has been fixated in language and thus set the preconditions for later conflict (with a dynamic scientific exploration). Better to understand that the language of the spiritual pattern is the language of poetry, a language of living symbols.

What, though, is the difference between that and a scientific language describing the quantum that must also be to a great extent poetic and symbolic since direct, immediate experience is problematic?

Did the actual acceptance of Copernican theory make a practical difference in the daily life of the medieval individual? Though dwelling on earth, did being the center and immovable or moving around a sun which was

7. Heisenberg, *Across*, 219–20.

8. Heisenberg, *Across*, 224.

itself the center and immovable affect the conduct of daily life? Most likely not but it wasn't a matter of indifference. Even though accepting that the theory was possibly correct, there was perhaps the concern (consciously or unconsciously) that the new theory would also engender a more dangerous shift in perspective—obscuring the whole with a partial new truth, eclipsing in human consciousness the living coherence of human spiritual community with an instability of estrangement of individual from community.

> In the images and likenesses of religion, we are dealing with a sort of language that makes possible an understanding of the interconnection of the world which can be traced behind the phenomena and without which we could have no ethics or scale of values. This language is in principle replaceable, like any other; in other parts of the world there are and have been other languages that provide for the same understanding. But we are born into a particular linguistic area. This language is closer akin to that of poetry than to the precision-oriented language of natural science. Hence the words in the two languages often have different meanings. The heavens referred to in the Bible have little to do with the heavens into which we send up aircraft and rockets. In the astronomical universe, the earth is only a minute grain of dust in one of the countless galactic systems, but for us it is the center of the universe—it really is the center. Science tries to give its concepts an objective meaning. But religious language must avoid this very cleavage of the world into its objective and its subjective sides; for who would dare claim the objective side to be more real than the subjective? Thus we ought not to intermingle the two languages; we should think more subtly than we have hitherto been accustomed to do.[9]

Science, itself, has been compelled to more subtle consideration, especially with regard to quantum physics. Immediate experience is no longer the object of research, as this new world can only be penetrated by instruments of modern technology. The language of daily life is no longer adequate here, too. We can represent it in mathematical forms but if we wish to speak of the quantum world we must be content with images and likenesses, much like we do in religious language. In both cases, language itself is inadequate. And in both cases, we find increasingly the interconnectedness, and corresponding abstractness and difficulty of understanding.

As technological ability increases with new discoveries and applications, there are also new ethical problems that arise that are not easily solved (the researcher's responsibility for the practical application of a discovery, or

9. Heisenberg, *Across*, 226.

the prolongation of the life of a dying patient with new medical discoveries and abilities). The answers to such questions are not to be found in the pragmatic consideration of scientific inquiry but in the source of ethical principles in human attitudes, expressed in the language of religion.

The impulse toward unity, whether in science or religion, is focal as is the abstraction that results from pushing this impulse to its limits. In religion, the clash between Judaism and Christianity was and is the unity of God, the result of millennia of struggle with the idea of many gods who seemed more immediately accessible. At the same time, as with abstraction in science, this impulse can lead to a divorce from lived experience as Christ maintained that the abstraction of God could only be separated from the immanency of God active in the world at the peril of our human bond in community and commune with God.

As later chapters will indicate our exploration of a new understanding of the cosmos offers a world that inspires us to see it as a whole, rather than through a dualistic lens. The attempt to fashion a unified vision ultimately shows the world as multifaceted. Our world is open, pluralistic, and ever evolving, and the struggle to reduce the vast array of perspectives, historic, cultural, religious, individual, scientific to a singular approach would be intellectually dishonest and simplistic. This is not a negation of the scientific enterprise but a recognition that a reductionist position, that the "world" can be reduced to a "simple," "absolute," "fundamental," irreducible "thing" is, perhaps, not the only way of looking at our world.

Chapter 8

God's world and revelation . . . must not be understood mythologically or in a fundamentalistic sense, but historically. . . . God's revelation takes place in and through the history . . . through the *experiences* that believers have had of their God in very varied ways in the course of history. . . . They are and remain human words.

—HANS KÜNG[1]

The very symbol or idea of God has history, writes Karen Armstrong, since it has always meant something slightly different to each group of people who have used it at various points of time. The idea of God formed in one generation by one set of human beings could be meaningless in another. Indeed, the statement "I believe in God" has no objective meaning, as such, but like any other statement only means something in context, when proclaimed by a particular community. Consequently there is no one unchanging idea contained in the word "God"; instead, the word contains a whole spectrum of meanings, some of which are contradictory or even mutually exclusive. . . . When one conception of God has ceased to have meaning or relevance, it has been quietly discarded and replaced by a new theology.[2]

In the same vein, Hans Küng argues that such symbols, paradigms, patterns, terms and expressions as is our topic "stem from the world of experience and language of that time, and for the most part they are not directly accessible to us today. Consequently, all of them must be continually brought home to us in new ways, must be distinguished for the better

1. Küng, "Paradigm Change in Theology," in Musser, *Whirlwind*, 102.
2. Armstrong, *History*, xx.

understanding of the reality they are meant to convey, and sometimes must be replaced."[3]

Küng's point is that replacement is necessary so that the reality to which the experience and message point may be perceived *and* understood.

The intellectual and emotional turmoil arising from the collision of religious thought, of "God language," and the spirit of secularism has brought about a variety of responses as theologians, clerics, and laity have sought to come to terms with the modern world, seeking a consistency between the way we live and religious faith by trying to make faith intelligible and relevant to secular life. Before turning to those responses, let us look at "God."

As noted in chapter 2, "God" is a "catch-all" term which has come to designate the divine, deity, or Supreme Being. The problem with a word representing such a wide range of meanings is that, in the end, what has become a syncretic term "God" means too many things to mean anything. To ask, in the Judeo-Christian-Islamic tradition, "Do you believe in God?" begs the question: Which God?

An extended discussion of the history of "God" can be found in Karen Armstrong's *A History of God: The 4000-Year Quest of Judaism, Christianity and Islam* and, as noted in the quotation above, the term, in its referent, has been quite malleable. Charles Hartshorne and William Reese present another, more comprehensive volume which presents the wide range, Eastern as well as Western, of concepts of Deity, with selections from a diversity from Plato to Lao-Tse to Spinoza, from Buddhist and Hindu writings to Whitehead, Schopenhauer, and Nietzsche.[4]

For purposes here, Mark Johnston's *Saving God* provides a more concise discussion of the confusing variety of referents often included in the word, "God."

Confining the discussion to the Western monotheistic traditions of Judaism, Christianity, and Islam, again as noted in chapter 2 the word "God" is not used in the primary texts of those religions.[5] Judaism itself begins with an ambiguous relation with the divine, using plural terms such as *elohim*, not necessarily as a proper name for the divine but as a title or indication of status, though often in a polytheistic context. Even the term by which the voice from the burning bush self designates, "Yahweh," does not mean "God," rather the divine being here is "I am" or "I am who I am."[6]

3. Küng, "Paradigm Change in Theology," in Musser, *Whirlwind*, 103.

4. Hartshorne and Reese, *Philosophers Speak*.

5. And, of course, even in Eastern metaphysics, that term, "God," is nonexistent in the languages and texts. The words used, and which in Western translations resolve to "God" or such divine referents, have other and deeper meanings.

6. Exod 3:14–15.

In the later intertestamental, Christian, or Islamic texts the divine being appears with a number of other appellations depending upon the language used: *Adonai, haShem, Theos, Kyrios, Pater, Abba, Allah*, and so on. None of which mean, as we use the term, "God," but are referents. And those referents really are different. Even within themselves. How else does one explain Yahweh who, during the Israelites' return, orders the extermination of whole cities and people down to their livestock, with the Yahweh who is gracious and merciful, slow to anger, and abounding in steadfast love (Ps 145:8)?

One would be hard pressed to reconcile Yahweh with the Christian Trinity or even Islam's Allah. They really have differing "personalities" which pose a dilemma for the questions posed: Which God? Whose God?

Why is this important? If we are to find language pertinent to our day we need to understand how and where our assumptions and worldviews have created false representations. We need, too, to understand how archaic language and conceptions, carried over into our times, have created the very dissonance we seek to remedy.

The basic problem, addressed in later chapters, is disentangling personal symbolism from a larger supernaturalistic theism. This supernatural theism became increasingly problematic within the scientific worldview which grew from the seventeenth century through to today. Already in the early eighteenth century the attempt to reconcile these two threads was becoming strained to the breaking point leading to the formulations of liberal theology.

Liberalism and liberal theology are vague terms which describe the trends in the late nineteenth and early twentieth centuries which sought to make faith intelligible in categories relevant to the secular mind. Liberalism saw the necessity for formulating theological understandings of traditional doctrines and creeds in the light of scientific, philosophical, historical, and moral ideas of culture. Building upon the new historical consciousness, liberalism sought to establish more immediate grounds for Christian certainty, locating "God" and "God's activity" in the natural, creaturely forces of history.

Not necessarily a single or united movement, some elements of liberal theology pushed for a metaphysic while others—especially Ritschl—denied metaphysics.[7] Intrinsic to this theology, however, was an innately optimistic notion of an evolutionary development of the cosmos from chaotic to

---

7. Albrecht Ritschl, German Lutheran theologian, b. 1822, d. 1889. Ritschl explicitly sought a "theology without metaphysics" emphasizing the moral nature of religion over doctrine and the religious practice of Jesus as opposed to later teachings about Jesus (Trinity, incarnation, and so on).

higher forms. "God's" creative work in time directed this development toward "God's" own far off goal.[8] Liberalism thus reformulated Christian doctrine on the basis of the contemporary scientific, immanentist, and progressivist notions. The belief in an ultimate progressive order, the harmony of things and "higher purposes," still helped to make "God language" intelligible at the time.

In the twentieth century, however, the philosophical and religious problems of liberal theology tended to erode this position. The metaphysical side of liberalism met with the anti-metaphysical mood of secularity; the possibility of metaphysical speculation became tenuous and ultimately meaningless.[9] Perhaps even more important was the religious problem engendered by the rationalistic and optimistic assumptions implicit in the evolutionary, progressive understanding. Though already questioned in the nineteenth century, the liberal theological faith in the goodness and perfectibility of humanity and the progress of history disintegrated in the face of human and historical evil, especially in the atrocities of world conflict in the early twentieth century.

In the midst of this increased sense of evil and the failing attempt to locate grounds for transcendent certainty in immediate experience, neoorthodoxy arose. Its response, though, differed from the conclusions secular despair drew from the collapse of liberalism's optimism. The response was found in "faith," a return to Reformation's justification through faith in the redemption accomplished by Jesus Christ.[10]

Neoorthodoxy located the grounds for belief in "God," in the goodness of life, and the meaningfulness of history, outside the "word of man" and secular experience. Healing truth about humanity and its destiny could only come from the "Word of God." In an attempt to be biblical and orthodox, and autonomous in regard to the world's truth, neoorthodoxy based its truth on revelation and tradition. Taking the secular world secularly (for example, interpreting biblical narratives such as creation, the "fall," and end times as "myth" rather than literal historical points) and the biblical and

8. Though liberal theology was a movement with a variety of expressions, even two such diverse theologians as Friedrich Schleiermacher and Ritschl, who influenced liberal theology, structure their thought along the lines of a historicizing and "progressivizing" of Christianity. (See the discussion in Gilkey, *Reaping*, 210–14.)

9. This assessment is admittedly a generalization. While many works document the fortunes of liberal theology, the assertion here is that the liberal rapprochement, though still offering important considerations for contemporary theology, finally suffered at critical points and was not successful in expressing the religious dimension of modern life.

10. An especially insightful discussion of neoorthodoxy can be found in Williams, *God's Grace and Man's Hope*, 27–32.

orthodox world religiously, neoorthodoxy agreed with the secular mind that "God" was not revealed in ordinary secular life. Humanity, lost and estranged from the all-sovereign and all-sufficient God, absolutely depended for truth and grace upon special revelation in the divine activity among the Hebrew people centered on Jesus Christ. Thus Scripture and tradition were normative sources for Christian theology and life. Though the relative thought patterns containing the "Word of God" communicated to faith needed contemporary translation, secular knowledge at best was supplementary to the core "Word" communicated to faith. Neoorthodoxy thus began and ended with faith.

Neoorthodoxy, though strong as a movement in the mid-twentieth century, ran into difficulty at this point because outside the circle of faith such knowledge and discourse were meaningless. The language of neoorthodoxy became equivocal by accepting a dualism—a naturalistically interpreted world and a biblically understood "God" who gives meaning and coherence to that world by "God's" activity. By accepting a scientific, naturalistic interpretation of the world in which events were explained not by miraculous divine interventions but by the causal nexus, how could one understand language denoting "God's activity" by action verbs to be anything but equivocal?[11] What does it mean for "God" to "act" at all if no historical conceptual content is given? And if "God's" action in ordinary events—floods, accidents, wars—is denied as counter to "God's" goodness and transcendence of finite events, what does it mean that "God" is sovereign ruler of history?

The naturalistic assumptions of neoorthodoxy undermined its theological assertions of "God's" activity in history. Agreeing with the secular mood that God was not revealed in ordinary secular life but only in faith, neoorthodoxy could point to no accepted secular, worldly evidence of God's action. If these mighty acts were seen by faith, what was it that was seen? By removing "God" from historical, cultural, and ordinary experience into sheer transcendence, into supernaturalism, and thereby agreeing with the secular spirit that its own existence was devoid of "God," neoorthodoxy provided the framework for the later declaration of "God's" death.

Further, identification of the "Word of God," the exclusive principle of "God's" self-manifestation to humanity, became problematic as a consequence of neoorthodoxy's acceptance of historical and scientific study of its Scripture and documents. They were sifted as any other fallible and relative words; indeed, scholarship led away from any absolute claims, shattering the

---

11. See Gilkey, "Cosmology, Ontology," 194–205.

unified, authoritative biblical view.[12] In result, the "Word" was subjectively localized in human experience, in the encounter of faith with "God" in the scriptural Word's challenge to our existential self-understanding and authenticity. Not in objective "Acts of God" did neoorthodoxy ground its language, but in personal "religious" experience which to modern secular existence was becoming problematic because it was separated from ordinary experience.

The dilemma posed by the secular spirit undermined the neoorthodox enterprise. The separation of church and world, belief and unbelief, the world of "God" and world of the secular could not stand for the secular penetrated even the church. Secular doubt gnawed at this belief. Was this language pointing to anything real at all? The split between actual existence and theological thought was, in the end, too radical, too unreal. With the elusiveness of the divine predominant in contemporary reality, such language became obscure, strange and empty.

At root, as Daniel Day Williams notes, both liberal and neoorthodox theologies, though both recognizing elements of truth, fail theologically because they have no place for, no way to account for, God's *redemptive* activity in human history.[13] Liberalism saw no need in the progress toward the creation of a new humanity, a new world, in which sin would be eliminated. Neoorthodoxy saw no need as redemption was for another realm, denying any transformational effect of God's activity in the world.

The privatized, interiorized, and individualistic emphasis of neoorthodoxy provided the basis for the radical critique of its theology. The radical theologies were critical of this theological enterprise and sought to interpret Christianity in the terms of the secular spirit. These radical theologies,[14] though not monolithic in character, incorporated secularity into their assumptions—the denial of an absolute, transcendent "God" (or any "God" in some cases), the acceptance of secular norms and thought, the rejection of appeal to religious authority in favor of personal honesty and integrity, an emphasis on the historical Jesus, a rejection of supernatural entities, and an emphasis on creative action rather than correct belief.[15]

Harvey Cox's *The Secular City* is emblematic of this "death of God" movement. Cox had argued that God's demise meant that rather than centering on the transcendent religion needed to find its focus on humanity and an ethos based in concrete humanistic values.

12. Gilkey, *Naming*, 97.

13. Williams, *God's Grace*, 32.

14. Represented in Gilkey's analysis by Thomas Altizer, William Hamilton, Paul Van Buren, and Richard Rubenstein, see *Naming the Whirlwind*, ch. 4.

15. Gilkey, *Naming*, 185.

Cox's argument was not new. Nietzsche had previously declared the death of God, the uselessness of the symbol against the cultural landscape of Western thought in the nineteenth century. Nor was Nietzsche alone in this evaluation. As noted earlier, the challenge to the traditional theism of the West goes back further than Thomas Aquinas. But in the nineteenth century, this movement against the traditional understanding of "God" picked up momentum from Hegel to Schopenhauer to Kierkegaard to Feuerbach and on. Even writers such as Tennyson, Dostoyevsky, and Matthew Arnold felt this loss.

Nor was Islam immune to this shift, though for different, economic, political, and cultural reasons.[16] The reaction there, though not within the purview of this work, took a variety of different although not dissimilar directions, including a fundamentalist reaction.

Throughout the 1960s and 1970s authors such as Thomas Altizer (*The Gospel of Christian Atheism*, 1966), Paul Van Buren (*The Secular Meaning of the Gospel*, 1963), and William Hamilton (*Radical Theology and the Death of God*, 1966) rejected the theistic models, even those of Bultmann and Tillich, in favor of an embrace of the secular world as the place where humans would ultimately find solutions to their problems. If "God" was to be meaningful again, only a journey through the silence of the secular would provide a basis.

Although prophetic in critiquing modern acceptance of past conceptualities, raising important issues for contemporary theology, and even creating an atmosphere conducive to the investigation of other, Eastern sensibilities, this "death of God" movement is limited in its usefulness to this discussion. Suffice it to say that the radical theologies are not helpful resources for addressing the current situation because of the considerable inconsistencies and problems in their formulation.[17]

Other, primarily Western, theological movements sought to address the challenge of a secular world in the late sixties. Theologians such as Jürgen Moltmann, Wolfhart Pannenberg, and Carl Braaten, to name just a few with disparate orientations, sought to deal with the discontent of the postwar culture, the rising political and social awareness and rejection of what was deemed the oppressive, racist, and imperialistic character of liberal culture and from the deepening sense of the eschatological and apocalyptic challenge to those structures.

16. For an extended discussion of both Western and Islamic development of this secular trend, see Armstrong, *History*, ch. 10.

17. For a longer discussion of death of God and radical theology see Gilkey, *Naming*, ch. 5.

The purpose here is not to explicate the theologies of each of these thinkers (and this listing is only a small representation of the alternative theological undertakings of the late twentieth century and the short treatment given is in no way to disrespect or dismiss their contributions) but to give some sense of the range and "flavor" of the wide-ranging theological reactions to modernity, and the postmodern age.

The range of theological outlook varied across this field with some focusing on a neoorthodox wholly other God of the future (Carl Braaten) while others rejected the wholly other God though unlike neoorthodoxy holding God's coming kingdom as a historical reality, juxtaposing the christological and eschatological limits to modern thought and seeking an authentically liberated humanity in opposition to oppressive Gods and inauthentic traditions.

Others such as Pannenberg seeking a rational orthodoxy with historical-dogmatic approach, found the locus of his theological historical investigation and his historical theological inquiry set ultimately upon a theological horizon, of the "end of history" in Jesus Christ. Moltmann, much like Pannenberg, constructs an eschatological horizon that combines an understanding of Christology and eschatology in Christ's second coming.

Just as the neoorthodox theologies were a reaction both to the growing influence of secular society and the liberal theological tradition, the eschatological theologies of the late twentieth century were a rejection of both liberal and neoorthodox theologies in favor of both a recognition of the modern emphasis on historicity and an anticipatory theological denouement in a teleological *eschaton*, or final event in a "divine plan" for the world.

Although not seeking to categorize these thinkers individually, overall eschatological theology finds ontological priority in the future, reversing the "common sense" conceptualization of historical causality. This eschatological orientation looks to the future as the decisive mode of time with the future determining the present in anticipation, rather than the past determining the future through extrapolation. The future, then, holds the essence of our existence, and contains the meaning of events in history, the source of the power to change things.[18]

God's *eschaton*, then is the creative power, the inner dynamic of the world in process, and only that future power can contradict the negativities of our present and free us to overcome them. Creation thus occurs from its end and comes from God as the power of the future, the power of hope.

These eschatological theologies also present problems both with intelligibility and meaningfulness for our postmodern world and

18. Braaten, *Future*, 24–25, and Braaten, *Eschatology*, 35.

self-understanding. Stress on the power of the future determining the present and themes of negation and contradiction create a devalued present in favor of a realm of future being. If God's contradictory eschatological kingdom is realized outside of history, then human social and political activity in the world have little or no enduring worth. If, as is also argued by some eschatological theologies, that *eschaton* is to be realized within history, as an authentic historical reality, then how can every present be in need of contradiction.[19]

Further, the future as the cause of the present yields other problems. The future, today, is not necessarily viewed a rosy place, rather it threatens, especially in ecological terms. If God's future is "something really new" does not that "new thing" arise in contradiction to the present and deny the very concern for responsibility, action, and freedom intended by these theologies? Can hope and future be experienced in the same way? Hope and future seem to be distinctly different things.

Lastly, by divesting the present of the divine, God thereby has no meaningful relationship, presence, in present experience. Contingent human freedom, too, is at stake. How is free human creativity to be understood within an eschatological realization of God's action? If history does not stop in the *eschaton*, in the fulfillment of God's kingdom, then free human decision must have affect, else such freedom is denied.

The theist models thus far presented all present a problematic character to the enterprise of finding language of ultimacy appropriate to our times. Especially problematical in our age where pluralism and a parity of religious belief has a much stronger position in cultural consciousness, though the liberal and neoorthodox positions admit to God's revelation elsewhere in creation—a radical relativity of culture as Langdon Gilkey notes[20]—Christianity still retained an absoluteness, a superiority of revelation in Christ. Therefore, any discussion of parity, of a pluralistic understanding of "the divine" has been truncated unless demanded by a cultural shift.

The problems that the secular spirit raises for Christian or for that matter all mono- and polytheistic theology cannot be dismissed. The problems presented by this mood set the context within which any theology must take shape in order to be relevant and intelligible. This context does not allow any easy assumption of an ultimate rationality to experience nor of the intelligibility of a faith encounter as a basis for talk about the transcendent.

---

19. These contradictions and the force of the arguments seem ambiguous at best. See Braaten, *Eschatology*, and esp. Braaten, *Christ and Counter-Christ*, 10–16.

20. Gilkey, *Blue Twilight*, 109.

These are in fact, when acknowledged at all, denied as "imaginary," or in the church uncomfortably held in a schizophrenic tension with everyday life.

The following two chapters examine first the backlash against both secularity and the modern world and the attempts to find new definitions and conceptualities, and second another approach growing out of the liberal tradition and the philosophical examination of the "God problem."

Chapter 9

This interweaving of religion and politics is not new. . . . A close union of the two has persisted during most of human history . . . whether we look at primordial tribal groups, at ancient societies, at the medieval Catholic world, or at most early Protestant nations. The so-called "separation" in the eighteenth century of these two . . . was a radically new departure scandalizing many amazed onlookers at the time.

—Langdon Gilkey[1]

Not everyone was or is willing to concede that faith born of tradition and worldview long past no longer has relevance. On one level some within faith traditions believed that the new scientific playing field could be amenable to traditional faith understanding and practice.

Often this view presents itself in attempts to equate the "big bang" with the Genesis account of creation or relativity and quantum indeterminacy, chance, with God's ultimate rule of nature. Such a viewpoint can be found in the "intelligent design" argument, which posits the need for an ultimate power, "God," in the orderliness that created such complex mechanisms as living organisms.

This attempt to reconcile religious belief and tradition with current scientific understanding, however, is misguided on at least two levels. First and foremost these meldings of science and religion interpret ancient religious symbols, metaphors, and stories which are mythic in nature literally while holding them up to their scientific "counterparts." Second, such attempts neglect or ignore the necessity for scientific rigor and proof and instead render a confusion of religious parable and scientific statement.

1. Gilkey, *Blue Twilight*, 44.

For a large segment of faith communities, though, this has become, conscious or not, the norm. This method of reconciling religious belief with life within a modern scientific world of computers, quasars, black holes, satellites, molecular biology holds an unacknowledged tension, or occasionally regarded with grudging perplexity. In the main these conflicting worldviews exist in their own domains without a serious examination within the religious community due not only to a lack of theological and philosophical sophistication but also to the very real internal dissonance such discussion engenders.

There are those, on the other hand, who were and are not willing to compromise or find any accommodation with modern science and the contingent, indeterminate world. This viewpoint arose in reaction to the logical positivism strain in modern intellectual thought—an intolerant fundamentalism which regards the natural sciences as the sole source of knowledge. This reductive position allows only for data and statements which could be tested and verified by means of sensory scientific inquiry and thus excludes questions incapable of definitive answers: beauty, justice, peace, mortality, and suffering.

This reaction to modern rationalism is most obvious in the Christian fundamentalism tradition.

Reform and reaction has been normative within religious traditions; witness the various sects, denominations, and branches of the world's major religions. Often these reactions take the form of faith renewal in the face of perceived weakening of moral and religious standards, such as in the "Great Awakening" movements of North America. More often these struggles have been over internal, doctrinal issues. Sometimes these issues are contained within that religion, from burning books and treatises to heretics; but often these sectarian conflicts spill over into cultural contests, the Inquisition, the Reformation struggles, the expulsion of the Jews and Islam from the Iberian Peninsula, the Sunni and Shia conflicts, the Wahhabist Islamic reaction, and on.

In the context of our age, this reaction has been an absolutist religious stance over and against both secularity and other religious understandings. Such reaction is not new; today's fundamentalist movement in the United States grew out of the Pentecostal movement of the early twentieth century, a Christian positivist reaction—evoking immediate sense experience—to modern rationalism.

The early fundamentalist movement that followed on the heels of the Pentecostal movement still espoused a rational, scientific basis for their beliefs, beliefs based upon the facts of their understanding of the Christian faith and on the verification of faith through speaking in tongues, healings, and conversions. The development of this movement follows closely the twentieth century's cataclysms of two world wars and a worldwide depression.

Fear seems to be large component, and perhaps a driving force, behind the fundamentalist movement.[2] Fear is found in the anxiety over changes in a culture or society. This is especially so for the profound transformations in community attitudes, laws and norms, and demographics that have increasingly characterized Western societies, the United States in particular (which will be the exemplar below), though Islam and other Eastern religions have not been immune to these reactionary movements.

This fear solidifies in an absolutist "zero tolerance" for the object or objects of that fear. This fear, this "zero tolerance," has a primordial appeal in that it seeks a simple Manichean worldview of a dualistic "good" versus "evil," "light" versus "dark."

The modern fundamentalist movement in the United States grew out of the general horror at the First World War's destruction, an apocalypse that took on a spiritual dimension for many religious conservatives. The Russian Revolution and the rise of the Bolsheviks did nothing to lessen the feeling of threat. Nor did a positivism, both scientific and Christian, which essentially closed off the metaphysical as any sort of component of reality.

The sense of threat to belief on that part of the new fundamentalist movement was also reinforced by the attacks, not necessarily biblically or doctrinally based, by more liberal theologians on their literalist interpretation and apocalyptic imagery. The fundamentalists averred that their liberal opponents themselves were the locus of all that had gone wrong in faith and values, instigating the evils of modernity. Suffice it to say that any exchange since then has left dispassion and logic behind.

That defensive and militant stance of fundamentalism, however, has been a hallmark whether in reaction to modern scientific knowledge or changing societal norms and values. The purpose here is not to rehearse the history of fundamentalism, whether the present-day Religious Right or other worldwide religiopolitical movements. In seeking a new language or conceptuality with which to approach the metaphysical, the "divine," in our time the literalist understanding is problematic and of no help as has been discussed above.

What seems to be most characteristic of these movements is their absolutist political nature, whether seeking to establish a "Christian America" or an "Islamic State," or other theocratic nation. This absolutism, beyond the

---

2. Indeed, Armstrong, *Case*, 271, makes just this point in relation to the various fundamentalist movements she has studied. Her discussion in *Case* and in *History* provide a more complete context to these religious movements, not only Christian but Jewish, Islamic, Hindu, and so on.

problematic theological premises and conceptualities, ultimately absolves the individual of any real responsibility to be thoughtful or discerning, to have a willingness to make distinctions, to have a sense of proportion or perspective.

There is within these movements an identification of their social and political agenda with what is considered by adherents to be the "real" version of religion. Concomitantly, there is a tolerance for racism and sexism with a nostalgic yearning for a "lost" age.

At bottom, this identification of "God" and "God's Will" with ourselves is idolatry. Even the literalist interpretation of religious symbolism falls within this camp. "God" has always been symbolic of indescribable transcendence and has, over the millennium, been interpreted in a multitude of ways, a whirlwind (to use Gilkey's phrase) called upon in many and different ways and names. To understand the symbol of God, to reconceive God conceptually so as to point to this symbol's relevance to our existence, we need another path.

Chapter 10

God is . . . the binding element in the world. The consciousness which
is individual in us, is universal in him: the love which is partial in us is
all-embracing in him. . . . All attainment is immortal in that it fashions
the actual ideals which are God in the world as it is now. Every act leaves
the world with a deeper or fainter impress of God. He then passes into his
next relation to the world with enlarged, or diminished, presentation of
ideal values.

—Alfred North Whitehead[1]

A re we, then, left with the choice of an empty, dead symbol, "God," or an
equally vacuous ancient conceptuality of power and control? The one
seeks what meaning there might be in a secular and technological world and
the other identifies meaning with conceptuality that is problematic, at best,
with an understanding of the universe within which we find ourselves. Certainly the past language of "God" has become impossible for many people,
not to mention the cultural baggage that has accompanied this struggle
through a white, Western, male dominated world.

One response to this impasse has been an interest in and a resur-
gence of the mystical traditions, especially the Western mystical traditions
of Judaism and Christianity. For those mystics God was conceived as a
Nothingness from which we came and to which we return. Although mystics such as the Christian Meister Eckhart have found a modern audience,
mysticism especially in Europe had been denounced as anti-biblical since
the sixteenth century and therefore existed, and still exists, on the margins
of Western religion.[2] The increased interest in and adoption of Eastern re-

1. Whitehead, *Religion*, 150–51.
2. Armstrong, *History*, ch. 7, has an extensive discussion of the mystic traditions

ligions in the West can be seen in this context, as a desire to find access to an ultimacy of meaning.

There was another avenue of exploration seeking a meaningful language describing the "Absolute" or "Ultimate." Whether the Ultimate was to be designated with the term "God" would depend upon the explorer. Some still found the idea of "God" to hold meaning, problematic though it might be. Unfortunately, this meaning often had limitations that closed off a relation to the modern world. Karl Barth's emphasis, for example, on biblical "knowledge" over and against the powers of the intellect as corrupt ("sinful"), and in denying any insight to other religious traditions was seen as an uncritical acceptance of biblical "truths."

Others sought, in spite of finding the concept "God" empty, to find language beyond a "personal God," God as *a* being, who interfered or controlled the natural world. The concept or "idea" of "God" expresses a transcendence beyond the mere phenomenological, evading capture or containment within human sensory knowledge. The Hebrew Bible acknowledges this sort of not knowing, incomplete apprehension, in the prohibition of images of "Yahweh." Yahweh himself protects Moses, whose relationship with God has helped cement a covenant with Israel, from actually "seeing God" in full as Yahweh passes by. Moses is to have only the briefest of glimpses the backside of the retreating God.[3]

Such an acknowledgment of incomplete understanding can be a corrective both to nineteenth and early twentieth-century rationalistic optimism which expected scientific explanation of the world and to the religious proclamation of dogmatic certainty in the formulation of belief. Seeking new ways to speak of "God" requires a wrestling with the ambiguity of Life and the necessity of humility in seeking meaningful language that expresses the claim of transcendence beyond ourselves and our self-interest.

If we are to avoid the pitfalls of fundamentalism or creationism, our language and concepts need to acknowledge the modern view of the world, of space, time, and nature. Not only acknowledge but find how such an understanding is, of necessity, present in our formulations.

The following discussion is limited in scope in order to provide a brief sketch of differing pathways charted by twentieth-century theologians and philosophers. This discussion is nowhere near to exhausting the various trends, thinkers, and thoughts, nor does it include such noteworthy names as Rahner, Whitehead, Derrida, Lonergan, Ogden, Cobb, and many more.

---

both Eastern and Western. Some of those themes will be referenced in later chapters in this work.

3. Exod 33:18—34:9.

Simply put, the intention here is to present some alternative ways of doing thinking about the "Absolute" or "Ultimate" which may be helpful in formulating a new way of speaking, thinking, and practicing an understanding of "ultimacy" for our time.

Paul Tillich stands out among the twentieth-century theologians and philosophers for both his commitment to coherent theological thought and his rejection of a "Personal God," the "God" of traditional Western theism. Tillich sought an ontology which accounted for and was accountable to a modern understanding of the world but also took seriously the religious experience of "ultimate concern," the structure of our being and knowledge of its essential nature, of being and nonbeing, of that which is prior for us, of *ultimate concern.*

God, in Tillich's view, did not tinker in the cosmos nor interfere with human freedom and creativity. Related to conceptuality which Tillich felt needed to go was the dualistic thinking that separated our objective bodies from our inner spirits. This dualism introduced in modern times through Galileo and Newton dominated Western thought and truncated our ability to grasp the essential unity of life.

Tillich described God as "the source, ground, and power of all being, including our being. God is, therefore, first of all Being-Itself and not *a* being among the beings."[4] God is the creative source and power of our being, of all being, the wellspring of creativity in the cosmos. This creative source and wellspring is no static or impersonal "Ground of Being." Tillich uses "spirit" to describe fullness of being, both that of human capacity to find meaning and purpose in being and of God as Being Itself. "God *is* Spirit. This is the most embracing, direct and unrestricted symbol for the divine life."[5]

Thus, for Tillich, "God" did not "exist" for that would imply a mere being among others, a controlling tyrant and threat to human freedom and dignity. Rather "God" *was* Being, undergirding Reality, pervading and inseparable from all experience.

Other philosophers and theologians sought new ways of imaging and imagining "God." The Jesuit Catholic Teilhard de Chardin wove an understanding of modern science, particularly evolution, into his theology. This evolutionary thrust to creation found its *telos* in the divine presence, God's incarnation and immanence. This *omega point* of the universe is the climax of evolutionary process, where the variety and complexity of the evolving world finds a meaningful unity in the animating divine power: love.

4. Gilkey, *Blue Twilight*, 102–3.
5. Tillich, *Systematic Theology*, 1:249.

In both cases, the divine rather than being transcendent to the world is existentially bound up in and experientially present in the world. The implications of such a redirection of focus in understanding the divine are profound and were not so readily accepted.

Not only Christian thinkers were exploring how to redefine the divine present in the world. Islamic scholar Ali Shariati, in a rejection of a Westernization of his faith, urged Muslims to reinterpret the symbols of their faith. Although producing more of a commentary on Islam for the faithful than a fully articulated theological argument, in developing a fuller appreciation of the *hajj* and Islamic faith Sharitai emphasized the existential nature of this journey towards God all the while realizing that the divine transcends human expression and cannot be captured within those symbols. The faithful needed to rediscover the meaning of "God" in their lives but should also be mindful that "Almighty Allah has no 'shape', no color and none is similar to Him. No pattern or visualization of Allah that man imagines can represent Him."[6] The Kaaba, the symbol of the *hajj*, has no direction, symbolizing the universality and complete immanence of the divine in all creation. Shariati's emphasis on the lived experience of faith, the living out of faith, however, left unanswered an ontological ground to that faith.

Within Judaism there was also a range of explorations of the relation of the divine to the world. Best known, perhaps, are Martin Buber and Abraham Heschel.

In *I and Thou*,[7] perhaps his best-known work, Buber argues for an understanding of reality as a duality of dialogic relationships between I, You, and It. Within these relationships of persons, animate objects, and deity lies a center of value; there is no isolated "I," only an "I" in encounter with another. However, for Buber this "encounter" takes on a mystical character of revelation without adequate discursive content. Though insisting on the ontological reality of this presence, especially that of the "Divine," the vagueness of such "encounter," "revelation," and "presence" clouds any philosophical or theological understanding. The tilt in Buber appears more to be mystical-ethical, existential in the sense of moral direction, than actual ontological explication of the underpinnings of faith.

Abraham Heschel found in the existential particularity of existence ("this person" as opposed to a "universal" person) a tie to Jewish faith and thought which, he felt, had a character distinct within, if not from, Western philosophy. "Judaism is a reality, a drama within history, a fact, not merely a feeling or an experience and claims that certain extraordinary events

6. Shariati, *Hajj*, 46.

7. Buber, *I and Thou*.

occurred in which it originated. Judaism stands for certain basic teachings, claiming to be the commitment of a people of God . . . and the term Judaism . . . used primarily as a subject" of philosophic examination.[8]

Judaism, for Heschel, was a self-comprehension in a call to a responsibility before God and humanity. In this way, the ethical is the fundamental self-understanding, founded upon a demand engendered historically by a relationship of a people with the Absolute, "God." Judaism, then, reverses the philosophic position of questions endlessly seeking solutions with "the mystery of the answer [which] hovers over all questions."[9] "Philosophy deals with problems as universal issues; to religion the universal issues are personal problems. Philosophy, then, stresses the primacy of the problem, religion stresses the primacy of the person."[10]

When philosophy or religion places its emphasis on investigating *being as being*, ontology and metaphysics, they misapprehend the true nature of the matter. Rather than doctrinal, religion is a way of thinking focused on *being as creation*, history and meta-history. "God" far from a *being* is a "being in and beyond all things,"[11] echoing the *panentheism* of many process theologians (which will be taken up shortly). Heschel does not really develop this point as the existential demand of the divine is his focus, God being an ontological presupposition. For him the spiritual response is a valid and universal insight to the ineffable Subject enveloping all, thus obviating the need for proofs and rational arguments for God's existence.

Although Heschel provides, at least somewhat, a structure to his "idea" of God, this structure in the end is based less upon our usual ways of thinking than upon a call to a recognition of a "spiritual response," a response that may not in the end satisfy the desire for cognitive articulation.[12]

Although not, perhaps, as widely known is Leo Baeck whose characterization of Judaism as "ethical monotheism" emphasized a departure from previous religious and spiritual responses, a "sharp break, a revolution." This transformation, Baeck posits, was the work of creative personalities, a discovery of and historical founding upon "One God" and the moral demands that historical consciousness uncovered.[13]

---

8. Heschel, *God in Search*, 22.

9. Heschel, *God in Search*, 4.

10. Heschel, *God in Search*, 4.

11. Heschel, *Man Is Not Alone*, 78.

12. A further explication of Heschel's theology can be found in Michael, "Abraham Heschel's Concept of God," 120–30.

13. Baeck, *Essence of Judaism*, 59–60.

Baeck, much like Buber and Heschel who followed him and owe much to his thought, found focus more upon the prophetic and moral demands of faith than an ontological explication of the "God" from which those demands flowed. Distinct from Buber's mutuality of relationship with the Eternal "Thou," though, Baeck's divine "Thou" is an unconditional demand on the human conscience which requires a response.[14]

Judaism is thus a social faith, prophetically influenced, under which social welfare is a matter of divinely imposed obligation. The "One God" cannot be wholly known and thus the religious experience and the ethical demand arising from that experience issues from that mystery. Given that God's essence was beyond human knowledge there is a difficulty with Baeck then of distinguishing metaphor and allegory from what might thus be the "essence" of the source of that encounter and demand. To spell out the moral obligations entailed within the human experience, an existential accounting of a divine command, was more important than systematic theological examination.

The strong emphasis upon the moral dimension and spiritual response, then, of religious experience as opposed to developing theological argumentation is a thread that runs through much of Jewish theological thought in the twentieth century, as well.

Throughout these trends in thought about "God," if a "God" there be, runs a thread of the entanglement of the divine within and throughout the world, as opposed to the estrangement of a self-contained, impassible, supernatural Being. This direction places the experience of the divine within the existential as a demand upon human conscience and behavior.

The identification of "God," in the foregoing, not with "substance" as in traditional theologies but with "expressive activity," a process of outpouring and disclosure within reality finds expression in the philosophical/theological formulations of process theology and *panentheism*.

14. Meyer, "Thought of Leo Baeck," 108–9.

Chapter 11

The aim of science is to seek the simplest explanations of complex facts.
We are apt to fall into the error of thinking that the facts are simple
because simplicity is the goal of our quest. The guiding motto in the life of
every natural philosopher should be, Seek simplicity—and distrust it.

—ALFRED NORTH WHITEHEAD[1]

Human reason tends toward oversimplification and only a disillusionment with "neat" answers can spur change. Whitehead's "Seek simplicity and distrust it" is apt to the intellectual, and spiritual, quest in which this work is engaged. The world, the cosmos, that confronts us is a complex system which we only partly see or apprehend and which we understand but dimly. As Whitehead asks, "Is not this the very truth? Should we not distrust the jaunty assurance with which every age prides itself that it at last has hit upon the ultimate concepts in which all that happens can be formulated?"[2]

The human notion of "God," of "deity," began not with analytic discernment but emotional and practical expression, poetic, feelings without analysis or definition. And yet, if not defined, those notions were exclusionary, tending toward a one-sided emphasis of the divine character, whether the Hebrew Yahweh, the Upanishads, or the monotheism of Ikhanaton.

Further analytical ruminations on divinity by thinkers such as Aristotle, Philo, Sanhara, and so on created a sorting of contraries: eternal/temporal, absolute/relative, cause/effect, permanent/contingent or changing. Whichever was deemed as the most positive attribute became the traits of the divine and foundational for Western classical theism, and also for Eastern pantheism.

1. Whitehead, *Concept of Nature*, 163.
2. Whitehead, *Concept of Nature*, 163.

> The difference between the two [Western theism and Eastern pantheism] is that theism admits the reality of plurality, potentiality, becoming—as a secondary form of existence "outside" God, in no way constitutive of his reality; whereas pantheism, properly so called, supposes that, although God includes all within himself, still, since he cannot be really complex, or mutable, such categories can only express human ignorance or illusion.[3]

Classical theism and pantheism are characterized by categorical contrasts, a polarity in which the more admirable or excellent is applicable to the divine whereas the contrary is by definition, then, excluded. However this then produces a reality of deity plus something else (not deity). By contrast, *panentheism* challenges this assumption of necessary, separate ultimate poles in understanding these ultimate contraries are correlative, mutually interdependent. Nothing real can be described by a wholly one-sided contrast.

In other words, rather than monopolar in conception, *panentheism* is dipolar, or better non-dualistic, in thinking about "God." Being as a factor in becoming, from which becoming being is abstracted. Unity entangled with plurality as an integration of the many or a member. Actuality as the realization of potential and the ground of further potentials to be become actual. In all cases, deity ("God") is the supreme case or supercase of these categories of contraries. The divine, then, in *panentheistic* understanding is referencing that change which is "coextensive with all change, whose actuality is to be coextensive with all actuality, and whose power-to-become is to include all such power."[4]

As such "God" is the ultimate, conceptually, of these various attributes; without any sort of qualifiers the ultimate fulfillment of these concepts. *Panentheism* as a conceptuality finds expression, in part or whole, in many philosophers and theologians in the twentieth century but can with some justification be traced back from such varied thinkers as Buber and Heschel above, through Whitehead, Niebuhr, Berdyaev, Schelling, Ramanuja, and Plato.[5]

Panentheism is distinguished from "pantheism" which identifies God with the natural realm. *Panentheism* asserts "that God is partly *constituted* by the natural realm, in the sense that his activity is manifest in and through

3. Hartshorne and Reese, *Philosophers Speak*, 2.

4. Hartshorne and Reese, *Philosophers Speak*, 5.

5. Hartshorne and Reese, *Philosophers Speak*, is an extensive resource on this topic with selections from thinkers from various traditions stretching back before the Common Era (BCE).

natural processes *alone*." But the reality of God "goes beyond what is captured by the purely scientific description of all the events that make up the natural realm. . . . [God is revealed] in the natural realm by disclosing in religious experience an ultimate form of the world" which is not at odds with the causal realm disclosed by natural law. As opposed to a classical monotheism which emphasizes God as substance, as the eternal, unchanging, perfect First Principle, *panentheism* is focused on the "expressive activity of that first principle."[6]

This understanding and identification of God with a universal process of outpouring and self-disclosure, of expressive activity, also places God at risk in the world through an interrelatedness, God needs the world as the locus of the potential sites of that self-disclosure. In this sense God is identified with Existence Itself, not as a standalone substance, but as actively exemplified in the world in the self-disclosure of Existence Itself.

The identification of God with self-disclosing Existence then contrasts with the Greek Ideal Form, timeless and self-contained, which is disconnected from the world in its own perfection. The tension of this disconnect, which is the basis for much of Western monotheism, creates the need for new understandings, a new language, which the concept of *panentheism* and the process emphasis in theology might supply.

One might question how the expressive reality of the divine can avoid entanglement with that divine reality, as many traditional forms of theism seem to tie together God's nature and God's activity. But in contrast "God's expressive activity," the mode of God's presentation, *is* the reality of the divine, not a Singular First Principle or Form but a Totality of complexity or an all-encompassing of the natural complexes that make up everything that is or might be.

At the least, all of natural reality constitutes part of the divine reality. To find such a reality an object of worship is to draw the worshiper into a relationship not only with the divine but the natural world in which the divine is invested. This relationship is, for the worshiper, agapeic in their creative self-expression as it is for the investment of the divine in humanity and the world.

The issue, here, is certainly philosophic (and theological, perhaps) as opposed to a question of natural science. For the concern is not a question of fact, per se, but of a fundamental concern with "meaning" or "principles" for which factual distinctions are neutral. In short, that of philosophy. The crux of the issue for *panentheism* is of "God" inclusive of the world but not thereby limited by it. In admitting a temporal aspect of the divine,

---

6. Johnston, *Saving*, 119–20.

panentheism, in a way classical theism and pantheism do not, allows for the relation of the supreme to awareness and to the world. This total reality, God-and-World, understands "God" as all inclusive, not just all of other things but having all other things literally in "God."

As a beginning point to re-understand, to reincorporate, the divine in the context of the modern world, *panentheism* (as we shall take up in later chapters) offers a new pathway for exploration. The process theologians of the twentieth century, following Alfred North Whitehead, have presented this conceptuality in a variety of ways.

Of the many such thinkers, Charles Hartshorne whose work has been encapsulated above and alluded to previously, presents an extensive catalog of writing (preferring the term "neo-classical theism" to "process theology") which explicitly examines the issues just discussed and makes a thorough-going philosophical and theological case for *panentheism*.[7]

It should be noted at the outset that there is more than a little "anthropomorphism" in play as Hartshorne describes the divine. Hartshorne believes that the Christian theological thought eliminated anthropomorphism incorrectly by removing the ability for the divine to "prehend" or have sympathy, take into oneself, the feelings of the world, creation. Although a conscious choice in his conceptuality, critics have pointed this out as a flaw.[8] Hartshorne would respond, with Charles Pierce, that one cannot express a thought, a human thought, about human nature non-anthropomorphically. Human thought has no alternative but to think, at least in part, analogically between human nature and nonhuman things. "Human thinking, even about God, cannot cut its human root."[9]

"God," more specifically in Hartshorne's conceptuality, is a dynamic process, in which God's relationship to the world is analogous to human mind-body. The cosmos is the "supreme body" of God who is supremely creative of the cells, we and all other individuals. As such God receives us, the cosmos, so that "For God, too, reality *develops* . . . there can be no end of the divine-creaturely process. . . . The world consists of individuals, but the totality of individuals as a physical or spatial whole is God's body, the Soul of which is God. . . . So, in a sense, even God evolves, but in a decidedly transcendent or divine sense."[10]

God for Hartshorne, then, is not a static entity, unchanging or unchanged but infinite *and* finite (in uniquely supreme and excellent ways)

---

7. Hartshorne's body of work is quite large, and exposition here is but a gloss.

8. Buchler, review of Hartshorne's *Man's Vision*, 245–47.

9. Hartshorne, *Omnipotence*, 29–30.

10. Hartshorne, *Omnipotence*, 94.

whose essential trait is love. This characteristic, love, is embodied "supreme-ly" in the divine but also is evident, actualized, within the world which itself contributes something to the divine. Love, here, also implies freedom but also chance and contingency.

God is not all controlling nor a consciously purposive being, in the sense of "holding the reins" of all that happens. Creaturely self-making, or freedom, is essential to a loving divinity else the divine become a tyrannical despot usurping creaturely responsibility and rendering worship let alone redemption as conceptually meaningless if not impossible. Much more ap-propriate an image of the divine, for Hartshorne, is the idea of a mother, "influencing, sympathetic to and hence influenced by her child and delight-ing in its growing creativity and freedom."[11]

Divine power, encompassing all potentiality but valuing those pos-sibilities they tend to increase or decrease "the beauty of the world (or the harmonious happiness of the creatures),"[12] is that which influences all that happens but determines nothing in the concrete particular. God's "influ-ence" is taken here to mean that God "appreciates and fully appropriates every feeling of value there is, sums up and integrates on the highest level possible what the creatures come to in value terms."[13] Thereby God seeks, as the Ultimate or Highest Value, suasion of every creature irresistibly to the extent compatible with that creature's freedom toward an agapeic relation-ship with the world.

While other process thinkers, such as John Cobb Jr.,[14] also addressed this new direction in theology, Daniel Day Williams, a student of Harts-horne, seems even more accessible to an understanding of a process (and I argue, *panentheistic*) conceptuality, particularly in his book *The Spirit and the Forms of Love.*

"What we need," Williams wrote earlier in *God's Grace and Man's Hope,*

> is a theology which will hold together the fact of the creation of the good world, the fact that evil invades that goodness, and the fact of a redemption which brings hope in the midst of tragic failure and loss . . . but it must be far more realistic in its under-standing of the continuing limitations of the life of the Christian than former theologies have been. . . . Yet either some break with sin in fact as well as in principle is possible or else the whole

11. Hartshorne, *Omnipotence*, 58.

12. Hartshorne, *Omnipotence*, 25.

13. Hartshorne, *Omnipotence*, 81.

14. There are many others, such as Schubert Ogden, Norman Pittenger, Paul Spon-heim, and Lee Snook, whose works deserve the reader's consideration.

of Christian experience is a delusion. That break takes place in
human experience, in history, in the process of life.[15]

Williams argued that philosophical concerns are integral to the work
of theology, stating, "The Christian faith has always been articulated in relation to philosophical concerns . . . the New Testament with the Greek and
gnostic background of the Logos doctrine . . . incarnation . . . the stoic elements in Paul's ethical outlook. To be a philosophical theologian is to carry
on the task of seeking that understanding which arises from faith and which
is coherent with the data of human experience and the rational intelligibility
which philosophy seeks."[16]

Both philosophy and theology have a commonality in the search for
the truth of "reality" and in the mutual support each renders the other's
shortcomings in that inquiry. He argues, rather than a singular and final
methodology for this search, this inquiry can only occur within the cultural
and philosophical context within which the questioner resides.

Thus to our twenty-first-century understandings of the world, science
does not present issues which contain the ability, or the need, to appeal to
a divine reality for resolution. The interplay of philosophy and theology is
needed to service the self-understanding of faith itself in the modern context, for faith to have a relevant concern for our everyday life.

Williams, too, believed that positivist critiques of assertions about "God"
were based upon those older, traditional doctrines. While those critiques had
merit (with regard to traditional understandings) he argued for a reconception of the metaphysical which holds both being and becoming, power and
participation, transcendence and immanence together in unity, and also recognizes the world's continuing evolutionary activity and human freedom and
originality, however limited, to shape existence and environment.

"God," in this sense as creative activity, enters into the processes of the
world, of human society, giving structure and value, the basis for ethical
judgment. Williams took it as his task to develop this understanding and
make it relevant to "living together and achieving a tolerable environment
for significant human living."[17]

Williams asserted a social understanding of metaphysical structure,
where God is to be understood as "an immanent structure-giving actuality,
participating all becoming, and moving from actuality to new possibilities
with the life of the world."[18] Contra Hartshorne's ultimately ontological ar-

15. Williams, *God's Grace*, 33, 38.

16. Williams, *Essays*, 1.

17. Williams, *Essays*, 3.

18. Williams, *Essays*, 10.

gument, though, Williams thought affirmations about the divine required some experience of what exists (an experience of the divine), acknowledging in every experience we are, however dimly, aware of a sustaining, value-producing, goal-ordering reality at work.

In this conceptuality "God" becomes that which binds life to life, that which transforms and is transformed through relationships and the creativity that flows from the life of the world, and which is the supreme standard of value for the results of that activity. We exist in the world and the question as to what is real, what is meaningful, is ultimately a metaphysical question for which the philosophical and theological in tandem are instruments for illuminating experience.

In *The Spirit and the Forms of Love* the basis of Williams's understanding is summed up in his phrase "love has a history."[19] That is, love as the expression of the spirit, the "concrete personal expression of living creative beings," and especially the continual expression always present in God's Spirit of love, is a creative force not a static form. This love, above all God's love which we can call Spirit, is present and participates historically, creates its own history, in the life of the whole world.

In tracing the traditional understandings of God's love within Christianity Williams critiques Augustinian, Franciscan, and evangelical (read Reformation) formulations as too static conceptually and not adequately accounting for God's creativity in the world which is God's self-revelation, self-giving (a concept which will appear in later chapters in this work), as agapeic love manifests in the concrete process of history.

Williams posits five categories as necessary for love—individuality (and taking account of the other), freedom, a capacity to be acted upon (in the widest sense, to suffer) and changed by another, causality in which the personal and the person is at stake, and an impartiality which transcends personal bias to assess both lover and loved and their relationship objectively.[20] These categories belong not only to creaturely love but also to the divine love, and thus Williams follows Whitehead and Hartshorne in understanding God as having "the capacity to be acted upon, to be changed, moved, transformed by the action of or in relation to another. The active side of love requires that we allow the field of our action and its meaning to be defined by what the other require. To be completed in and by another is to be acted upon that other."[21]

---

19. Williams, *Spirit*, 4.

20. Williams, *Spirit*, 114–22.

21. Williams, *Spirit*, 117.

This, Williams believes, has been misunderstood in previous conceptions. Fulfillment in human love means one's freedom is circumscribed, but not destroyed, by the freedom of the other. This is not only the understanding of love but of suffering, too. As it is true for the creaturely, for the world, so it is also true for the divine, God. To suffer is to be acted upon, undergoing pain, and thereby changed. No less is this true for humans than it is for the divine.

At bottom, for Williams, Love is historical, "time-full." God's Spirit, love, in history, requires a historical context. The concrete finite historical world is a necessary extension, as love needs history for expression and existence; the world is necessary because God is. Thus, also, "salvation," "God's kingdom," is time-full, not static, abstract, "out of time," a "state after time is no more." Time as we know and understand it may be altered, but historical passage will be the context of God's work of love for creation, thus necessitating a radical rethinking of our conceptions.

Within the foregoing, the point to be underscored is the conceptuality in *panentheism* and process theology or metaphysics of God understood in dynamic temporal terms. God "joined with his world in the adventure of a real history where both God and the creatures have freedom to act and to respond, God supremely, and the creatures within the limitations of their creaturely status."[22]

The argument might be made that there is no philosophy which can be sufficient for Christian faith which is an existential experience for the historical community of that faith. However, theology seeks to interpret the life of that faith and such interpretation requires a philosophical structure for the intelligibility of faith and its assertions—in other words to illuminate it in the concrete problems of life.

Process theology opens a way to conceive of God in historical and temporal terms. The God of the Bible (in the Christian, Judaic, and Islamic traditions) acts historically, even within the freedom of contingent reality that allows for human, creaturely, worldly misuse. Traditional conceptualities have not allowed for or encompassed this possibility.

Rather than argue the entire case for process metaphysics, the case will rest here as there are shelves of books on this topic to which the reader can turn. The foregoing simply establishes a starting point for the constructive portion of this work that appears later in this volume. However, there is still a matter that needs to be addressed: the assumption of a divine "dimension" to reality, the "will to believe."

22. Williams, *Spirit*, 9.

Chapter 12

Theology, in the broadest meaning of the term, is the attempt to place religious experience on the scale of reason, or at least to formulate it in the language of reason. (Many theologians . . . tend to confound their intellectual formulations of faith with the substance of that which is believed. This is one of several reasons why theological reflection should not be left to the professional theologians.)

—PETER BERGER[1]

The argument has been made that all the previous discussion of theological conceptualities, "God language," is based upon the presupposition of the reality of the "divine," that the "will to believe" is only an assumption, and a nonsensical and illogical one at that, without basis in fact. That argument is not without merit. However, the counter supposition—that only those things which can be measured, tested, and thereby validated—are real equally misapprehends the limits of reason and natural science to describe the world around us.

At base, religion is not about answers, at least not in the concrete phenomenological sense of, say, "What is the speed of sound in the atmosphere?"[2] Like art, religion helps us "to live creatively, peacefully, and even joyously with the realities for which there were no easy explanations

---

1. Berger, *Far Glory*, 135.

2. The speed of sound varies with the medium through which it travels (moving faster through water than air) and other properties such as the temperature of that medium. At sea level with a temperature of 68–70 degrees Fahrenheit (21 degrees Celsius) and normal conditions, the speed of sound is 770 mph (344 meters per second, 1238 km/h).

and problems that we could not solve: mortality, pain, grief, despair, and outrage at the injustice and cruelty of life."[3]

But isn't this "special pleading"?

The materialist positivism at the root of most of the criticisms of religion in the modern age would say so. In such a view only those matters which can be tested and verified, through rational, sensory experience, are considered; natural science, in this view, is the final arbiter of what would be considered real.

The most extreme examples for this argument may be, perhaps, Richard Dawkins and Sam Harris who, along with the late Christopher Hitchens, have argued religion is merely an evolutionary contrivance that modern scientific process has rendered vestigial. The choice, so represented, is thus between science and faith, facts with established rational bases and irrational and fanciful imaginings.

At least two problems immediately arise with that position. First is the counter argument that science's purview is not, perhaps, competent to comment on the existence or nonexistence of God as such a position would step beyond the limitations of natural science, that of natural explanations. This would be the argument made by Stephen J. Gould, himself at the least an atheistic agnostic.

More importantly though, second, is the dogmatic and fundamentalist approach such a forced choice argument is based upon. In the main, these arguments from science are predicated upon misunderstandings of, if not acceptance of fundamentalist and literalist religious interpretations of, biblical (and other) religious understandings. This interpretation is just as simplistic in mistaking belief as mindless credulity as is the literalist understanding of the faith they seek to criticize.

There is the mistaken notion that the increasingly expanding scope of human knowledge means a decreased area for faith or belief. But this is based upon the false equivalency of the concepts of *knowledge* and *belief*. The wide range of knowledge our modern age presents us with is mainly information over which no act of belief is called for (even in the realm of quantum physics).

I *know* things such as $1 + 1 = 2$, the boiling point of water at sea level is 212 degrees Fahrenheit (100 degrees Celsius), my social security number, my dog's name. I need not say "I *believe*" those things.

The word *belief* has different qualities depending upon the circumstances of usage. *Belief* in the sense of "I think such and such might be so" is a weaker use, as "I *believe* these mittens are warmer than those," or "I *believe*

---

3. Armstrong, *Case for God*, 318.

that Schröedinger's cat is still alive in that box"; I may not be sure but I do have some reason to think so.

There is a stronger sense of *belief*, however. I *believe* in justice; I *believe* my friend is truthful. These statements, perhaps, also carry an element of not knowing, but the element of *belief* is more than just a probability. Such statements are acts of commitment or investment in something important, something which matters to me or is of concern (ultimate or not). This sense of *belief* is what might be termed "faith."

The argument made here is that *belief*, "faith," "religion" is not supposed to answer questions for which reason, thought, provides answers. One can argue against "God" as something that does not exist, but then one might as well argue against "justice" or "beauty," "forgiveness" or "democracy" as they too do not truly exist even as we seek their incarnation. If they are present at all they are only present imperfectly. In the same way, "God" becomes a promise, a "desire beyond desire," a hope beyond hope, a promise which lurks within the cosmos but can never be defined or definitively captured in human word or thought.

For science, unambiguousness is paramount and language as the method of communication needs structures of reasoning. Science looks "to derive the particular from the general, to understand the particular phenomenon as caused by simple general laws. The general laws when formulated in the language can contain only a few simple concepts—else the law would not be simple and general. From these concepts are derived an infinite variety of possible phenomena, not only qualitatively but with complete precision with respect to every detail. . . . Concepts of ordinary language, inaccurate and only vaguely defined as they are, could never allow such derivations."[4] Most often this precision in language takes the form of mathematics and thus a necessary level of abstraction.

Not just theological or religious language and concepts, however, but scientific study, too, has had difficulty with new understandings or data necessitating new conceptualities about the phenomena surrounding us. Most problematic contemporaneously has been the use of language to describe quantum theory. Here there was no simple guide to correlating ordinary language with mathematical symbols. Common concepts especially did not apply at atomic and sub-atomic scales. As in the case of relativity the reference scale makes a difference in the ability to use ordinary language and the quantum scale had no referent analogous solutions in ordinary language.

Perhaps, given the questioning nature of the scientific enterprise, there has been less objection overall with novel conceptualities but there has been

4. Heisenberg, *Physics and Philosophy*, 171–72.

strenuous objection nonetheless. Great discoveries from the time of Newton to Hubble to twenty-first-century cosmological study have been met with strong resistance. Even the great Einstein rebelled against the uncertainty inherent in the nature of quantum mechanics famously declaring, "[God] does not play dice" to express his opposition to the role chaos and randomness played in that theory. This is a bit of an oversimplification of both quantum physics and Einstein's objections, but quantum theory has stood the practical test of experimental study and much of our modern computer and telecommunication technology is based upon the theory's application.

With the introduction of special relativity and then quantum physics this orderly system was stressed. The assumptions that the order of events in time is entirely independent of their order in space and that the influence of the observer could be minimized to negligibility were swept away. But new structures, new language, were lacking to speak adequately about the new reality. Was the structure of space and time really different from what had been previously assumed? The old language could not communicate the new reality, offering only unambiguous old concepts which experimental results proved inapplicable in all cases.

In a sense the conservative reaction to new conceptualities has some justification. From a scientific perspective up until the dawn of modern science, let us say the early seventeenth century, human knowledge of the world around us was not much more than a systemization of ideas carried forward from ancient times filtered through authorities such as Aristotle and the Christian church. C. S. Lewis in *The Discarded Image* characterizes this cultural mindset as an "organizer, a codifier, a builder of systems," constructing broad images of reality and concentrating on universal issues and ignoring experimental and experiential details as irrelevant. Thus were medieval humans able to achieve a synthesis of science, theology, and history within a harmonious and clearly articulated model of the cosmos.

But the result also allowed superstition of various kinds to inform that understanding and precluded the advance of experimental science through experiential data. The details of the suppression of such "alternate" understandings, from Kepler and Galileo and on, are well known. Even with the success of the scientific revolution that carried forward from the seventeenth century, the appeal to "authority" to oppose such experiential study still holds sway today in many quarters.

On the other hand, positivists in the scientific community, those who find valid only that information generated through experiential data derived from strict scientific methodology in the study of phenomena, in reaction to that tension draw a line separating specific facts and ignoring and denying a discussion of universals or wider connections within and among groups of phenomena. In Newton's words, "I do not know what I appear to the world, but to myself I seem to have been only a boy playing on the seashore, and diverting myself in now and then finding a smoother pebble or a prettier shell than the ordinary, whilst the great ocean of truth lay all undiscovered before me"[5] This is the ethos of modern science, expressing fundamental laws governing natural phenomena in mathematical terms but of anything more, "one must remain silent."

> It is quite understandable that, in their rebellion against author-ity and superstition, scientists should often have gone too far. There were, for instance, many old reports about stones falling out of the sky, and several monasteries and churches had even preserved such stones as relics. Now in the eighteenth century all these reports were dismissed as rank superstition, and the monasteries were asked to throw their worthless stones away. . . . I mention this fact merely to draw attention to the mental attitude typical of the dawn of modern science.[6]

The argument, of course, from a scientific perspective is that the need for precision in scientific conceptuality requires a rejection of the imprecision of early philosophy. The positivist insistence on conceptual clarity, though, comes at the cost of a discussion of wider issues not only in "metaphysics" but also at the heart of modern science where "clear cut conceptuality" and "complete understanding" preclude an understanding of quantum theory (complementarity, interference of probabilities, uncer-tainty relations, separation of subject and object, and so on). Even from a scientific perspective there needs to be a recognition of a difference between the predictive ability of experimental data and a "complete understanding."

Within the scope of the philosophical or theological enterprise, there is very often a disconnect between claims of what "Reality" must be, com-plete understanding, and the phenomena the reality of the "world" serves up. This disconnect may be the result of the rejection of any relevance that modern science may have to believer or belief, or may reflect an inattention to or disregard of the implications that advances in human understanding of the cosmos hold for the believer and belief.

This lack of humility on the part of positivists of both science and reli-gion (here in the latter I do not refer to August Comte's positivist philosophy but to an attitude which, like the scientific positivists limiting conceptuality, seeks to restrict the acceptable range and content of knowledge to a closely defined metaphysics) in the face of a "cosmos" which far outruns our ability

---

5. Heisenberg, *Physics and Beyond*, 207–8.
6. Heisenberg, *Physics and Beyond*, 208.

to grasp has led to, on the one hand, a dismissal as infantile or ludicrous of any ideation resembling religious or spiritual thought and, on the other, a rejection (whether consciously or not) of the results of scientific study.

In both cases, a militant stress on the completeness and superiority of one's conceptual framework and a lack of humility to see the inadequacy of one's own description of nature creates a restrictive environment in which we close our minds to ideas and problems simply because of the imprecision of language and conceptual clarity.

One must, as Tolstoy avers, be willing to get past preconceived notions of reality in order to encounter what that reality actually might be. To recognize this we need look no further than the previously mentioned perception of our daily encounter with the sun. We "sense" that the sun traverses the sky, rising in the east and setting in the west, each day. But we now know this phenomenon is only the result of our planet's daily rotation and that earth also orbits the sun.

Recognition of these facts alone took millennia to be accepted, not to mention the condemnation of many individuals, and even their death, which stemmed from the steadfast belief in what our "common sense" and prior authority told us and not what experiential observation found to be what truly was happening. There are still those today who do not "buy" this understanding, even in the face of photos from orbiting spacecraft or such craft launched into the outer solar system.

At the same time, it wasn't until the early twentieth century that the scientific community understood our solar system within a larger body, the Milky Way galaxy, was one of millions, then billions, of other galaxies all speeding away from each other. Edwin Hubble's discovery in 1925 that the Milky Way was just one of a multitude of similar galaxies, "nebula" so called at the time and considered phenomena within our galaxy, was vehemently opposed by many in the scientific community, notably Harlow Shapely. His further observation that these galaxies were rapidly receding from our galaxy and that the universe was expanding, in 1929, even contradicted Einstein's earlier (1917) belief in a static universe.[7]

Overcoming what we have traditionally believed to be the case, what has been handed down as wisdom, a scientific fact from a previous century, or even as religious truth and understanding is extremely difficult. Quantum physics, quantum mechanics, as an understanding of "how the world works" faced that headwind to acceptance. Quantum physics as a concept is very difficult to understand let alone explain in "simple language." The

---

7. Einstein later thanked Hubble for this discovery which supported what his general relativity theory indicated but which Einstein, at the time of the formulation, did not believe.

description of reality quantum physics provides is counter-intuitive to our everyday senses. And yet quantum physics is the basis of much of our modern life from computers to cell phones to GPS navigation. Quantum physics, as obtuse as it can be to the average person, works and our lives today depend upon our understanding, such as it is, of the mechanics of that working.

In a sense, the scientific exploration is just as much about self-discovery as is the theological/spiritual enterprise. Both really are about our place in the cosmos and the perishable nature of the world around us. Humans desire order and stability, an explanation of the obvious contingency that surrounds us. Einstein's belief in a static and stable universe are reflected in his conceptual models. And yet, those models were upset by Hubble's discovery of an expanding and changing universe and new explanations were sought to recreate equilibrium.

The shift of cosmological understandings from mythos to physical science still reflect this intense desire for order in a worldview whether religious or philosophical (and here I include the underpinnings of the scientific enterprise). Every culture has a unique view of the cosmos whether ancient storytellers or modern cosmologists, each in turn channeling mystery, awe, and the fear and terror of uncertainty and ultimate ending.

Even with modern scientific and mathematical underpinnings and a reliance on "immutable" physical laws there is still a mysticism, and element of trust in that which is unknown, in modern scientific thought and formulation. For instance, in astronomy and thus the cosmological pursuit, most of the information upon which our understanding is based. Even as data gathering instrumentation has become more and more refined, most of that information is indirect, second-hand. The information is gathered from observing radiation that has arrived on earth (and now orbiting satellites and telescopes) filtered through unknown media that can distort, disrupt, and change the message.

Even as we are able to create a consistent view of how the universe operates from that data, we need to acknowledge with humility the speculative and incomplete nature of those models. As much as ninety percent of the matter in our cosmos, and through which our observational data has flowed to us, is invisible, dark matter, dark energy which we are still struggling to understand.

Beyond these considerations the cosmos that we can "see," whether by enhanced visual or other means such as microwave, is only a fantastically minute portion of what most likely exists. Our knowledge of the universe is limited; there is a "cosmic horizon" beyond which we know we cannot see due to the speed of light and cosmic expansion. The light we can "see" by these various means has been traveling for millions and sometimes billions of years. At the same time, this universe we see is expanding, pulling away from us and from the phenomena we see.

There are therefore causal and technological limits to our knowledge of our cosmos. Within that limited body of knowledge it is tempting to construct a worldview, a worldview that as with past historic constructions will be inaccurate and false.

Thus is humility even in our quite remarkably successful scientific exploration of our world necessary. Science is always "recalibrating" understandings of that world through experimentation and experiential data. But just as often, scientific understanding comes about through a revolution which overturns current scientific worldviews. Aristotle was wrong, as was Newton (though, to be fair perhaps, in Newton's case this was a matter of scale); we can be, too.

The same is the case, I would assert, in the matter of religion and spirituality today. The mental model of our cosmos contains, for many of us, a religious, spiritual, or theological component that has passed from generation to generation without change, without a consideration of our knowledge of the world in which we actually live. There are, of course, also the extremes of belief and nonbelief with the cases each makes to their own adherents and which make no sense to their opposites.

And there is the vast middle, of whatever religious or spiritual understanding, who do not give much thought to the matter. They operate with those traditional beliefs or thought patterns handed down through generations with only the odd occasion where a vague notion of doubt creeps in. But any sense of dissonance between those traditional beliefs and a modern sense of the world is quickly tamped down. Such dissonance, a feeling that those traditional beliefs might not be "true" faced with a modern worldview, is disconcerting if not downright scary for most people.

Religious or theological language though reflecting on the transcendent as its subject is nonetheless rooted in ordinary reality. Therefore, such reflection is of necessity fraught with intellectual uncertainty and the possibility of doubt. There are those for whom religious reflection has the character of certitude. Often such certitude occurs in traditional cultures without the interaction with modernity. But this taken-for-granted certainty also has occurred with increasing frequency within modern societies.

This neo-traditional point of view, especially as it exists within modern societies, necessarily must deny or repress uncertainty in the face of the contradictory knowledge that the complexities of the modern world present. Such a neo-traditional stance need not only be religious as social and political movements have also been built on this appeal to authority, a surrender to authority of one's freedom.

The argument made in this work is that rather than religious or spiritual belief being at odds with a modern understanding of the "world," or the "cosmos," this is also a case where our philosophical and theological "sense," the intellectual constructs we have built to explain the religious and spiritual dimension of life, needs to be overturned, reexamined, and a new understanding of "what is" created to more fully and richly describe that experience.

Conversely, a positivist perspective that disallows any discussion of metaphysical problems or formulations, of "wholeness" or "consciousness" and so on, as relics of prescientific or animistic thought needs also to be reexamined in the light of the "looseness" of quantum conceptuality. Perhaps a better conversation would be how to avoid the mistakes of metaphysics, to allow for a subtler and nuanced understanding of the processes of the cosmos, and so not superficially talk the "deeps in which the truth dwells" out of existence.[8]

At bottom then is the argument that, on the one hand, humility in science and the scientific pursuit with regard to the metaphysical is warranted and, on the other hand, even with the shortcomings of Enlightenment objectivity humility in metaphysical inquiry and formulation calls for a need to acknowledge and take seriously the positions staked out by science and the consequences thereof.

8. Heisenberg, *Physics and Beyond*, 211.

Chapter 13

To open our eyes to the true nature of the universe has always been one of physics' primary purposes. It's hard to imagine a more mind-stretching experience than learning, as we have over the last century, that the reality we experience is but a glimmer of the reality that is.

—Brian Greene[1]

In seeking a reconstruction or reformulation or, perhaps better, a new metaphysical understanding the contention in this work is that the results of scientific inquiry cannot be taken lightly or ignored. But it is also the case that the humility called for in the last chapter works both ways, in terms of understanding the limits of our knowledge and apprehension.

The argument, thus, is for an approach which recognizes the legitimacy of both the natural sciences and a metaphysical context to life. There is a moral and practical foreground to life that must be acknowledged—human concerns of sorrow and joy, suffering and love—for they are also a dimension of human life. By the same token, there are inconsistencies within traditional religious understandings that modern scientific investigation has made more pronounced, if not obviated all together.

To be intellectually and emotionally honest any beginning to the reformulation of metaphysical thought must begin in humility, uncertainty, and contingency in the face of the world as it presents itself to us. Therefore, the basic understandings of modern science need to be respected and accounted for within that reconstruction. Any argument that posits a miraculous, or special exception, suspension of those understandings in favor of a "divine intervention" must be considered "special pleading" and as such rejected as logically and theologically unsound.

1. Greene, *Fabric*, 12.

What is attempted in the following chapter is not a complete accounting of the scientific view of our world (as if *an* accounting, singular and all inclusive, was possible) nor even an outline. The development of our current position is also better left to others as the focus, if not the space, here is limited. In the following segment only the broad brush strokes of our understanding of the underpinnings of our world currently perceived are presented.[2] I ask the forbearance of the physicists who might stumble across this work; as a book aimed at a general audience, most likely not conversant in the science and physics referenced, I attempt by these broad strokes to give a sense of the vast and non-intuitive nature of reality without, I hope, reducing the same into simplistic misconceptions.

Why is engaging in an understanding of current scientific investigation of the universe important at this point in reconstructing a metaphysical sense? The purpose is twofold: first, as noted in previous chapters the world as we understand it scientifically has increasingly made past religious formulations untenable, and second, any future formulation, because of the naturalistic approach in this work, ought to honestly confront and account for our present knowledge of this world.

What is real? That question lies at the heart of the struggle to interpret, scientifically, philosophically, and theologically, the world around us. For those of us who live in the early twenty-first century that question encapsulates the debate over the interpretation of quantum mechanics. Since the early twentieth-century physicists have faced the conundrum of quantum mechanics, the fact that something real is described but *that* "something" is "nothing material."

That sounds really weird but in fact it actually describes what is happening at the foundation (as near as we can measure) of reality, of what makes up our universe. Nothing is what it seems.

Our understanding of how the universe works has evolved from ancient times as we have seen in earlier chapters. Seventeenth-century Newtonian physics worked fine at large scales until eclipsed by Einstein, and other early twentieth-century physicists, who found that at smaller scales Newton's laws did not quite fit. Even Einstein's formulations, which worked fine at certain more minute scales, were found wanting as quantum physics asserted a new and stranger dynamic in operation at the base of reality. And, strange as the newer models seemed, they have been verified in experimentation and have led to the explosion of practical applications in computing and communication technologies we are experiencing.

2. The reader is directed to works by Brian Greene, Sean Carroll, Marcelo Gleiser, and Fritjof Capra, not to mention earlier primary works by Werner Heisenberg, Niels Bohr, and Erwin Schrödinger as indicative of the influences at work here.

In the same way we have grown up with religious and spiritual images and metaphors that are inherited from an ancient and no longer valid
understanding of creation, we still carry, in popular culture, descriptive notions of scientific understandings which no longer fit. To move forward we
basically need to change the way we look at the world around us.

Space and time is the arena in which we exist and form our reality. Our
understanding of space and time is foundational to our concept of "what
is real." As noted previously, we do not need to be restricted by a materialist positivism, but we cannot, by the same token, base our formulations
on premises that violate the data, observations, theory, or mathematics of
modern science.

In a later section of this work, the self-understanding of science, the
relationship between the part and whole for understanding the universe,
will be addressed. The contention there will be that there is a symmetry
between whole and parts and it is in the understanding of that interplay
where a fuller understanding can be reached. The part contributes to the
understanding of the whole, certainly, but it is the dynamics of the whole
that is primary and gives the ground for deriving the properties, patterns,
and principles of the part. Here, the major concepts of science are outlined.

Whether we begin with the unimaginably large, the universe itself, or
the equally unimaginably minute, the level of quantum mechanics, we will
find interrelated conceptualities that function, with effect differing to some
extent on scale large or small, in ways critical to how we interpret what we
perceive. What then are the basics, the outline, of what we need to take
into account from modern science as we move forward in an attempt to
reconstruct our metaphysical conception?

First is the understanding of our universe as continually expanding at
an increasing rate (although as it seems today in an uneven manner) from
a point some fourteen billion years ago, in a process deemed the "big bang."
To be clear, the "big bang" does *not* designate a firecracker like explosion in
a particular spot which begins the universe. The "big bang" is the term used
to describe the expansion of the universe from an initial state, incredibly
small but not a zero size "singularity." The idea of an initial singularity arises
from Einstein's relativity theory which itself breaks down at small dimensions. In this description the initial inflationary period from this non-zero
point is not discussed, nor is the status of that initial non-zero state.

Another common misconception treats our position on earth as a
special vantage point from which to perceive and measure the universe.
In reality we exist in only a tiny "bubble" of perception of that universe,
limited by the speed of light. Even the "cosmic background radiation" we
detect from the early moments of the creation of the universe is merely that

portion of the expanding universe from which light has reached us. The visible universe is likely ninety-two billion light years across, with the entire universe being infinite for all practical purposes, and light from such extreme distances will never reach us.

Fun fact: Although it does not impact the argument made in this book, the size of the universe is dependent upon its shape—flat, open, or closed. You can read about this bit of cosmology elsewhere but in a nutshell if the architecture of the universe is flat or open the universe is probably infinite. If closed like a sphere, say, then the visible universe centered on the earth and factoring in expansion is ninety-two billion light years and the entire universe which includes what we cannot see is at least 250 times wider than that. Pretty big in any case.

All that is exists in, to the best of our measuring capability, an infinite universe. We really do not know for certain how large that universe is because we are limited in how far we can see into the cosmos. In reality, looking into the universe, we can only see back in time to the limit that the energy emitted by the stars, galaxies, and other phenomena, what we perceive as light and other electromagnetic energy, has traveled. They are so incredibly far away that light has been traveling millions and sometimes billions of years before reaching us.

A corollary of this is understanding that the constraints of the speed of light, the expansion of the universe accelerating away from us and all other points, and the vast distances involved create a cosmic horizon which limits our ability to perceive that universe. Those energy sources we see (and many we cannot) are traveling away from us in a cosmic expansion. Light, or other electromagnetic energy, from some sources has not had time to reach us, and some of that energy never will due to distance in space/time. Beyond a certain limit we cannot know, cannot see, at least with present technology.

To the best of our understanding, the galaxies and so on themselves are not moving away from us, the space intervening is expanding and pushing everything away from each other. In the case of, say, our galaxy the Milky Way there is enough gravitation to hold this object together as a unit.[3]

Second, the universe, even that portion considered "empty space," is a lively matrix of fluctuating fields and "particles," moving and interacting, changing, rippling in relation to those fields, especially the electromagnetic field called "light." In truth, what is revealed is that the universe exists not in separate axes of space *and* time but a combined matrix *space/time*. This

---

3. In coming to terms with the cosmic horizon, the inflationary period, and "big bang," a variety of theories have arisen including the idea of the multiverse. These concepts, while intriguing, are not a focus here.

is important to understand as the interplay of the forces which govern the universe play out within and influence the nature of this *space/time*.

On larger scales gravitation and the Newtonian laws of motion have been understood, modified through observation, and in the case of gravitation reconceived by Einstein in an attempt to better understand another fundamental force: electromagnetism. Gravitation binds all masses together; gravitation governs the "attraction" of bodies, the interplay of orbits, and how objects of mass interact with one another. Newton's laws are predictive indicators of how gravitation affects those objects.

Electromagnetism, or better electromagnetic radiation, has been at least rudimentarily understood since the nineteenth century when HC Oersted discovered that electrical current produces magnetic fields in 1820 and later in 1831 Michael Faraday found that changes in magnetic fields can induce electrical current. This interaction led to the conceptuality of the combined electromagnetic field.

The electromagnetic radiation with which we are most familiar is "light." Light (which will be used as shorthand for electromagnetic radiation) is a mass-less, self-propagating disturbance of fields comprising space that carries energy. Unlike other generated disturbances with which we are familiar, such as waves spreading from a rock tossed in water, light needs no medium as it propagates. Light travels at a defined, and not to be exceeded by itself or anything else, speed of 186,000 miles/sec or more precisely 299,792.458 km/sec.

Light "carries" information, interacting with and produced by ordinary matter. This information has allowed us to examine the makeup of distant stars and planets, in addition to matter closer to home in the form of chemical testing of substances in the laboratory.

However, it is the strange nature of light that has led to a number of refinements, indeed revolutions, in our understanding of the underpinnings of the universe. Light behaves such that it can be described in two very different ways: as a particle (called a "photon") and as a wave (of electromagnetism), depending upon how it is observed. The photon, the mass-less particle, carries energy at the speed of light and are characterized by the energy they carry in proportion to their frequency. The higher their frequency the more their energy; this proportionality was discovered in 1900 by Max Planck (Energy = frequency of the light times the Planck Constant) and is the basis of the quantum world where matter and radiation are energy having the properties of particles and waves to which we turn shortly.[4]

4. At this point, discussion of the nuclear forces which are also fundamental to our understanding of the operation of the universe are deferred.

Third, another process in play helps define and intellectually support our understanding of a crucial component of *space/time*, the process of time. Called the laws of thermodynamics, this process posits three main characteristics: the conservation of energy and matter, the increase of entropy, and the inability to achieve an absolutely zero state where all energy stops.

At most concern here is "entropy" especially as it applies to the operation of the universe in general, and with regard to the *arrow of time* in particular.[5] The main understanding for purposes here is that the *arrow of time*, space/time, has a direction: the "past" is the "past" because of entropy, space/time decays or decomposes to constituent parts of discriminate points in space and in time.

High or increasing entropy indicates the presence of more ways for a physical situation to occur; low entropy indicates fewer ways. Overall, physical systems tend to develop toward higher entropy. Often described as a movement from "order" to "disorder" within the universe, this process could also be characterized by an increasing number of potentialities, possibilities, or contingent outcomes—more ways that things could happen or evolve toward the high entropy outcome.

Entropy is, then, a measure of the ways things, in this case the energy of the fundamental constituents of the universe, can be arranged and rearranged, while leaving the overall system (the universe) unchanged (first law of thermodynamics, conservation of energy).

The key understanding to entropy, and thus time, is that energy always flows from hot to cold and not the reverse. This is because the greater energy, movement, of hot atoms has a higher probability of striking a cold atom (and not the reverse) and thus leaving or distributing some of its energy behind.

Whether it is a glass of melting ice, a burning fire, a shattering egg, all present a perceivable direction, *arrow*, to the flow of sequence in time. The shattering egg presents a larger number of constituent parts ("disorder," contingencies), a higher entropy which cannot un-shatter. The direction here is from the simpler, easier to the more complex, more difficult and that direction seems to be unidirectional.

---

5. The discussion here is encapsulated for space and clarity of purpose. For an extended discussion of the direction of time, see Greene, *Fabric*, ch. 6, or for an extended discussion of the "arrow of time," Carroll, *From Eternity to Here*. There are multiple "arrows" but the most relevant are the entropic (thermodynamic), the psychological (we remember the past not the future), and the electromagnetic (electromagnetic waves move away from moving charges not toward them), and even that of quantum mechanics.

The directionality of time, from low entropy to higher entropy, seems to be a function of the creation of the universe, the "big bang." The universe began in a dense, hot, low entropic state and that is what created the order, the *arrow of time*, we currently observe. This does not mean that orderly structures cannot form—they do as, evidenced by stars, galaxies, and life around us—but that in so forming that order an even greater disorder is created.

Another way of looking at this, beyond the terms "order" and "disorder," is that even as one thing is actualized out of a myriad of contingent possibilities, that one thing contains within it not only those past contingencies but also even more contingent future possibilities for actualization in interaction with the rest of the contingent universe. Complexity dissolves into "simplicity" which itself is in reality an increased complexity.

All this, however, does not address the question of beyond the entropic *arrow of time* "What is Time?" This question resolves into "What is Past?" "What is Present?" "What is Future?"

These may, again, seem intuitive but as has been previously noted our intuition can be immensely misleading. As we shall see shortly, special relativity indicates the "present" is subjective, relative to the observer. Our intuition says that time "flows," that it "passes" going through the "present" from the "past" to the "future." But this intuition is based upon our limited, as we have seen so far, experience of reality. Is time itself fundamental to reality? Perhaps time itself is a function of the limitations of our "consciousness" to the finer details of the reality surrounding us.

Fourth, the process of the evolution of life on our planet, the proposition that all life on earth arose through a natural process. That process includes occasional changes or mutations of DNA affecting future generations, that such mutation can be beneficial, harmful, or neutral and that beneficial changes tend to be preserved and reproduced (natural selection), and that such changes occur over long periods and are the proximate cause of new forms of life.

This area of understanding has been fraught with misunderstanding and misdirection, particularly from the more conservative or fundamentalist religious perspective, which obscures what the theory of evolution, indeed the process of scientific inquiry, entails. It is, however, important to point out that evolution as a category is neutral per se as to theological questions. Evolution seeks to explain, as a secondary causality, how present life arose out of previous forms of life, not to explain any sort of "First Cause."

The present work is not intended as a tutorial on evolution as other works offer such explanation in better detail and at an appropriate length. The purpose here is to point out that evolution as an account of the proximate causes for life on our planet has an experiential basis in research and experimentation. Is it a "final" explanation? No. The canons of the scientific method rule such a finding out, understanding methodological limits. But the tenets of evolutionary theory are testable and provide relatively certain conclusions.

At the same time an assumption of the self-sufficiency and absoluteness of scientific inquiry has left a blind spot with regard to other ways of "knowing," whether historical inquiry or the understandings of self and culture in art, morals, philosophy, and religion. This is not to argue in favor of the infusion of "supernatural" explanations into the scientific method (that should be categorically ruled out) but that aspects of our cultural life are in need of creative reflection beyond the empirical.

Fifth, general relativity. Einstein's general theory of relativity grew out of his 1905 journal article that presented his theory of relativity (today known as the theory of "special relativity"). Again, the following narrative is not meant as an exposition of the relativity theories but an affirmation of their importance to our understanding of how the world, to which later philosophical and theological conceptualities are addressed, works.

Einstein's special theory of relativity posited that time does not pass in the same way for everyone: for example, time slows down for a person in motion relative to another at rest, a notion that has been experimentally verified. However, Einstein discovered that his theory did not fit with the current understanding of gravity, how things fall, as formulated by Isaac Newton three centuries before.

In an attempt to solve this dilemma Einstein, in 1915, published his general theory of relativity which provided a different perspective on the nature of gravity and the reality in which we live.

As has been the case in previous scientific breakthroughs, Einstein broke with traditional Newtonian notions of gravity that perceived gravity as a "force" that drew material bodies toward each other. Space, for Newton, was an empty arena through which objects moved until acted upon by this "force" which then curved the objects' trajectory. But by the nineteenth century the presence of electromagnetic fields as a real entity diffused through space presented a new factor.

Einstein's breakthrough was the understanding that gravity itself must also operate as a field, a "gravitational field"; not diffused throughout space the gravitational field *is* space itself! Space is a gravitational field. Space is a material component of the universe, curving, flexing. The curving of space around objects causes them to fall toward each other. Even light bends through this twisting gravitational field. And not only light, but time!

Strange as this sounds, these effects have been experimentally verified.

In addition, the theory of relativity predicted the existence of black holes long before they were verified. More importantly relativity predicted the expansion of the universe before Edwin Hubble observationally confirmed such an expansion (as noted above called the "big bang") from an initial extremely hot and condensed condition.

Sixth, the quanta and quantum physics. If detailed explication of the prior necessary understandings of the processes of the universe were better left to works outside this volume, due to space, clarity, and full understanding, then quantum mechanics is of necessity left to the shelves of books detailing current scientific understanding, The basic premise for foundational work in physics, "The Standard Model," is thus left to those other more focused and complete works.

Anyone interested in the Standard Model would do well to gain at least rudimentary acquaintance with the components: quarks (six "particles"), leptons (six "particles"), and the nuclear forces—strong and weak. Twelve "particles" of matter governed by three forces (the weaker gravitational force is left off the preceding enumeration as, well, really weak) that are caused by the exchange of four particles (from the enumerated nuclear forces, again gravitation being really weak and gravitation's agency unclear).

And yet, some sense of the very strange "activity" that lies at the heart of all that exists is necessary. As before, there have been common misconceptions regarding quantum reality and misleading metaphors such as Schrödinger's (of undetermined animation) cat,[6] which were used to convey early understandings of quantum activity. They are still sometimes found in works by popular authors.

Basically, the quantum in quantum mechanics refers to "quanta"—the smallest bit of something, such as the quanta of a sand beach is a grain of sand, the quanta of an ocean is a molecule of water. "Mechanics" simply refers to the action, movement, or behavior of this discrete something as referencing quantum physics.

Traditionally the conceptuality and image we have inherited from Aristotle through Rutherford (in 1911) for the smallest component, the smallest "somethings" of existence, was the atom, and later protons and electrons as the smallest of particles. The popular image for these discrete items was

---

6. Schrödinger and his "cat" have been the source of numerous jokes, memes, and other commentary, but in actuality the metaphor of the cat was Schrödinger's ridiculing reproach to the clash between Einstein/Podolsky/Rosen (EPR) and Niels Bohr over quantum physics, a theory Schrödinger helped found, as it was being extrapolated to the macroscopic world in an attempt at "complete understanding." Although quantum physics does create a paradoxical entanglement of observer, observed, and measurement, the quantum effect on the macro scale is negligible.

and often still is that of a minute solar system, really tiny, tiny balls, like planetoids, whizzing around in an incredibly small space.

The problem was: this isn't at all what is going on.

In attempting to describe the activity of these atoms, and their constituent makeup, as time went on these ordinary visual referents no longer worked. The electron and the nucleus (positron and neutron) took on more of a "fuzzy," indeterminate aspect. These super small components do not have a marble or pebble-like reality but were understood to be "quanta" of fields (such as the photon being a quanta of the electromagnetic field). These quanta were excitations in the most basic structure of their field.

Ultimately these fluctuations, these quanta needed to be described mathematically in terms of "wave functions." And even there, in the excited or fluctuating field vibrations at the heart of nature, the cosmos refused to give up its secrets instead presenting a fundamental limit on what could be known.

"Quantum mechanics" refers to the action or movement of the super small components of the universe. Describing activity on the sub-atomic level quantum mechanics operates in the realm of photons and electrons, using what is called the "Planck Constant," an extremely tiny number. On this level, the action of such "particles" can only be explained (i.e., "measured") mathematically in what are called "wave functions." These "wave functions" describe the range of possible locations for quanta that the quanta could be until a measurement is actually taken, at which point the "wave function collapses," actualizes.

In other words, the quanta is everywhere until specified by measurement; it is the activity of measurement that actualizes what is going on. This "uncertainty" in the quantum world was first expressed by Werner Heisenberg (1927) in describing the behavior of an electron and has led to our current understanding. But even that understanding is limited. What the "wave function" really is, well, nobody knows for sure. There have been plenty of conjectures but no resolution other than the "wave function" model works.

As strange as this might seem, quantum mechanics has been verified through experimentation and has "real world" applicability in computing, digital communications, chemistry, engineering, and more upon which our modern world depends. So, weird as all this might appear it is real and finds effect in our lives.

Another point also needs to be made: although quantum effects for the vast majority of interactions and measurements made on the macro scale are negligible, current scientific investigation is beginning to blur the line between classical physics and quantum, including experiments on nanotechnology, quantum computing, quantum interference experiments aimed toward molecular and larger matter, and "mesoscopic" manipulation of groups of atoms.

Finally, experimental verification of nonlocality, the quantum instantaneous action-at-a-distance, has added to the strangeness of fundamental reality by confirming influence between things spatially separated but entangled. Something influencing something else, exchanging information, far away without communicating is indeed "spooky action at a distance," but real just the same. Although such a state of affairs is beyond "reasonable," the temptation to stray into a variety of crazy speculative areas ought to be resisted. Just the same, how such a foreign understanding relates to our everyday perception is matter not to be ignored.[7]

The point in this brief narrative on modern scientific understanding is:

First, that the world in which we live cannot be accepted at "face value," what we "see" is only a miniscule version of what really is happening around us, in excited and fluctuating fields throughout the universe;

Second, relying on "common sense" or intuition without sound factual basis leads to misapprehension of that world;

Third, quantum mechanics' new understanding of the structure of reality has led to a complexity and subtlety of expression (mathematical) to describe what is going on. That understanding includes probability, not certainty, of events and contingency or chance woven into the fabric of reality;

Fourth, any reconstruction of a metaphysics for today must take into account the nature of our world as we understand it, always allowing for methodological limitations, uncertainty, competing theories, and openness to new understandings arising out of future investigations (for example, What is dark energy? What is dark matter?);

Fifth, the universe is less about isolated objects than it is about interactive relationships.

There is a subtlety to the fine structure underlying the universe. At the most fundamental level, we and everything around us are a community of interrelated vibrating energy. At the base, this interrelated community of vibrating energy that makes up us and all that exists itself is the result of excitations or vibrations in "fields," the Higgs field being the most basic as we understand things now, that give substance and eventually mass as we "scale up" to what we experience through our senses, aided or unaided.[8]

The laws of quantum mechanics may operate most clearly on smaller scales, effects being much more minute on large scales, but as we are made

---

7. Or, we could, as some physicists insist, "Shut up and calculate!" accepting the science and ignoring the implications.

8. Mass comes from the interaction "particles" with the Higgs field; in other words, the Higgs Field *gives* mass as a consequence and to the extent of interaction.

up of quanta, as is everything, what we learn about the quantum level can also tell something about us and the reality in which we live. Perhaps physical space is not an inert container for the universe but is itself made of "quanta of space," interrelated and creating the texture of what we deem "space." Perhaps even time itself is only a function of the interaction of these quantum events.

This is, of course, quite simplified (and as Whitehead said, mistrust simplicity). But such a truncated description will do for the present purpose of challenging and redirecting our thinking as we reformulate conceptualities of the "divine," the self, consciousness, and the ultimate interrelation and interpenetration of all reality, the cooperative nature of reality.

Chapter 14

Yet my study of the history of religion has revealed that human beings are spiritual animals. Indeed, there is a case for arguing that *Homo sapiens* is also *Homo religiosus*. Men and women started to worship gods as soon as they became recognizably human; they created religions at the same time as they created works of art . . . these early faiths expressed the wonder and mystery that seem always to have been an essential component of the human experience.

—Karen Armstrong[1]

"Religion" is nested within the roots of human nature. This impulse is a sense that living is intended to be good but with an understanding that it definitely is not; life is a mixture of pleasure with pain, fortune with misfortune and accident, joy with fear and sorrow. Historical social and political movements often are described as religious in nature, but are more involved with an existential commitment to the ideals of particular human structures.

"Religion" in the sense used in this work has a "cosmic demand." This demand is not nested within the particularities of human institutions but concerns what we count within ourselves as worthy of reverence, as eternally "true" for all, and especially encompassing the deepest bond with our neighbor. "Cosmic demand" indicates an urgency, a seriousness, that something is at stake, a truth of vital importance. Not an individual, solitary, or ego satisfying demand but an understanding that there is a "right" way to live that preserves us within the flux of disorder and futility present in our experienced existence.

Religions, *per se*, have historical roots—places and times, cultures and civilizations—within which they developed. This is just as true for

---

1. Armstrong, *History*, xix.

Christianity, Judaism, and Islam as it is for Confucianism, Hinduism, Buddhism, and on. Whatever belief, or lack thereof, in the divine origination of particular religions one might have, those particularities that shaped the growth of world religions cannot be denied. The intention of this work is not to overcome, replace, or amalgamate those communities of belief. There is too much sociocultural history to overcome, even if such a task was possible in a world of over seven billion people.

And yet an understanding from the wide range of religious experience and expression may provide insights that can aid and clarify a reconceptualizing of the metaphysical dimension to life. From the perspective of Christian faith the commandment to preach the gospel to all nations has been both blessing and curse. On the one hand such a demand has led that faith into diverse cultures and societies and led at least to the attempt to learn the folkways, the language, the thought patterns of others in order to tell faith's message in an intelligible manner. On the other hand, this path has also led to stylizing conceptualities, creating dogma, around philosophical categories such as those Greek ideals which have become so problematic for the modern age.

The task this book calls for is to share in, from whatever religious, philosophical, or theological vantage point, the interreligious quest for universal humanity, to seek a new understanding of the metaphysical "divine" in a plural society. In this quest there can be no monopoly on the "truth," only a limited franchise, as we seek to uncover the roots of what is meant by the religious or spiritual quest.

The approach taken toward this task is not necessarily to, as John Dunne and others have termed it, to "pass over" (from a Christian perspective) and "come back."[2] That is, to "pass over" into the faith understanding of another, to know from "within," and then "come back" to one's own faith world, changed but still within the original faith world but with new insight gained from the other.

Indeed, the author's own initial perspective is that of the Christian faith; however, whether affirming the root message of that faith in "passing over" and "coming back" I make no assurance. Nor is there a compulsion to render one and only one faith message as the standard. The journey here is make existential sense, if such sense there be, of not only the root message of my initial faith but to understand the meaning of that faith in the context of the pluralistic spiritual world. If the cosmos conveys, as posited above (and

2. See Dunne, *Way of All the World*, Robinson, *Truth Is Two-Eyed*, and Snook, *Anonymous Christ.*

to which we will return), a sense of moral demand on us, then a metaphysical "divine" has a core meaning beyond our parochial interests.

Beyond the inter- and intra-religious arguments over the particular theological understandings, noted in previous chapters, metaphysics itself as non-measurable, non-verifiable, non-testable is ruled out as a scientific category and not within the purview of scientific investigation. But too often metaphysics is mistakenly deemed, in scientific circles, as solely "supernatural" and overriding scientific knowledge, as it is often used in non-scientific, common parlance, too. Such a "straw dog" only confuses the issue and frames abandoned and uninteresting dead-end conversations. We should not confuse the focus of these inquiries just as we do not seek a scientific basis for beauty in art and music, or truth in ethics.

The meaning here, the conceptualization, however, is not a symbolized *goal* in terms of an answer or definition. That is too Western, too Greek, too post-Enlightenment, too static for the reality to which the metaphysical "divine" points. The modern concept of "God" as a personal creator/power, supernatural personality, and so on is a phenomenon of the modern, or more the Enlightenment, age arising from the belief that the indescribable or inexplicable in life would succumb to the scrutiny of scientific inquiry and control, which is reason. "God" in this view is a projection of the will to human mastery over the environment and to human resolution of the universe's mysteries.

And it does not do justice to the reality of nature which our modern scientific understanding finds. As has been argued throughout this work, "God too must really change if his reality is to respect the nature of all reality as modern man tends to understand it. God too would become."[3]

The implication thereby is that the metaphysical divine reality, however symbolized or termed, is not about a *goal* but about the *journey*, both in terms of conceptuality and manifestation. This *journey* is perhaps the ultimate meaning of the Christian term *Parousia*, indicating the arriving or presence of God. Theologically, *Parousia* has been used as a term for the "second coming." I prefer a more present perfect progressive understanding of the verb: arriving, of activity, past and continuing present.

The idea of "God" is a symbol pointing to an indescribable transcendence. "God" is not an "object," or objective reality which "exists" in the same way a banana "exists." "God," as Paul Tillich recognized, is not an object of cognition. We need to look through and beyond the symbol to the pervasive ground of all becoming and recognize the transcendent (but *not* supernatural) reality built into our human condition: that of love, peace, and

3. Lee, *Becoming of the Church*, 15.

understanding, the "compassionate" mind of Buddhism, the self-emptying of *agapé*. To anticipate the argument to be made:

every act of love is a transcendent experience, an experience that recognizes the Other/other which is a part of the pervasive, all present, nature or "field" at the center of not only the universe but our self.

For the most, when people talk about transcendence they talk about something supernatural. This is not how this term is used or understood in this work. Transcendence indicates going beyond ourselves, in the sense of a call to us or a demand from us, something which draws to seeing, understanding, or being in a new way, on a new level. Transcendence, here, is understood as that life encounter or event that occasions something new in me—growth, conversion, death and rebirth, my becoming someone, something, new.

The arguments made in this book present themselves, at least initially, in response to the theological traditions and understandings of the Judeo-Christian-Islamic faith communities and their understandings of "God," in whatever linguistic form. In addressing a reconstruction or reconceptualization of the metaphysical divine present to us it is helpful to understand that they each offer a salvific message which is tied into their respective conceptions of "God." That salvation is most coherently understood in terms of life reconciled to the large-scale defects that so vividly present themselves to us.

I acknowledge Walter Kaufmann and Leo Baeck's arguments, from the Jewish perspective, that Judaism is not itself salvific (which they equate with reward) so much as being based upon the (behavioral) admonition to live righteously within the living tradition and ever fresh demand presented by the Torah and the Prophets to every contemporary moment. For them the Torah itself was the "Tao," the "Path" or the "Way" as those latter terms are understood in the East. I do, however, think even such a call to obedient service contains a salvific element. "Religion" as Kaufmann points out, "is rooted in the human aspiration to transcend himself."[4]

That life which should be good and is just as obviously not is something truly a part of everyday experience. Whether arbitrary suffering, corrosive aging, untimely death, self-involvement which separates us from community, ultimately the vulnerability of everything we care about, the list goes on. More times than not we are ignorant, willfully or not, of our true condition.

The tragic and horrific are often without any kind of psychological remit or balm within the context of everyday experience. Placing such events within the operation of the "other worldly" succeeds only in discounting or denying the nature of the offense to life that they are.

4. Kaufmann, *Critique*, 253.

The salvific message in the midst of these events, in the midst of life itself, is that there must be, that there is, a way forward. In the midst of suffering there is a release, a freedom, which allows us to gain and retain a faith in life itself. The goal of that salvific effect is a new, transformed life, a new orientation which redirects the saved toward a different awareness and action in the world.

I have framed this salvific message in more general terms than the Judeo-Christian-Islamic traditions would because these religions are not alone in having a salvific nature. For example, though not theistic, Buddhism also offers a salvific message, the Four Noble Truths, not so far removed, a theme to which we shall return.

Thus I argue "religion" is a moral challenge, an aspiration to transcend oneself, woven into the cosmos, that embraces suffering and contingency not escaping it. The transformative action is not a "supernatural" escape, a flight beyond and away from this life, but is in that embrace, not expecting more. Jesus after all suffered and died with the cry on his lips: "My God, my God, why have you forsaken me?"[5]

It is instructive to remember that Mark, as the earliest gospel, ends with the empty tomb, no resurrection and no glory, only confusion and fear on the part of Jesus' disciples, in line with Mark's characterization of the disciples as utterly misunderstanding what they have been taught. The later resurrection narratives are indicative of the Pharisaic belief in personal resurrection amid the intellectual context of the intertestamental period in the Middle East and are not the sole resources present in the Judeo-Christian tradition for finding meaning in human existence.

Moving forward, the main initial issues surrounding a reconstruction of the metaphysical divine are directed at: the language used to describe this "God," the self, salvific action, and how these are set against the backdrop of an understanding of life and death. The reconstruction within this work is set in a framework of philosophic theology, which itself is within the naturalism orientation of philosophy and theology.

As has been argued throughout, traditional religious (and thereby theological) language is ill suited to the task of communicating let alone making understandable a metaphysical viewpoint, "God" language, to a modern age. There are so many connotations and associations with the archaic conceptual language used, especially for the Judeo-Christian-Islamic traditions, that popular usage makes misunderstanding, misinterpretation, miscommunication, and confusion inevitable.

---

5. From Ps 22 and quoted in Matt 27:46 and Mark 15:34.

The point of view here *precludes* a supernatural interpretation and affirms nature as a knowable and instructive arena of reality, especially with regard to human values and fulfillment. Naturalism, here, references a model of thought that is biological, developmental, and process oriented—that is, based upon temporal "becoming" and interrelational in nature.

At the same time, even though the conceptualities and methods present in this work require thoughtful effort, there must also be a pragmatic effort at clarity and comprehension for those not steeped in the philosophical or theological enterprise. Religion describes, after all, the belief and activity of people who are religious; religious language cannot become so far removed or abstracted as not to be understood. This is not to say that the following arguments will be elementary or easily reasoned. Nor will it be argued that definitions and conceptualities cannot change; they surely have over the millennia but the task of rejecting certain understandings and encouraging others should not be seen as mere preferences, either.

The argument here is that the limitation of the divine, "God," to a personalized, supernatural being no longer fits either the modern scientific world or the robust understandings of the various world religions and a new set of definitions and conceptualities is necessary. The task, then, is "to reinterpret and redefine religious terms and to revise doctrines. However, there are boundaries beyond which unnecessary confusion is created and where clarity requires a vocabulary other than that of traditional usage . . . modernity requires a deep rethinking of traditional theological categories . . . rethinking necessitates a deliberately selective use of traditional terms and concepts."[6]

6. Milligan, "Limits," 300.

Chapter 15

The first thing to understand is that "God," if it is a name at all, is not an ordinary proper name like "Judas Maccabeus," "Samuel Johnson," or "Kurt Gödel."

—MARK JOHNSTON[1]

As I have argued in previous chapters, "God" is a word, and a concept, fraught with so much cultural baggage that what it references is simultaneously confusingly vague and yet inconsistently specific in ways that make communication about a metaphysical divine unintelligible. "God" most often is taken to mean if not a proper name then a descriptive name, an appellation inclusive of a variety of meanings and attributes.

A number of words in Hebrew, Arabic, and Greek (the basic languages of the Judeo-Christian-Islamic traditions) have been translated as "God" (or "god of" in the variety of Hebraic forms), some as titles, some as honorific descriptors. A specific proper name for "God" only appears as the vaguely communicated "Yahweh" (יהוה) in Hebrew and "Allah" in Arabic. Even in Hebrew, "Yahweh" was not vocalized as being too sacred and other words were substituted. "El" (אל) was the most common usage referring to "God" or "god of," even in referring to the Jewish people of God as Israel (ישראל "God contends/struggles").

"Yahweh," "Allah," the "Holy Trinity," all are named and in common usage become confused into the word "God." "Confused" because those three—"Yahweh," "Allah," the "Holy Trinity"—are not all pointing to the same monotheistic source, any more than the ancient Egyptian "Aten" or the Zoroastrian "Ahura Mazda" would be considered within the scope of "God" by those three traditions. The confusion or intermixture is the result of a

1. Johnston, *Saving*, 4.

process called syncretism in which such terms become conflated or blended without a discrimination of crucial differences.

Such syncretism often dominates modern discussion of theology or religion in the laudable desire to harmonize and/or respect the beliefs of others, that we all worship the same God. But such worthy intentions do not make a merger of "gods" true as a study of the particular traditions named above will inevitably show, that to which the appellation points differs from tradition to tradition. The issue of idolatry, worshiping a false god, is intrinsic to monotheism, a charge each tradition above could and would level against the other since it is one's own god that is "God."

Related to the issue of idolatry raised within differing traditions against such syncretism is the idolatry that is present within and among these, mostly, Western religions. The charge of idolatry lodged against another religion, that only my "God is God" is in itself idolatrous. Such an attitude assumes that contingent humanity understands, has tamed, Religious Ultimacy—basically an egocentric, magical manipulation of that Ultimate. The attempt to domesticate "God" for one's own human ends is all too obvious in the world, at least in others so that one might not see "the mote" in one's own eye.

This is in a way understandable. The Religious Ultimate can only become actual to us through an "object," something actualized but pointing beyond itself. These "objects" are not the Religious Ultimate in and of themselves but only mediums; in negating themselves the "object" points toward the Religious Ultimate. The problem is that often the "object," whether a word or concept and so on, becomes for the believer that divine itself, the seat of ultimate concern, and so becomes idolatrous and demonic.

This idolatry is present in the religious fixations on the supernatural, the other or next world, egocentric obsession with a personal afterlife, apocalyptic punishment of evildoers, and final reward given to those whose actions are worthy. To be blunt again, "God," the metaphysical "divine," is *not* a personal being and such a concept is a result of idolatry.

In contrast to these elements of deeply rooted individual or group self-worship, the argument here will be that what is considered under the canopy of religion is the appropriate life-orientation toward a metaphysical divine in which only a radical self-abandonment to the metaphysical divine manifested in the unselfish turn toward others, working toward their well-being, can be considered as a proper and non-idolatrous conception of that Divine.

How, then, is this metaphysical divine to be conceived, on what basis, and why? This latter question is best answered first. Why should one bother with any conceptuality of a metaphysical divine, whether old, new, reconstructed, or traditional?

Supernatural or idolatrous responses aside, and leaving sectarian traditions of the metaphysical on hold, throughout human history people have expressed immediate and pressing questions of ultimate concern: what is it to live rightly, where is justice (however that concept is expressed) in a manifestly unjust world, why is there capricious and unmitigated suffering?

Is a metaphysical divine necessary to answer such questions, to establish what should be of value as an object of pursuit, of the ethical? If our reconceptualization proceeds from naturalistic view of the world, why should reason not be the basis for what we should desire and do? Is not a philosophy based on *this* world enough to answer the need for a reconciliation to its defects and to work out a trust in the ultimate virtue of goodness?

In answer I think we need to look first to what might be considered the "human condition," and return to the initial human concerns raised throughout our history, and articulated within various traditions, East and West, but most familiarly to readers here in the Judeo-Christian tradition. We live in a fractured world, are ourselves fractured by the motivation to self-interest or self-will (our inclination to pursue higher consideration for ourselves at the cost to others' welfare), oft times even in the pursuit of "the good" and most times we are either unaware of or blind ourselves to such failing.

The answer to this state, from those traditions, is a transformative encounter that enters and guides us to a new understanding of life and its meaning. And it is the Source of this transformative encounter to which the metaphysical divine points, but a Source which is more than the monotheistic, and perhaps the nontheistic, traditions allow.

This state of "self-love," Mark Johnston argues, has its roots "in the very structure of consciousness . . . the arena of presence and action in which and out of which each one of us lives, presents itself as a fundamental context for the worldly happenings that make up the details of one's life. So long as we are alive, we ourselves are always around; every time we wake up in a chair or a bed, there we are, coeval with the appearance and reappearance of the world. And so we operate as if the world just wouldn't be the world unless we were *here*, as it were, in the center of it."[2]

Though we will return to this "arena of presence and action" later, for now the basic point is that such an understanding of consciousness helps demark the Being Here, of the center of our arena—the property of being me—and a "There," which distinguishes the rest of the world. The asymmetry of the two presents "Here" as the center of the self value, noted above,

---

2. Johnston, *Saving*, 183.

and the "There" as opportunities and obstructions to the satisfaction of the "Here."

If this is the state in which we operate, then the deliberation that other-regarding action, that the "Other" "There" is worthy or deserving of our regard and positive action—a "conscience" demanding such benefit toward others—is required. As noted earlier, the cosmic demand seems to be a historic hallmark of the human quest for a life shaped to some meaning.

Those values of the worthy and the good can only be disclosed from within the "landscape" of the world, from our interaction within the world and those around us, providing some directional sense of the "worthy" life. In such case, then, the "conscience" (or perhaps "self-conscience") which creates this felt demand must be a feature of human existence since it exists not only "Here" but "There," too.

But even if we internalize those other-directed conceptions of the worthy and good, the strength of self-will or self-love acts to overpower that communal sense of obligation, to tip the scales to favor ourselves. Such a failure in the face of the felt demand toward others creates a dissonance within the "conscience," a feeling of guilt and failure to live up to the felt standard and a promise "to do better in the future." And yet . . .

This is a familiar behavioral cycle, even to those not committed to any religious outlook. The problem is exacerbated in that the internalized conception of the worthy and good communally received also contains elements of the very "self-will," which we are trying to avoid, that arise "There." The foundation is compromised at the start by conflicting interests which distort the basis for the communal sense of obligation.

In the existential need to answer "how should I live," internalizing and accepting the communally received and communally enforced "law," however flawed, in the process becomes the bulwark against failure and an uncertain conscience. Living within such a framework however results in a false righteousness and rigidity which lives within the letter but not the spirit, respectability but not necessarily ethical.

Within the Judeo-Christian traditions the critical commentary of the Prophets, Jesus, Paul, through to Martin Luther and Karl Barth highlight such shortcomings, returning to what they considered a "higher law," that of loving God foremost and one's neighbor as oneself.

What of the virtuous life, without all the religious trappings? Cannot the life of a virtuous person be considered ethical?

Even from outside of those religious traditions, Immanuel Kant's critique of human nature as turned in upon itself posited the self by nature in radical opposition to the other, to the ethical life. I think one could also posit the concurrence in Buddhism if not of a *homo incurvatus in se* then of a radical ignorance or misunderstanding of our condition, a flaw which too leads to suffering and the opposite of the ethical life.

If this inward curve to human nature is to be overcome so that we can recognize our arena of concern is not our inward self alone but all others on an equal footing, their interests and our interests of equal legitimacy, where then is such transformative, salvific, "grace" to be found? The variety of sources bidding for that role have been mentioned. What could be this unity, a highest common "source" for that transformation, which respects that diversity of forms of grace?

If, as has been posited throughout this work, there is a cosmic, existential, demand at the root of reality, one of ultimate concern and none higher for us, this would be the basis for a metaphysical "divine." This metaphysical "divine," and this alone, would be deserving of our loyalty, as that to which we could turn as a source of salvific grace from our "bent" self-will.

If a part of this metaphysical "divine" is an actualized, distinct reality, say a cosmos, this actualized reality would share in the perfections of that "divine." Such a joint reality would itself be more correctly the aim of our fealty and worship. This metaphysical "divine" itself need not be singular or a "simple" (in philosophy, an atomistic irreducible unitary) but could include or comprehend within itself a diversity. The parts, it may be said, are actually dependent upon the whole rather than the whole being subordinate to the parts of which the whole is comprised.

At root, the metaphysical "divine" can be conceived rather as a complexity, with traits that "can never be regarded as fully and finally ascertained or completely circumscribed."[3] In this way, the metaphysical "divine" might be considered a "natural complex," in the words of Justus Buchler.

The metaphysical "divine" thus holds in unity a diversity, a "complex," of traits and inexhaustible paradigmatic values which itself "preserves overwhelming contrast with the finite . . . perpetual consummations of a related kind—delimiting all other complexes, opening human ways beyond prevailing limits, and constantly renewing in the experiential orders of the world (in the perspectives of man) that sensitivity to the similar and the different which lies at the base of query."[4]

Thus, the question "Does God exist?" itself becomes deficient as the concept "existence" is ultimately problematic, as it too contains categories of distinction or application. The issue might more straightforwardly be stated that "God" (the metaphysical "divine," as a term for the present) prevails as a

3. Buchler, *Metaphysics*, 5–6. The use and explication of "natural complex" here is necessarily truncated for space and clarity of mission. See Buchler's work for the extended argument toward just such an understanding of "God."

4. Buchler, *Metaphysics*, 7–8.

complex varied in scope and discrimination of understanding and relation. Such a metaphysical "divine" is not, then, a single, indivisible reality, nor a divisible composite or compound, but a complex containing possibility *and* actuality in a contingent relation within reality. The metaphysical "divine" has a unitary (but not "simple" or irreducible) aspect in its integrity as belonging to or apprehending the multifariousness of its relationships.

If this metaphysical "divine" is considered to be the highest or most worthy, with nothing higher or more worthy, then whatever else may be good or worthy can only be modes or manifestations. Thus the metaphysical "divine" also then "includes all beings as . . . modes or manifestations"; leading to the "premise to the effect that all being is good."[5]

The preceding discussion has slipped past the traditional arguments and conceptions of "God" to posit the metaphysical "divine" as being complex, comprehending attributes without singular identification or predication. This allows for an understanding of the "divine" in terms other than traditional monotheisms or even polytheisms.

5. Johnston, *Saving*, 96.

Chapter 16

God must be viewed as *necessarily* all-inclusive, incapable of a genuinely 'external' environment. . . . All actual things must be actual in God, they must be constituents of his actuality, and all possible things must be potentially his constituents.

—CHARLES HARTSHORNE[1]

In each atom of the realms of the universe,
There exist vast oceans of world systems.

—FROM *THE GREAT FLOWER ORNAMENT*, ANCIENT BUDDHIST SCRIPTURE[2]

What does it mean that this metaphysical "divine" is the highest in terms of worthiness and goodness? All forms of theism would find that "goodness" or "worthiness" at its ultimate would be a descriptor of "God." Does "goodness" describe a benefactor state, a relationship of favor toward humans and/or the world? Such an understanding is the basis for the "problem of theodicy," "God's" responsibility for evil in the world.

Or, does the highest "goodness" mean that the metaphysical "divine" is most desired among all there is? No special pleadings to make, or levers to pull in order to achieve a worldly advantage. In this latter, we, the cosmos, are called as part of the actualized metaphysical "divine" to share in, to participate in the meaning (the "self-disclosure") of that "divine" disclosed, revealed in creation. In so doing, we enter into, to the extent contingent actuality can, the life, the orientation or direction, of the cosmic demand that the metaphysical "divine" entails. This outpouring, this "self-disclosure"

1. Hartshorne, *Natural*, 20.
2. Quoted in the Dalai Lama, *The Universe*, dedication page.

in creation exemplifies that "end" or "will" of the metaphysical "divine's" cosmic demand as *agapé*, the highest relational form of love.

Here, then, we touch on the theological characterization for our reconceptualization of the metaphysical "divine." In an earlier chapter we alluded to process theology and *panentheism*, and it is to this we shall now turn.

Panentheism argues that "God is partly *constituted* by the natural realm, in the sense that his activity is manifest in and through natural processes *alone*. But his reality goes beyond what is captured by the purely scientific description of all the events that make up the natural realm."[3] This is to contrast with *pantheism*, which identifies "God" with the natural realm. The difference is important.

A useful but limited analogy is H_2O and water. Water is only one state in which H_2O appears, ice, steam, snow being other states. H_2O constitutes water, but not the opposite. To clarify a bit more, in arguing for naturalism as has been the case here the natural sciences are recognized as complete in explication of natural processes. But such naturalism does *not* argue that *only* the natural realm exists.

Even though, as argued above, there is complexity to the metaphysical "divine" which includes the actualized cosmos the metaphysical "divine" is not identical with the world. At the same time nothing in the natural realm is outside that metaphysical "divine" or the *expressive activity* of the metaphysical "divine." The *expressive activity*, "God's" outpouring and self-giving power, underlies and suffices the world but not in way that is at odds with the scientific understanding of the world. The emphasis on *expressive activity* instead of *substance* is what distinguishes a *panentheistic* understanding from traditional theism. In this *expressive activity* "God" becomes, as was indicated earlier for the metaphysical divine, "at risk" in the world, needing us as instances of "God's" self-disclosure as much as we need the "divine" as the "orient-er" of salvific grace.

Panentheism as a basis for reconceptualizing the metaphysical "divine" not only includes an inclusive understanding of that "divine" as an object of worship or veneration but also as *expressive activity* which provides the basis for the new orientation called forth in the cosmic demand of self-outpouring toward the other, in common terms: love as the basis for all interrelationships. "In particular, the identification of the Highest One with the all-inclusive process of the outpouring of Existence Itself into existents for the sake of self-disclosure, makes the old Self-Complete Being of classical theology just one pole of God, the activity of outpouring and

---

3. Johnston, *Saving*, 119.

self-disclosure, and to that extent overcomes the dualism between being and becoming."[4]

By this a lived sense of "Being" is returned to the world of reality as a counter to the *incuratus in se* (life curved inward on itself) which envisions "Being" only in terms of instrumental power and advantage especially as applied to stultified deities from whom we seek favored treatment. Variously in the Judeo-Christian-Islamic traditions has "God," who is closer than breath and will not let us go,[5] rebuked such idolatrous behavior and called for a change of heart, whether the jealous Yahweh or Allah's demand of all-encompassing devotion or call to repentance of the Gospels and Letters of Paul. Traditional theism has allowed these calls to slip back into transcendentalized and anthropomorphic conceptuality which hides the presence of the metaphysical "divine" in the world.

In a reconceptualized metaphysical "divine" of *panentheism* the *expressive activity* of Self/self-outpouring continually recognizes the making and remaking of the world as "holy ground" in the "divine's" presence. Even with the defects, that the world isn't as it "should be," and our profound ignorance of our condition (from a Buddhist perspective), the recognition that the ground of our nature, the highest and most worthy good, is found in self-outpouring, self-emptying promises healing. Not in a salvific future personal history but in a transformed understanding that we are a part of this reservoir of life.

All of this, though, still provokes the question of what do we mean by a metaphysical "divine" that is partially constituted but not wholly encompassed by the natural realm? From a practical standpoint this still sounds like an argument for something supernatural. How are we to understand this metaphysical "divine" which also lies beyond the natural realm?

The problem inherent in all descriptions which seek to distinguish the realm of nature and that of *expressive activity*, the outpouring of "Being," is that such explanations wrongly become dualistic. In reality these are not separate realms but interrelated. Coexistent with the processes of the natural realm is potency or potentiality of Being and Becoming, encompassing the disclosure of actuality. Reality consists of both the actual existents and the variety of ways in which those beings may be presented.

There is a connection between what made something present and that which is actually present, an essence that at least partially defines what is present. This is not some sort of argument for "intelligent design" nor representational thinking about states *of* or *about* what is present. Such a view

---

4. Johnston, *Saving*, 121.

5. Pss 46 and 145, Surah Qaf [50:16].

would have us as producers of the world whose psychological processes precondition that which is actualized or disclosed.

Being and Becoming are a preexisting presence to our perception and thus present in a fundamental self-disclosing *expressive activity* in the actual existents of the cosmos, independent of individual intellectual assent or recognition. The cosmos itself exists independent of our experience of its presence. All existing things and all the possible ways they could be thought about or sensed are carried into being with the things themselves.

We only consciously partake or access the contents of what is already fully actualized. Rather than producers we are, as Mark Johnston argues in *Saving God*, "Samplers of Presence."[6]

In contrast, in the Western philosophical tradition the notion that we are "Producers" of presence has predominated. As "producers" our inner mental states created by brain function are themselves representational states of and about the external world. The logical consequence of this "natural representation" position is that without a brain or other site of representational states there is no presence; there is a necessity for the external to have a subject to be present else presence disappears.

The alternative suggested here is that there is no gap between the mental representation and that item in the world the mental representation makes present. The modes of presentation are themselves objective, a part of the object itself accessed by us, made present to us. This is just as true for abstract objects.

All of this is a fairly complex way of saying: the world still exists even if you do not see it or are not personally present. The world may even be perceived, made present, through senses we do not possess (think cats, dogs, bats, Klingons). We, at most, selectively sample what is already objectively "out there." Seen in this way presence is not subjective, not conditional on a psychological process, but objective and accessible in many ways.

To return to the earlier question: Why is this important to the reconceptualization of a metaphysical "divine"?

The argument was made that the metaphysical "divine" is partially constituted by the natural realm, but is not contained by it. The further argument was made that while things are made present through the processes of the natural realm they are not products of our mental acts but have objective status in themselves which we only "sample" in the modes of presentation grasped by us—their presence is mind-independent.

This objective realm of presence or disclosure which makes up the realm of sense has itself structure of necessity. Given the various modes

6. Johnston, *Saving*, 132.

of thinking about things, the limited modes of experiencing, and even the *incuratus in se* as universal affliction, there must be an idealized value, if not maximum at the least fully adequate, of the most complete modes of presentation of reality. This ideal limit could provide a basis for understanding the self-disclosure of the metaphysical "divine," the *expressive activity* which draws us toward our own better grasp or approximation or understanding of the "cosmic demand."

This, then, is Being/Becoming-making-itself-present to us. The realm of sense and the realm of nature are not separate but a unity where every creature that exists is a finite expression of the metaphysical "divine." In a *panentheist* understanding of reality, this "God" exists; exists for the sake of this outpouring of Being/Becoming which finds expression in the reality of ordinary creaturely life (understood broadly, not just in human terms).

Is this Being/Becoming thus exemplified in the ordinary existents sufficient to remedy the *incuratus in se* and other defects of life noted above? Not in and of itself. This "divine" is not, as has been argued, an all-controlling, superpower that negates the very creation which is the *expressive activity* of the outpouring of Being. In our finite and limited "horizon of self-regard" we can and do create roadblocks to fully appreciating the gift presented to us. The self-disclosure within this outpouring, the nature of this agapeic activity, although available is not necessarily obvious or readily accessible to all given the conditions of finite life noted above.

But there is "grace" in this; Being/Becoming outpoured, expressed, disclosed, available through no merit or action on our part. The understanding and acceptance of this grace can be the beginning of recognition of our state, our *incuratus in se*, and propel us toward a different, corrected course to the arc of our life.

Chapter 17

The absolute is the absolute and the relative is the relative, and yet the absolute and the relative are completely interdependent.

—MASAO ABE[1]

To speak of "Ultimate Reality" is to reference human life and its essential relationships and purposes, because it is in the ultimate relevance for human life that the words "Ultimate Reality" take on meaning. The sense of this phrase is not found in some subjective choice or formulation but in what is taken to be the true nature of reality, Tillich's "ultimate concern," the "Highest One" (in Mark Johnston's Saving God).

Such a term has a spiritual, if not necessarily religious, connotation. Implicit in the spirituality of a person or a group is the desire to align or conform life and action to the perceived "Ultimate Reality." Along with various methods to create such alignment there is also the acknowledgment of the obstacles or impediments in contingent life to reaching such a harmony.

While engagement with ultimate concern in some form is a part of being human, holding something as the most important of all concerns does not necessarily carry a religious connotation. There are many orientations toward what might be considered a meaningful life directed toward the most important valuation of reality, whether truth, social justice, or the well-being of the human or the wider created world.

This work focuses on the spiritual and religious sense of "Ultimate Reality." As has been implied earlier religion has a cultural component that forms the various systems and their understandings of "Ultimate Reality" and human/worldly standing toward it. These systems have transmitted a variety of messages, traditions, and activities all directed toward fulfilling

1. Abe, *Zen and Western Thought*, 247.

the desire to align or conform one's life with "Ultimate Reality." And because they are cultural and thereby historical these transmissions are contingent and changing, whether subtly or radically, and give rise to a plethora of schools, sects, or strains within those traditions. In particular, speaking of "Christianity" (and other religious traditions, in particular for this work of "Buddhism") is itself misleading given the wide range of such understandings or shades of conceptualities within that tradition (or, really, traditions).

What is attempted within this work is a deconstruction of what has traditionally been accepted as the understanding of "God," the "Ultimate Reality" within Western Judeo-Christian-Islamic faiths. As has been argued previously, the modern scientific understanding of the world has made the traditional images of the "divine" increasingly problematic. Even before this situation, however, there were intimations in the mystics of these traditions, and the traditions themselves, that created images of the "divine," of "God," were insufficient and reifications—the immaterial made material, or a reality among a totality, just the utmost and greatest. The referent was to be considered beyond being something, beyond being nothing, that encompassed and dissolved such dualisms as being/nonbeing, finite/infinite, past/present/future, immanent/transcendent, ultimate/mundane.

In this ineffability of ultimacy is a touch-point, I believe, between Christianity and Buddhism which can be a source for beginning transformative engagement of both understandings of "Ultimate Reality." The understanding of human existence which underlies the arguments here flows from that engagement and will, hopefully, help clarify the arguments made or at least give a framework for understanding the words and conceptualities as used.

Like Christianity, Buddhism has a variety of traditions, sects, and traditions, many of which have differing approaches to their understanding of reality and ultimacy. In the following pages the point of view characterized comes from Zen Buddhism. The Zen (Chan) branch of Mahayana Buddhism arises from the Taoist Chinese encounter as Buddhism spread from India eastward to China and Japan.

A crucial distinction between the Western and Eastern mystical traditions can be seen in their differing views of the "absolute." This is most evident in the contrasting Judaic-Christian-Islamic and Buddhist traditions. For the Taoist (Zen Buddhist), the "Tao" is a "thing"—that is, not a "person," not having an independent, objective form. Thus the approach to the Tao is meditative, intuitive, and more adaptable to a broad mystical speculative approach. As the Taoist is in union with the absolute, the "Tao," which is no longer thus a "person," the Taoist in turn is not a person, an ego "self," either.

In the Western tradition, both philosophical and theological, the absolute is almost always a "person" or has the aspect of the "personal." Thus such union with the absolute takes on the aspect and always is "personal" and "relational."

These are two differing ways of dealing not only with the understanding of "Ultimate Reality" but also with the central dilemma of ego, either resolving it or strengthening it. Both Christianity and Buddhism, as religions, have been fairly eclectic in composition as they have moved within the world as seen from their encounters with the various cultures and philosophical patterns in their path. However, the Western traditions—especially as they have interacted with and drawn from Greek thought—are imbued with Greek categories which tend toward the rational, geometrical, and mathematical for cosmological norms. The Taoist outlook orients more toward change, flux, movement, the non-stable, and non-rationalist, and therefore the intuitive. Such an orientation finds expression even in their differing aesthetics of art. As these aesthetics have grown closer together in the modern setting, so, too, has the opportunity for transformational spiritual and religious understanding.

The lack of a concept of "God," a theistic understanding of reality, comparable to the Judeo-Christian-Islamic tradition need not be a hindrance to the transformational enterprise. Early in the Buddhist tradition, the Buddha acknowledged the Indian deities but found they had no salvific role in or ultimate meaning for human liberation. A hermeneutical mistake is made in comparing the nontheistic approach of Buddhism to "Ultimate Reality" in Christian theistic terms. As will become clear in the following chapters, Buddhism and particularly the Mahayana Buddhist view of "Ultimate Reality" reveals a religious and spiritual understanding that can be transformational for Western faith and belief.

Taking a non-reified approach to comprehending "Ultimate Reality" for the Christian tradition will alter our point of view of that tradition, giving a new perspective for grasping meaning, creating new wineskins for the new wine of understanding. Such a new point of view will require, at many points, redefining how the words of that tradition are understood, creating transformational points and conceptual reconstructions in the language used in both traditions.

This is especially important since language can often have differing meanings to others and the arguments here are quite dependent upon a definite understanding or direction. The problem that confronts such clarification is the plasticity of language in multiple and often changing meanings. Initially the word which I wanted to use but found to be problematic was "dimension." "Dimension" can be so fraught with misunderstanding and taken to depict some other realm or locale that I chose "pole" to better frame the descriptive aspects of existence.

Human existence has two aspects or poles. First, we live in a socio-historical context of space and time. This pole might also be called the "secular." Here the temporal, the particular, the contingent—all people and things—exist in distinction one from another. This is the realm of scientific inquiry, laws, and processes. The distinctiveness of all things one from another creates non-chaotic conditions conducive to the orderly investigation of science, even considering the chaos and uncertainty of the quantum.

The distinctiveness, however, also has a negative aspect in that when such differences are substantialized or reified they become grounds for conflict and strife, particularly so in human existence. To a large extent the religious and spiritual quests have their basis in coming to terms with and trying to understand if not overcome what are seen as the consequences of such distinction, suffering and struggle.

The second pole of human existence is metaphysical. Where the first pole might be considered immanent this second is transcendent. In this we find not distinction but nondistinction, in a dialectical relation which is inclusive and all-encompassing of Being/Becoming. But it must be immediately said that though these two poles are essentially and qualitatively different they are connected inseparably with one another within human existence. We live physically and metaphysically. Understanding of this intersection and of the two poles in which we live occurs not objectively but existentially.

While these two poles are both indispensable the second, the metaphysical, is the more fundamental as the ground or source of human existence whereas the first, the sociohistorical, is the condition or occasion of that existence. Overcoming the conflict in the sociohistorical, contingent is possible only by turning to the metaphysical, transcending distinction for dynamic equality. Metaphorically this dialectic of fundamental and occasional is found in the Christian sense of the kingdom of God within (Luke 17:21), Jesus Christ as true human and true God, and the nondiscriminating love of God who makes "his sun rise on the evil and on the good" (Matt 5:45). From a Buddhist perspective this dialectic appears in Śūnyatā, in which emptiness and fullness are dynamically identical and inclusive.

Thus in the two poles we have not only independent, distinctive existence but also a fundamental source of that contingent in interdependence, the nondiscriminative realm or pole where equality without distinction is realized. Everything that is exists dynamically within these two poles.

Within the framework of these two poles and their intersection the work of reconceptualization in this book takes place. Whether or not a sufficient ground for this task, that of taking the metaphysical seriously as a necessary component of human existence and understanding I leave to the reader. To continue forward under this grounding how are we to conceptualize the metaphysical, "what language shall I borrow" to speak of this ground?

If the word "God" is so filled with cultural and psychological baggage as to impede our reconceptualization of that to which such a descriptor points, what can replace it?

Paul Tillich's "Ground of Being" captures some of the sense described in these pages but itself carries Tillich's philosophical baggage and perhaps a dualism we wish to avoid. Mark Johnston finds "The Highest One" best describes, for him, this metaphysical "divine." Metaphysical "divine," by the way, is really too awkward as a phrase, abstract and lacking at least a bit of the anthropomorphic flavor which engages the mind and emotion. "Mystery," too, plays a large part in the various religious traditions throughout the world to describe the feeling, intellectually and emotionally, of awe and wonder. As a word and concept "Mystery," "Great Mystery," finds expression in many cultures and has the attractive sense of the unknown, of the incompleteness of our own knowledge and understanding.

The objection is often made that past language or words were adequate, just tweak the content. Language is powerful and sometimes certain language, words, and concepts contain content that overwhelm anything new, or have elements that really are toxic to the conceptualities that we try to express. The various movements by women and people of color have stressed the power of words and the often negative cultural contexts that they carry. Sometimes a new way must be considered; new wineskins fashioned to hold the new wine.

A splendid metaphor for exploration is found in the concept of paths, or trails.[2] A trail is a series of markers that structure our travel, guiding our way toward our goal with confidence and reassurance. We humans have blazed trails in the wilderness of the universe in which we find ourselves in order to make sense of our place, to understand the far country through which we travel, and provide insight into our journey's end. "Losing one's way" or "finding one's way," "finding direction in life" are all trail metaphors for self-understanding, or the lack thereof. The lack of a trail is by turns

---

2. This metaphor comes from Robert Moor's *On Trails*, which describes the place "trails" and "paths" have in both our consciousness and our history, metaphorically and physically.

"scarcely less bitter than death,"[3] and "horrible wilderness, rivers and lakes unspanned by human art, pathless swamps, dismal forests that it made the flesh creep to enter."[4] The trail gives definition to the way through the wild places, piloting us through a so often romanticized "wilderness."

Trails are made in the walking. The experience of traversing a piece of geography creates the pathway which will come to be used. Armchair speculation, and often even map reading, is not a substitute for the firsthand comprehension of the ground to be covered.

In like manner, the trails that humans have blazed in the search for the understanding of self and our place in the cosmos have also been most successful when experiential. This is not to denigrate intellectual rumination but to emphasize the necessary connection between experience and thought. A metaphor can be strained, too, when there is a disconnect between what we experience and "what actually is."

I don't think it is accidental that the Chinese word used to describe the negotiation of the transcendent and the secular is "*Tao*" (the "Way" or "Path"). "The philosophers of China hold that the highest life of all, that at which philosophy aims, is both this-worldly and other-worldly; and that the men who are in possession of this highest life are the sages . . . to transcend the world does not mean to be divorced from the world . . . [but to] synthesize the two sides, the sublime and the common."[5] The *Tao* thus harmonizes the sublime and "common activity," a trail to which this work will return later.

The trails toward understanding self and our world created by humans have taken many forms from magical to intellectual. In each stage trails have formed based upon the current conceptualizations of the world as we experienced it. And at each stage those trails were modified by new concepts introduced by novel experience, more persuasive information and experience, and intuitive "leaps" which yielded new and better explanations.

Not every "old" trail, though, was erased. Often well worn trails, though seemingly discredited, are still utilized and deemed the "only" or "best" way despite evidence to the contrary. Proponents of those trails can become increasingly shrill in their promotion of their trail, even as evidence of their obsolescence is seen in the retreating "hikers."

---

3. Dante, *Inferno*, canto I, lines 1–7, "Midway upon the journey of our life, I found myself within a forest dark, For the straightforward pathway had been lost. . . . What was this forest savage, rough, and stern, Which in the very thought renews the fear. So bitter is it, death is little more."

4. Edward Everett Hale at the 1851 Boston Railroad Jubilee, quoted Moor, *On Trails*, 30.

5. Yu-Lan, *Spirit of Chinese Philosophy*, 5.

The words we have used over the millennia for the metaphysical "divine" are likewise "signposts," markers that structure our travel through life, our experience of the "Mystery" of life, sometimes providing insight. Often time, though, those markers have led us astray, especially when the trail and markers have become overgrown, the path has washed away, or (to strain the metaphor even more) the signposts have been turned away from our goal. At times like these, new markers need to be considered and new pathways need to be named.

Many terms have been used by other philosophers and theologians over the millennia, but the one that has traction for me is: "Spirit." "Spirit" may also be an old marker; but "Spirit" seems to have a wide enough range to allow us to point to our path, as long as we clean out some of the "undergrowth of misunderstanding." "Spirit" in many ways, culturally and intellectually not just religiously, is a word indicative of power and animating influence. Oftentimes "spirituality" has a more friendly reception than "religiosity" as a more neutral in tone.

The word "spirit" encompasses a variety of meanings. Leaving aside the definition of "spirit" as intended in an "other-worldly" or "non-corporeal" sense of a "soul" or entity separate from "body," "spirit" refers to something beyond the immediate self, or even group. "Spirit" refers to something distinct from yet immanent in the concreteness of our being. But to be clear: the "spirit" to which this work refers is neither "other-worldly" nor an additive to existence, something which describes or encapsulates a personality for a post-death experience.

In the Western world and especially in Christianity (and most likely Islam, though that is not the focus here) the term "spirit" has for millennia been associated, through the apostle Paul, with an "immortal soul" and the concern for that "soul's" reckoning after death. This New Testament conception of soul or spirit, however, is more influenced by Greek thought, particularly Plato, and Zoroastrian influence than arising out of the Judaic scriptural tradition.[6]

"The conception of an immortal soul, imprisoned in the body, and with its earthly career but an incident in its ultimate destiny, is Platonism not at its best; it exhibits the partly life-hating and life-fearing Plato, or the legislator Plato, who is tempted to think of providence as an extension of our earthly legal codes."[7]

---

6. For an excellent discussion of the intellectual foment of so-called intertestamental times, which added "immortal soul," "resurrection," "apocalypse," and more to our religious vocabulary, see Jenkins, *Crucible of Faith*.

7. Hartshorne, *Natural*, 107.

The realization that such Hellenistic and Platonic baggage has so pervasively influenced the direction of modern thought is not something of which we are even aware. This is especially true in religious thought (whether Christian, Judaism, or Islam). Our cultural inheritance, the milieu of thinking into which we live and move, creates many of the intellectual, emotional, and spiritual problems we have as we try to examine the meaning, if any, of religious and theological language in a postmodern context— that is, separating mind from body, spirit from matter, sacred from secular or ordinary.

Humans are spiritual beings. The impulse toward religion comes from the same innate drive that creates art. This is not necessarily a desire to appease powerful, extra-human forces but an expression of a sense of the wonder and mystery that lies at the heart of our experience of a beautiful and yet terrifying world. The drive to discover a coherent and unified, an overarching, understanding of our world, the "cosmos," is a quintessential part of what it means to be human. When we speak of a "human spirit" we are describing that quest for ultimate meaning. Our desire to reconcile all too real suffering in the world, and our ultimate annihilation, with a mystical sense of unity that not only defines the spiritual quest but also, we come to understand, permeates modern quantum physics.[8]

But what, today, does the word "spirit" mean? What if anything stands behind that word, gives the term "spirit" any sort of identifiable character that is understandable in our world today? The human quest for meaning in life, whether philosophic, religious, or artistic has diverged from the human quest to understand life and the world in scientific terms. A chasm has opened betwixt the two modes of reflection and interpretation so that language from one side becomes gibberish to the other.

This state of affairs, especially with respect to theology, religion, and "God language," may be in large part a Western intellectual problem. Western religious thought begins with just that—*thought*, thinking about "God," "spirit," or what other terms are related to spiritual practice. "God language" is just that—*language*, words ("The Word") and the rumination on the written, historical encounter one has with those primary document(s), the Bible, the Qur'an. The way of meeting "the spiritual" in the West is most often, then, in thinking and not experiencing,[9] a theme more fully developed

8. Paraphrasing Werner Heisenberg. This is ultimately what Werner Heisenberg's uncertainty principle engenders: the unity and interrelatedness of matter, that the material world is not a collection of discrete and separate objects but a network of relationships that create a unified whole. See Heisenberg's discussion of Wolfgang Pauli in *Across the Frontiers*, ch. 3.

9. Theologian Lee E. Snook provides an excellent insight into and discussion of the

in other chapters with regard to the many ways of meeting that mystical dimension of the cosmos, whether our meeting place is on the grounds of Buddhism or quantum theory. We find that what we "think," what we "perceive," is often at odds with what actually "is."

And yet any language of the "spirit," whether deemed religious, theological, or philosophical, must arise necessarily in relation to and be intelligible to our understanding of the world around us. If not, if the "spiritual"—"God" in any of the many forms that concept can and has been formulated—is not accessible to our concrete world of thought and action, then such language really holds no meaning for our life, for our world. However, that requirement needs also to be tempered by the aforementioned understanding that often our perceptions and intuitions of the world are not necessarily reflections of what is actually taking place.

As we reconsider how we conceive of the metaphysical "divine" or "Spirit" we need to reconsider how we approach our understanding of human self-identity and examine the range of human spirituality by looking at Buddhist insight into the relativity and tenuousness of human self-identity along with the Hebrew Bible's insight that the sole indispensable self-identity is not found in the ephemeral individual self.

To return to the use of "Spirit," I think the definitions of "spirit" can be useful descriptions of the *expressive activity* of Being/Becoming which has been argued here is the essence of the "divine":'

The nonphysical inner character of a person, thought of as different from the material person we can see and touch;

Those qualities regarded as forming the definitive or typical elements in the character of a person, nation, or group or in the thought and attitudes of a particular period;

Temperament or disposition of mind or outlook, activating or essential principle, feeling, quality, or disposition characterizing something.

At bottom, I must agree with Daniel Day Williams that "Spirit is the best word we have to indicate the concrete personal expression of living creative beings. God is spirit. Man, created in God's image has spiritual existence, not as something added to his bodily substance, but as the expression of that concrete body-mind unity which he is as a person."[10]

This is *not* to equate "Spirit" or the metaphysical "divine" with a super- or supra- (this latter in the sense of over, above, not touching) natural entity as has often been the case over the past millennia. Rather, creation is

---

juxtaposition of thought, experience, and presents a way of bringing these together in the context of understanding and explicating spirituality in our postmodern context in his book *What in the World Is God Doing?*

10. Williams, *Spirit*, 3.

the self-communication of the divine (in the Judaic and related traditions), not in a dualistic or reified understanding of separate identities but as the dialectic expressed by Masao Abe in this chapter's epigraph. In the Christian tradition "God's" Ultimate Reality is not static, sufficient within itself. This is, in a more developed way, what the concept of "Trinity" expresses: the self-communication, emptying presence, of that "Ultimate Reality."

There is in this way of understanding a cycle or circle of selfless self-communication, self-emptying, deconstructing or de-ultimizing in order to affirm creation. For the Christian, this self-communication in human creation takes the form of Jesus Christ, "who did not regard equality with God as something to be exploited; but emptied himself" (Phil 2:6–7). This is, this cosmic interplay of self-emptying, truly the Christian Ultimate Reality. Spirit is the life of the divine in which the created world participates.

"Spirit" is, here agreeing with Johnston's definition, "the highest outpouring of Being by way of its exemplification in ordinary existents for the sake of the self-disclosure of Being" *to us* as actualized but contingent in creation.[11]

The constant problem which arises when speaking about this "Spirit" or metaphysical "divine" is that thought and speech, the only tools we have to interact and engage with the actualized world, rely on analogous symbols for communication. Thought and speech about the ordinary contains analogy as we represent our experiences to one another. How much more so in thinking and speaking about that which can encompass all reality?

That our thought and speech (and thus religious language and conceptions) proceed by analogy is not in doubt; no religion, especially the monotheisms, would claim that "God" could be contained completely in the "earthen vessels" of thought, word, and deed. But in reconceiving the metaphysical "divine," "Spirit" henceforward, the idolatrous modes and analogous way of thinking and speaking need to be left behind.

In many ways this transition or change will be intellectually and emotionally difficult, finding new words, new thoughts, new "paths" to consider "Spirit" for our world. But in other ways this change has, perhaps, already been anticipated in the conundrums where previous theistic explanations have been found wanting. Prime among these conundrums must be the answering of prayers.

What does it mean for "Spirit" to be active in the world, this *expressive activity*, this outpouring and disclosure? What does "Spirit" do and how does it affect the cosmos, and by extension—me?

---

11. Johnston, *Saving*, 158.

Chapter 18

Consider—

"My God, my God, why have you forsaken me?" (Ps 22:1, repeated in Matt 27:46 and Mark 15:34).

"See he [meaning God/Yahweh] will kill me; I have no hope; but I will defend my ways to his face" (Job 13:15).

"Into your hand I commend my spirit" (Ps 31:5, repeated in Luke 23:46).

The questions ending the last chapter are paramount to our understanding of Spirit. The second, "What does 'Spirit' do and how does it affect me?" contains the seeds of the first idolatry of past millennia that needs to be discouraged, the implication of a cosmic fixer who intervenes to "make things right." A host of issues follow from hoping for, or framing "God" as, the One Who Changes Things to my advantage, not the least being the question of theodicy—why does "God" permit evil? Positing "God" or the metaphysical "divine" as a supernatural personal being is the incoherent root cause of the "theodicy problem." If there is a Cosmic Intervener why does this Intervener, who by definition could impede the occurrence of bad things, not set things right?

Such a capricious and arbitrary "divine" who acts in those intermittent "mysterious ways" is not an Ultimate or Highest "divine." Nor worthy of worship or regard in allowing randomly rampant evil while having the power to prevent such evil. Within that conception are millennia of philosophical and theological gymnastics seeking to explicate, define, and justify a needless conceptuality. Rejecting such a supernatural personal being as an all too human projection allows for a clearer and more thoughtful experience of reality and search for moral and spiritual truth.

Looking at Spirit in a new way, removing an interventionist cosmic fixer, changes our orientation to a new way of seeing what may have already been before us. Bad things happen; people pray for a different or better outcome. Most times such intervention does not come. Thus the question of why some prayers are "answered" and some are not. The usual answer is the mysteriousness of God's "Ways." But really this is just special pleading, advantage-seeking, on our part; when it happens we feel "blessed" and when the result is negative we feel let down, not worthy, or somehow to blame for lacking faith. Or, we rail at that mysterious, silent "God" who failed to save us!

Consider, again, the biblical quotations above. In our new perspective, each is both asking why this bad thing is happening, the existential angst we all live with, and answering, "Even so, I shall persevere." In this way all three are examples of the denial of a cosmic intervener, a fixer, by living without the expectation of an intrusion from "outside." The Power and Meaning of Spirit lie not in the remediation of present circumstance, rendering such fixers irrelevant.

At base, what Job is questioning and what the role of cosmic intervention creates is the debasement of the "divine." How can one abused as in the story of Job find relevance in "One" that tests us in such a cruel and ultimately meaningless way? How could anyone "buy into" a "God" that lacks the compassion and love even one *incuratus in se* human can have? The answer is: no one. One need not affirm a faith in a "God" such as that to be faithful to the "divine" reality.

In finding our way to a new conceptuality of Spirit, we discover that Spirit is not an Intervener. Spirit is understood in a new way. The "Power" of Spirit appears in the totality of the laws of the natural realm. The "nature" of Spirit, analogized in "outpouring" or *expressive activity*, is Love, the intricate interrelatedness present in all the cosmos. Such interrelated outpouring, Love, is expressed both divinely and humanly in continual self-emptying, agapeic activity, which itself characterizes the "Will" of Spirit. Through this intimate, interrelated dance we come to understand that Spirit has a stake in creation itself in the outpouring of Self into self and receiving self into Self.[1] Encompassing the totality of the cosmos and lying at the source of the cosmos' Being and Becoming is Spirit.

The second idolatry is defining "faith" as dogmatic belief, an estrangement of "faith" and "reason." If the cosmos, and by extension us, is the concrete, if contingent, expression of the outpouring of Spirit then our ability to reason, the mind (a concept which we will explore later), is also an existent of that "divine" grace. The adherence to dogma is not the primary place of

---

1. "Self," capitalized, to be clear, is understood as analogy as expressed previously. Self and Mind are topics to which this work will return later.

belief. Dogmatic "faith" implies a denial of reason, the mind, the very gift given to us in the *expressive activity* of Spirit.

Placing Spirit at the heart of reality as argued in this work serves an important purpose—the affirmation of a creative and dependable order to the cosmos (strange and counter-intuitive as that cosmos often found to be) capable of rational understanding. The element of a rational, dependable order is foundational to the scientific method. Lest such an emphasis on reason seem to some as antithetical of "faith" and "religion," this is the essence of the Augustinian tradition in Western Christianity—the respect for intellectual values, the rational structure of the mind as reflective of "God's" being. For Augustine faith in reason found the "truth" of God's existence in the very structure of that rational understanding.

Over time such an understanding of reason has needed considerable clearing out in the face of modern thought and scientific inquiry. Prescientific views, limited knowledge and understandings, all became shortcomings in the paradigmatic shifts that have taken place over the past five hundred years. "Faith" too, unfortunately, as a concept became misdirected as belief in dogma, a metaphysical framework, rather than an outlook which sought understanding, trusting in and depending upon divine grace, that "outpouring" into the world which is the premise of this work. Here, too, a new point of view is called for.

Reason, and by extension faith as trust in working toward understanding in the light of the *expressive activity* of Spirit, seeks to comprehend the relations and structures of reality. To be sure there are abstract characteristics to these structures and relations but these comprehensions derive from the concrete, the actualized, through reflection. The abstract "form" or structure is not the "real" or "pure" being as Plato argued; that distinction belongs to the concrete and actualized.

At the same time reason also has its own context and limitations which are recognized in modern science's necessary self-critical and tentative valuations. In a contingent and finite world of existence, reason can be distorted by those defects so well defined by various world religions, but especially pride of intellect along with real and felt estrangement. "But it is men who are prideful, not reason."[2] True rationality recognizes its own limitations and finds truth neither in selfish assertion or domineering behavior but in submitting its judgments to the constant revision of reflective experience.

The limits of reason or rationality can be seen in previous chapters' discussion of Einstein's relativity theories and Heisenberg's uncertainty in quantum physics. Both point to the subjective, contingent factors that play

2. Williams, *Spirit*, 283.

a part in our attempt to scrutinize our world. Kurt Gödel's incompleteness theorems also indicate the ultimate limits of abstract rational judgment—whether in logic, mathematics, philosophy, or any other field—to a complete system of understanding.[3]

What this requires of us is humility in reaching for understanding and the necessity of reaching out beyond the *incuratus in se* self to the richness and complexity of the concrete experience beyond that self.

In positing Spirit as we have in these pages, encompassing, undergirding, and self-disclosing the cosmos, yet not identified with any particularity, the point to be stressed is: our encounter with Spirit is in the interrelatedness, the cosmic entanglement we have seen reality to be, in Self into contingent self as at the same time actualized self is taken into Self enriching Spirit's complexity, and, changing the horizon of potentialities of Being/Becoming Spirit contains. Not in a supernatural relationship but in a supremely natural expression of that interrelatedness. For Daniel Day Williams, and here I agree, that expression is most properly understood as "Love," a Self/self-giving outpouring that finds concrete, human expression in the concept of sacrificial "*agapé.*"

Agapé. Before proceeding this crucial concept needs to be clarified, so that the meaning of this activity is clear. *Agapé* is not the ethical life of ordinary virtue. The large-scale structural defects of human life obstruct or destroy the significance of such contingently based virtue. Even within the philosophical tradition itself there is a form of life which surpasses the virtuous life. This is the ethical life truly lived toward others, in which the "self" is counted as only one among many with no special standing. The interest of those others are on par with your own as equally legitimate.

This radical altruism is *agapé.* But to make sense of this life of *agapé* the necessary religious or spiritual framework within which it operates must itself be clarified if it is to have meaning and power in our lives. Religion itself is a moral challenge, an aspiration to transcend oneself—the "cosmic demand" woven into the cosmos. As a bit of foreshadowing, this is a demand which embraces suffering and contingency. This challenge is not an escape but a call to transformation without the expectation of more for the "self." Jesus, as human, died—"My God, my God, why have you forsaken me"—in this embrace. And it is the nature of this embrace that is the mission of the narrative moving forward.

"But," I hear someone asking in exasperation, "what is the *point* then of Spirit—what does Spirit *do*?!"

3. See Nagel and Newman, *Gödel's Proof,* and Goldstein, *Incompleteness,* for explanations and discussions of Gödel, his theorems, and their impact on mathematics and philosophy.

The query seeks a clarification of an admittedly complex and abstract new understanding of the relationship between "divine" and the world, aka "me." The unstated but underlying assumption is that this is activity "for *me*," my own self. Asking this question also balances precariously on the edge of that cosmic agency which itself is the idolatrous image of a metaphysical "divine" intervener we wish to eradicate. "What does Spirit do?"

Foremost we are graced with being, with existence, without any necessary action on our part. Is that not enough? Even so, the follow up query must surely be: "What good is being if it is also infested with suffering which stifles, shortens, and ultimately erases that being?"

And here we come to the crux of our dilemma in understanding the metaphysical "divine," Spirit: suffering. Our past conceptualities have expected something "outside" of us to effect change, to intervene on our behalf. But to what do these questions of "What does Spirit do?" and "What is the point of Spirit in the face of suffering?" ultimately point?

The religious, spiritual, and existential questions that we all face are:

How should I live so that I can be a happy, good, and decent person in a world and so to find meaning in life?

Why is there suffering? Why does the world seem so antithetical to the desire for happiness and meaning?

These questions themselves raise a myriad of related questions about why things are the way they are and how we can cope with the world as it is.

Why do we desire the outside change agent? We seek a cosmic intervener mainly because we recognize the defective quality of our own (and others') response: that our fears, our shortcomings, doubts, insecurities, self-absorption, all effectively short-circuit our intentions and attempts to live in a right manner. We can recognize Paul's lament, "For I do not do the good I want, but the evil I do not want is what I do. . . . For I delight in the law of God in my inmost being, but I see in my members another law at war with the law of my mind, making me captive to the law of sin that dwells in my members. Wretched man that I am! Who will rescue me from this body of death?"[4]

Our desire for something better, a different way, understandably drives us toward an intervener, a change agent. However, if we are arguing for a new way of thinking, for a conceptuality based in a naturalism, a *panentheistic* cosmic "divine," how do we approach this? What is the remedy?

The struggle in which we here engage is not an avoidance of the pain present in the world, or our own pain and self-absorption. The confusion we experience in this struggle is the beginning of our journey; it is a signal

4. Paul's Letter to the Romans 7:19–24.

of our own deepest yearning for freedom and happiness. Yet this struggle is also indicative of not only the potential present in Spirit's *expressive activity* for the instantiation of this new direction but the continual presence of our *incuratus in se* self. The recognition of this conflict is the beginning of our journey with Spirit.

Chapter 19

God lets himself be pushed out of the world and on to the cross. He is weak and powerless in the world, and this is precisely the way, the only way, in which he is with us and helps us.

—DIETRICH BONHOEFFER[1]

Too often when we consider suffering, polar answers are offered. There is the pessimistic or nihilist determination that this world offers only a negative, "fallen" state. Or, there is the "idealist" viewpoint that says in the end everything will be as it should be—this is an especially traditional Christian assurance. But neither outlook offers a real understanding of the world we actually experience nor a path to realistically understand and address the suffering present to us.

To understand this experiential, and existential, struggle with the world in which we live, we need to consider "suffering" more deeply. What is "suffering"?

Suffering is not an emotion, though it surely can be a component of many emotions we have. Suffering itself, as a concept, has many levels, many meanings and functions. Suffering at its core involves an experience of the world, an experience which in some way shapes or has the potential to shape us, to affect us.

To understand the range that suffering can take consider not only the obvious examples of privation, injury, and death but the more mundane experiences, too. As a child I was required to practice a musical instrument for a definite period of time, and struggle again and again with a musical piece to achieve a correct performance. Or, to go without television or some other favored activity until a chore was accomplished.

1. Bonhoeffer, *Letters*, 360.

Certainly this state of suffering is not equivalent to the suffering of illness or wrong, nor is it the same as a more accomplished performer might experience, either self-critically or at the comments of others, after a performance. But these, too, are suffering—at differing levels, but suffering nonetheless.

Suffering means to be acted upon. Suffering also can involve conforming to another in a relationship, whether parent-child, lover-loved, or one to another in the world. Suffering needs, then, to be understood within the personal context, the history, in which it happens. Suffering thus has both an existential and a situational context, and that context is communicative, between entities. Suffering, in light of the childhood instances noted above, might be considered on some level to have possible positive aspects, too.

Understanding the context and meaning of suffering is worth an extended quotation from Daniel Day William's *The Spirit and the Forms of Love*:

> Human suffering is always a symptom of a problem, a difficulty, a tragedy, a commitment, or a hope. Suffering discloses a need, a yearning, or a disruption. The power of suffering is the power to communicate the spirit's anguish. The truth here is so familiar it seems a commonplace. Yet we know that the deepest discovery in love is that the other suffers for us, and we discover that we love when we suffer for and with the other. Suffering's greatest work is to become the vehicle of human expression [and even at its worst suffering] has the potential of self-disclosure and knowledge of others.

With this in mind we can also find that far from always having a function that is constructive, suffering at times has the character of the self-destructive, the accidental, the senseless. But even amid the tragedy of suffering, such suffering can open up or expose both the true nature of suffering's source and yet become the wellspring from which understanding, growth, and selfless *expressive activity* can arise. Nothing in this latter result of suffering in itself necessarily implies the "peace and harmony" most often associated with that *expressive activity* understood as "love." Growth and understanding, especially as it relates to the uncovering of iniquity, reveals a conflict between the cosmic agapeic demand and contingent reality in which we live.

But even that conflict can become a source for a different response both to suffering and its causes. Understanding the communicative nature of suffering and its contextual setting in our personal experience, suffering's incorporation of the other into our own existential reality, taking the attitudes and emotions of the other in our self, offers new possibilities. We can recognize the weaknesses, hatreds, and frustrations present in both ourselves and the other. In this dynamic flux of interaction we can also recognize, through a continual self-reflection on this communicative experience of self and other, the possibility of personal interaction through the outpouring of Self/self which is the response of love.

In this way suffering has the positive transformative power in love to reconcile, to create new community. If Being/being (and concomitantly Becoming/becoming) entails continual *expressive activity* in the outpouring of Self/self, namely "love," which by definition is interrelational then suffering is necessarily a part of Being/being. This is no longer about human existence but also indicative of the nature of Spirit. Suffering, change, interrelation is a consequence of Self/self-outpouring, is a part of love's definition. The traditional theisms have kept "God" apart from change and suffering, in a sense isolated from the very world "God" created. Those theisms created elaborate conceptualities for the "in but not of the world" nature of "God." In Christianity Jesus' suffering became a substitute, a price paid for "God's forgiveness."

But if love is to be understood in this new way, the metaphysical "divine," Spirit, is already involved with the history of the world, in the story of the creatures of the world which are the existents of Spirit's *expressive activity*. This communion of Self and self, of Spirit and contingent existent, already exists in the continual consequences of the activity of that love in the world, Self into contingent self as at the same time actualized self is taken into Self enriching Spirit's complexity, and, changing the horizon of potentialities of Being/Becoming Spirit contains.

The communion of Spirit and human is revealed visibly in the love communicated from Spirit in and through the human. Absolute and Unlimited love, which is the love of Spirit, is poured out into contingent existence, is at risk to the vicissitudes present in the moment, shares in the profoundest of human experience, and suffers, is affected by that relationship of communion. This is the lesson of the Christian cross. Absolute love, *agapé*, does not shrink from suffering but is Spirit at work, disclosing a salvific intent, uncovering, reconciling and creating relationships anew even as contingent reality attempts to disrupt and separate the result of that *expressive activity*.

The cosmic demand of Spirit in self-disclosure and outpouring, the new orientation toward a Highest Good namely agapeic love, reveals to us that our attitude toward suffering, our own self-will and self-privileging, and our commoditization of how to live (as if it could be taken off a shelf) have been misdirected. Love, agapeic relationship, is experiential, concrete, contingent in the sense that each moment will require a response crafted to suit, not ready-to-wear, a response which will thus add to and change Love in turn presented to the future. In that Love which denies self-privileging in favor of outpouring toward the other, the suffering, the real suffering, of contingent reality is acknowledged.

Let's step back a bit in this topic of suffering.

That suffering is real there can be no doubt. But what, really, is that which we call suffering? If we free ourselves from what we want the world to be like and accept it as it really is in our most thoughtful experience of it, we can gain a different attitude toward the reality in which we live. Much like the Buddhist acknowledgment of the world as it is and that suffering drives from a misapprehension of that world. In both cases there is a salvific, redemptive action in that change of viewpoint.

Suffering takes two forms—natural (including aging and death which are natural and inevitable) and psychological which is, as has been argued previously, the result of "self-love" and "self-privileging," inauthentic "selfhood" whose consequences are desire, ignorance, thirst, greed, and so on.

The cause of suffering occurs on many levels. We tend to focus on those large-scale defects of the world—war, natural disasters, epidemics, terrorism, and pass perpetration of evil deeds. While these are real enough and important, for the most part the suffering that the individual undergoes is much more prevalent, if sometimes subtle, and often more disastrous.

"We are all heroes of our own story." This phrase has made the rounds of popular culture from such authors as Mary McCarthy and John Barth to more recently Rebecca Solnit, Jon Quitt, and George R. R. Martin. When we look at ourselves, we want to see someone special, not an ordinary human subject to the ordinary vicissitudes of life. This is the self-privileging, the self-importance, noted above that finds affront at aging, disease, pain, and death. There is a selfishness in thus seeking escape for ourselves from those realities of contingent, mortal life.

This clinging to an image of self-importance, self-privileging, itself imprisons us by looking for an invulnerable self that does not exist instead of seeing the reality of our actual vulnerability. We look for ways, interior, exterior, supernatural to protect us from the truth of our situation. In the same way that this book argues against a supernatural conceptuality of "God," the metaphysical "divine," in favor of a different, naturalistic, *panentheistic* understanding of that "divine," we need to look at this "self" for which much of the outmoded language, conceptuality, and ultimately religion and spirituality have sought to serve.

Buddhist understanding, a contributing outlook helpful to the task of this work, is aimed at what Mark Johnston (in his *Saving God* and *Surviving Death*, previously referenced) also views as the illusion of self—an abstract image, bifurcated mind constructed from memory or the amalgamation of experiences, the "arena of presence and action." Such inauthentic self, for which mortality is an affront, is a projection of bifurcated consciousness objectifying "self" which does not exist outside of experience, of events experienced. Authentic "self" is not "self-referential" but understands that it is only "cast up" from the flow of experience, constituted by the "myriad of events in the world."[2]

Stated another way, as will be argued going forward, our understanding of our world, and thereby we ourselves, needs to change. The world we experience is in fact a psychological and social construct that creates a "self," ego, as subject contra the "objective" world. This isn't to deny the operation of a "self." A developed sense of "self" is healthy and necessary to functioning in daily life, what in Buddhist terms is considered "conventional" knowledge. The problem arises when our sense of "self" objectifies and separates us from the rest of the world.

As a construct, the "self" can be deconstructed and reconstructed in a more fully integrated and interrelated whole. A whole without dualism. A whole which is the ever-changing process that characterizes the world and by extension an actualization of Spirit.

Returning to the problematic nature of our present conceptuality, the basis of the Western religious outlook, that of "fallen" humanity in need of salvific remedy, is that something is wrong with the condition of being human itself. This is, in essence, the Garden of Eden story. But if we look at the apparent defect of contingency another way, as the tendency of humans toward self-importance, to self-privileging, which is rooted in our very consciousness then the matter may be looked at differently.

Consciousness, Mark Johnston posits, "the arena of presence and action in which and out of which each one of us lives our lives, presents itself as a fundamental context for the worldly happenings that make up the details of one's life. So long as we are alive, we ourselves are always around; every time we wake up in a chair or in bed, there we are, coeval with the appearance and reappearance of the world. And so we operate as if the world just wouldn't be the world unless we were *here*, as it were, at the center of it. In this way it can seem as if we are the fountainhead of the very reality we inhabit."[3]

Each of us find ourselves, as Johnston points out, in the center of this arena of presence and action, "a composite psychological field, consisting of one's perceptual field, the field of bodily sensation, and the field of

2. Abe and Cook, "Response to Gilkey," 95–97.

3. Johnston, *Saving*, 83.

imagination and thought."[4] This arena seems to imply a position or center from which and to which sensation, presentation of the environment, mental and other activity, "self-awareness" occurs. The implied position seems to be within our own head, at the virtual center of all that occurs. This virtual center appears to be the very definition of "me," the "me" *here* as opposed to all else *there*, which encompasses "you" and all else. This virtual position of "me," this arena, presents itself as a special object in need of protection and special treatment, because it is "me."

The argument here is that what most determines our "personal identity" is a unification of our concrete actions, our will toward living—the aspirations we have and put into practice, those activities in which we engage, and the influence we wield in contingent existence—instead of an abstract metaphysical concept which has, in the past, defined, personhood. The concrete precedes, as noted earlier.

Examine, for the moment, the "self," looking deeply into what "self" is and where the idea of "self" leads. There are volumes, and careers, built around trying to define, to "pin down," "self." But self shifts as we try to catch hold; by its nature self is ungraspable.

"When we say, 'I'm old,' we're referring to our body as self. When we say 'my body,' the self becomes the owner of the body. When we say I'm tired,' the self is equated with physical or emotional feelings. The self is our perceptions when we say 'I see,' and our thoughts when we say 'I think.' When we can't find a self within or outside of these parts, we may then conclude that the self is that which is aware of all of these things—the knower or mind."[5]

In positing the non-reality of "self," "non-self" is *not* a nihilistic concept. Rather, as is understood here and throughout later chapters, "the doctrine of non-self means that we are not embodiments of an unchanging self-entity that remains self-identical through time. Permanent selfhood is an illusion. What we 'are' is a system of interdependent relationships—physical, psychological, historical, cultural, spiritual—that, in interdependence with everything else undergoing change in the universe, continuously create 'who' we are from moment to moment throughout our lifetimes. We are not permanent selves that have these interdependent relationships; we are these interdependent relationships as we undergo them. Because these relationships are not permanent, neither we nor anything else in the universe is permanent."[6]

---

4. Johnston, *Saving*, 83.

5. Kongtrül, *It's Up to You*, 5–6.

6. Ingram, "Buddhist-Christian-Science Dialogue," 169–70.

The basic structure of what we call "mind" or "consciousness" is more an orientation toward, a way of organizing, the phenomenological, concrete, and contingent events happening in the world, both "inner" and "outer" states. This structure, the arena of presence and action as Johnston terms it, presents itself in an asymmetrical way with a *here*, which becomes the seat of "self" importance and protection (since this is "me"!) and a *there*, which includes everything else, good and bad, beneficial and detrimental, in opposition to the "self."

The argument here is that "pure experience" (William James's phrase) is the fundamental unity of experience prior to any subject-object distinction. It is

> in the selflessness of pure experience, one finds the ultimate reality that grounds our derivate experience of subject or selfhood and the objective world . . . all subjective and objective realities of conscious experience are forms of this unified state of pure experience.
>
> The self is the "place" where this dynamic of expression and unification happens. At its deepest level, the self just is the "unification" of pure experience.[7]

The mind we call self seems to control what we do, but where and what is it really? If we are to take seriously the naturalism posited in the argument of this book, then we have to conclude that "self," as a separate entity beyond the physical processes of our corporeal body, does not exist. (The argument made for a "soul" or "essence" separate from our physical body will be taken up later but the short summary here is that such a conceptuality is also nonsensical and idolatrous.)

If we then let go of this objective or privileged "self," this "ego mind," we can experience the world around us openly, intelligently examining the phenomenological events presented to our awareness without being tied to a "self" in need of protection or special privileging. This is also a step along the path toward the agapeic outpouring of Self/self which is "self-less-ness," where the appreciation of the world outside the dichotomy of *here* and *there* is possible. Letting go of this self-privileging, self-importance, position allows us to reflect on the world of events without everything in our thoughts and emotions becoming personal to a "self" with regard to pain, or anger, or shortcomings.

This is not to deny that thoughts and emotions arise within our arena of presence and action. But as they do and we allow a selflessness attitude toward them, we can experience reality without the distorted filter of

7. Mitchell, *Spirituality and Emptiness*, 10.

"self-possession," "self-importance," "self-privileging." Of course the fears and reactions of the never-far-away privileged self will arise. They, too, can be examined from that selflessness perspective and become opportunities of further understanding and realization.

In this range of experience comes a sense of a history to this arena of presence and action, a remembered past moving toward an anticipated future shaped by one's own deliberative acts. That life is to be *lived*; but in what manner? According to what direction?

From a practical standpoint, whether we follow it or not, the sense of a meaningful or worthy life is derived from those around us, our community. Other regarding behavior and conceptions, a "conscience," again whether or not faithfully adhered to, seems to be a widespread human value for what is deemed worthy in life. This altruistic viewpoint occurs in the religious and non-religious alike and is a basis for moral behavior.

That self-regard, self-importance or self-privileging, creates a dissonance, a sense of shortcoming in trying to "tip the scales" and creating suffering for ourselves and others is a fundamental truth of the variety of religious expressions around the world. Often the remedy is the establishment of a set of rules or law to correct self-privileging behavior and enforce other-directed actions. But this, too, sets up a cycle of attempts at adherence, failure, recognition and repentance, resolve to improve, and repeated relapse.

This is the source of another idolatry into which we easily fall—the existentially terrified conscience in need of a rigid instrument, a code, to which one might adhere, absolute in its form and delineation of behavior. Such idolatry, in Christian terms, is often seen as "works righteousness," a respectability in following the law but often at the expense of the "letter" or intent, the objective of other-directed activity.

In removing "self" from the place of importance and privilege, one can thus encounter yourself (your arena of presence of action) and the other in egalitarian terms. The legitimate interest of the other is no longer obscured by "self" and is considered as equal to your own. You, the one you "know" most intimately, is only one among many others. As noted above, this radical altruism is known as *agapé*.

Chapter 20

Let the prince then empty himself of his power and supremacy in his heart and concern himself with the needs of his subjects as though they were his own needs. For this is what Christ has done for us, and this is a genuine work of Christian love.

—MARTIN LUTHER[1]

Thou must love God as not-God, not-Spirit, not-person, not-image, but as He is, a sheer, pure absolute One, sundered from all two-ness, and in whom we must eternally sink from nothingness to nothingness.

—MEISTER ECKHART[2]

We live in, have lived in for quite some time actually, a period in which religious or spiritual thought and conceptuality face a range of challenges. The context for this crisis of religion and spirituality is the sociohistorical cultural ethos of the modern world in which the question of how to authentically express such a message is challenged by the very investigation, knowledge, and insight which has made this technological world possible.

From the standpoint of Christianity the consequence of the faith's historic deep tie to the "pure transcendence of God," a transcendence of transcendence, is a profound alienation from the historical and cultural world.[3] But Christianity is not alone in being challenged. The wider sociohistorical context mentioned above provides the backdrop for the variety

1. In Brown, *Divine Humanity*, 28.

2. In Huxley, *Perennial Philosophy*, 32.

3. See Altizer's "Buddhist Emptiness and the Crucifixion of God," in Cobb and Ives, *Emptying God*, 72–73.

of present irreligious ideologies from Marxism to traditional Freudian psychoanalysis to nihilism, but especially "scientism"—the claim that the "scientific" method provides the one and only criterion for truth, that anything "nonscientific" is false. In many ways those challenges were brought on by religious thought itself.

The backlash of fundamentalism, a retreat from science and modern intellectual introspection, poses a significant challenge, too, if from another direction. This latter may be a more intractable problem in that reason and intellectual discovery seem antithetical to the expression and transformation of faith and spirituality. One cannot overlook such a challenge. But the arguments made by many contemporary theologians, and especially those made in the present work, would be seen from a fundamentalist perspective nothing less than a (thinly) veiled atheism.

The issue always at hand but always elusively difficult to address to the satisfaction of all is that of adequate evidence or argument. Whether the arguments made in these pages are useful in reconceiving and reconstructing is left to the reader.

Too often assumptions and paradigms from which previous religious language and conceptuality arose are stultified, calcified, rigid in outlook, and not able to transform in a cumulative way with the growth of human knowledge and understanding.

The lack of such progress, or process, has led religious thought to a point in which fundamental and radical transformation of basic assumptions is necessary so that a new paradigm or new conceptuality can emerge. Thus the argument in the direction of the past few chapters. Such transformation is crucial if religious and spiritual thought is to be seen as a valid and viable component of modern life.

From the preceding chapters the prominent status of science in our understanding of the cosmos should be clear. Religion and science do not in themselves necessarily contradict each other either. There are points of difference but not in mutually exclusionary ways and religion and science at least have the potential of being compatible with each other.

However, scientism's absolutist claims for the "scientific method" as the one and only basis of truth, that anything nonscientific is false, is definitely not compatible. Under this rubric, religion, being nonscientific, is by definition false and dismissible as an anachronistic fossil of pre-scientific thinking. As we have seen in past chapters, though, even the "scientific method" is not a paradigm without challenges.

Scientific understanding of our cosmos has evolved over time. Classical physics based on mathematical rationality and a mechanistic "objective" view of nature has given way to a contemporary physics much more relativistic and process oriented in its "objectivity," complexity, and richness of aspect and patterns. There is, however, a difference between critical rationality (and thereby autonomous reason) that examines not to produce truth values but to appraise theories critically and is itself open to criticism, and the rationalism which absolutizes and mysticizes the rational factor dogmatically.

In reconceptualizing the metaphysical "divine," Spirit, as totally *kenotic*, a self-emptying to absolute "nothingness" which is itself the fulfillment of Being/being, Becoming/becoming, in agapeic embrace of the concrete, contingent cosmos there is no longer the dualism of worlds, natural and religious, and autonomous reason and modern rationalistic subjectivity are preserved.

This fundamental understanding of the metaphysical "divine" was aptly framed by Masao Abe,

> God is not God (for God is love and completely self-emptying);
> precisely because God is not a self-affirmative God, God is truly
> a God of love (for through complete self-abnegation God is to-
> tally identical with everything including sinful humans).[4]

God, the metaphysical "divine" here termed Spirit, becomes "not God" through that self-emptying outpouring and by that activity God is thus truly God. The necessary corollary is in the existential understanding of the human "self" in agapeic outpouring from the previous chapter that the self is not self and precisely because it is not, self truly is self. By this latter, as will become clearer in this narrative, "not self" is not an emptiness but a recognition of the interrelatedness, interdependence, interpenetration of the cosmos so that there is no "thing" as "self," singular and independent.

In both cases "emptiness" does not refer to a *static* state but a *dynamic movement*, not a noun form but a verbal form of "dynamic and creative function of emptying everything and thereby making alive everything."[5]

The object in these formulations is to step away from dualistic notions of self and other, absolute and contingent in a way which allows for the interplay of the ceaseless movement of emptying Self into self and self into Self continually in the present moment, right now, right here. Emptiness, far from being negatively understood, finds in this a positive salvific meaning by defining the new orientation in life which holds the soteriological promise of spiritual life.

The meaning of "emptiness" needs to be quite clear here because language itself can be and often is limiting and full of ambiguity in expressing thought, particularly when such conceptuality does not originate within

---

4. Abe, "Kenotic God and Dynamic Sunyata," in Cobb, *Emptying God*, 16.

5. Abe, "Kenotic God and Dynamic Sunyata," in Cobb, *Emptying God*, 33.

a given cultural structure. "Emptiness" is not a nihilistic concept of void-ness, nullity, or the like. "Emptiness" is better understood positively as the interdependent and interrelated pattern of order that runs through nature. "Emptiness" is interdependent being as contrasted with the atomized "self," the independent "ego-self." So that, rather than nihilistic concept, "empti-ness" expresses the creative potential lying at the heart of the phenomeno-logical world.

Neither formulation limits nor denies the place of autonomous ratio-nal thinking. Intellectually, in Western thought, reason and rationality has had a less suspect stature as compared to Eastern and specifically Buddhist tradition. However, beginning with Christianity's accommodation with Greek thought for the purpose of evangelization the categories and con-ceptualities of rationality have become increasingly problematic since the sixteenth and seventeenth centuries as a modern scientific understanding of our world has grown. In contrast to the traditional Christian conceptuality of divine revelation which is perennially at odds with human reason, the *panentheistic* Spirit presented in this work rather than negating the contin-gent or human rationality intentionally embraces the contingent, the object of and the subject for human rationality, as the arena of dynamic activity.

Having hung with me thus far and enduring what at times seems ob-scure and esoteric, the reader might rightly ask, "So what? Why is all this really important? Why is a concern about religion, spirituality, or whatever something I should care about? What does it really mean for me?"

There are three aspects to consider in order to answer this challenge.[6] The first aspect, and perhaps the most obvious, is that of the world as ex-perienced through the scientific investigation and engagement, "natural" science so to speak.

In this first perspective on the cosmos natural phenomena all have co-equal status. Tidal waves, earthquakes, the sun shining, viruses and bacteria growing (and dying), rain soaking the earth enabling life to grow, mate-rial decaying, and so on. All these result from necessary natural processes, neither desirable nor undesirable. Absent the human context the world "is," without evaluative qualifications of "good" and "bad." Even the struggle of life as wolf eats lamb or cow eats grass is not considered malicious but a part of the instinctive cycle of survival. No more than the wind blowing gently or at hurricane force, or a flower blooming or withering.

Without the projection of human values and feelings, these events just *are*.

---

6. Abe's discussion in Cobb, *Emptying God*, 46–50, is very helpful in clarifying these questions and is the basis for the narrative that follows.

But layering on a human perspective these events take on a different, "valued" shape within our "minds." Events, like the tidal waves or viral growth noted above, take on negative definitions as they cause suffering and damage to the human community. Sunshine may be welcome, except when excessively it is a cause of drought; solar storms can cause worldwide electrical outages and other unfavorable events. Spring rains may provide necessary moisture for growing food crops but torrential monsoons cause untold damage and death. One event, from a human perspective, is "good" while the other is considered "bad" due to its effect on human life.

Taking a further step considering human interactions we arrive at the second aspect which is interrelational or communal concerns of human morality, ethics, and social engagement.

In human interactions the judgment of "good" and "bad" in unfavorable or damaging results of human activity as well as positive outcomes take on some clarity. In terms of ethical behavior the qualities of honesty, kindness, responsibility, and so on are considered "good." Lying, dishonesty, stealing, willfully harming or killing, and on are considered "bad" or "evil." One only needs to look at the Bible's "Ten Commandments" or the strictures raised by other world religions to understand these judgments. On the level of community interactions, too, such human communal interactions as peace and war find their place as "good" and "evil."

But humans are not always quite so simple, so easily delineated, in their behavior. Human inner motivation also enters into the ethical equation of whether an action is "good" or "bad," "right" or "wrong." And complicating the matter further is that *incuratus in se* self, the dilemma of the brokenness or defect to which all human endeavor falls prey. Ethics and moral judgment in themselves, as contingently operative, easily become relative.

What, then, could be more fundamental than the ethical or moral dimension?

A third aspect concerns the religious or spiritual dimension. Not a supra- or supernatural state but a perspective which grasps the essential nature of reality in a different way. In this religious or spiritual aspect the natural phenomenon of the first aspect is incorporated experientially and subjectively, not objectively, without the hierarchy of human valuations superimposed by our "personal" interests.

In this the division of sacred and secular/profane, "divine" and "human," or in Buddhism "emptiness" and "fullness," are overcome. True emptiness is identified with true fullness in the outpouring *expressive activity*, the "divine" and the "human" find a dynamic interrelation in the self-emptying, kenotic nature of Spirit and human of the cosmic demand. The whole web of creation, interrelated and interconnected, *is*, grasped subjectively and experientially as a unitary whole.

This realization of the essential nature of reality does not thus preclude the working of that *expressive activity, agapé*, to pull creation through compassion and love toward a better future, only not through self-interest but by its very denial.

What of human "free will" and responsibility for human actions?

None of what has been said thus far negates responsibility for one's actions. In one sense because of the interrelatedness of all things we share in one another, in the totality of actions good and bad whether we have a direct, phenomenological connection or not. In a deeper sense, casting the responsibility for the "bad" or the "evil" on an abstract "sin" or "sinful nature" is only a protective cover for our "self" protection. Whatever the ground, occasion, or opportunity for an action we are not free from responsibility; we bear responsibility in commission as part of the "self" will to be.

This is what raises the very issue of "free will." The literature on human "free will" spans religions and millennia, from Western Judeo-Christian-Islamic traditions to Eastern traditions of Buddhism, Taoism, and Hinduism, and philosophical works, most notably in the West, Kant and Nietzsche. A thorough discussion of these traditions, thoughts, and conceptualities would take more space than available here, and are much more competently done elsewhere.

However, the basic direction argued for in this work is that what is commonly termed "free will" is just as illusory as the ego-minded "self" of self-importance and self-privileging. In the abnegation of this "self," the self-emptying outpouring of *agapé* (the death in Christ of Rom 6:8, 2 Cor 4:10 and 13:4; the Great Death of Buddhism), arrives or is realized the fulfillment of a new orientation of life (the resurrection to new life of the foregoing; the Great Life of Buddhism).

Human free will is realized as a new pure form unattached to "self." Not in a transcendental or "formal" way of pure reason as in Kant nor transcendent "divine" will divorced from contingent reality. This free will is "pure" and "free" by the very act of self-emptying and self-negation without subject or object. It is free will in the kenotic Self/self, the *expressive activity* of Spirit.

This free will is still one's free will but at the same time it is not one's free will but the free will of Spirit, breaking the duality of sacred and secular, transcendent and temporal into a dynamic unity, an intentional focus on the other through agapeic compassion and activity. In turn, this dynamic unity becomes the criterion for value judgment in the third aspect mentioned above.

Chapter 21

As a dialectical existence, each of us is identical with and living at the intersection of temporality and eternity, particularity and universality, immanence and transcendence. This is why in Christianity Jesus said, "The Kingdom of God is within you" (Luke 17:21).

—MASAO ABE[1]

We live in the intersection of two poles or aspects to our existence: the sociohistorical which is contingent and which is filled with distinctive existents—what in Buddhist terms is called "conventional," and the transcendent or metaphysical in which such distinction falls away to nondistinction and equality. Both are intimately tied together as occasion or condition (in the former) and ground or source (in the latter) of existence. Neither occurs without the other. Both are necessary and interdependent if the conditional is to avoid the trivialization of meaninglessness without fundamental grounding—Buddhist "emptiness" which is dynamically empty and full, and Christian kingdom of God within and Lutheran *simul justus et peccator* (simultaneously saved and sinner)—and if the metaphysical is to avoid abstraction without its occasion in the particular—Christianity's Jesus Christ as true human and true God; Buddhism's *Śūnyatā* in which emptiness and fullness are dynamically identical.

The metaphysical as a "pole" or aspect to our existence is often thought of as unreal since it is not "test-able" in the sense of scientific inquiry. As has already been argued, such an absolutism over scientific method becomes a "scientism" ideology which is itself counter to the scientific methodology and even modern scientific understanding. Beyond that, however, consider

1. Abe, in Cobb, *Emptying God*, 174–75.

that not all things that are real are themselves concrete, even if connected or related to something contingent.

Potential is real, material, in the sense that it is the necessary predicate for actuality: Being and Becoming. Acorn and potential oak tree. The *change* from one to the other is also real; *process* is also material and real, involving the interrelation of various existents to produce. The division between immaterial and material is, perhaps, an illusion. A word appears on paper, it is made of something. A word or concept appears in your mind, it too is made of something.

Consciousness is real, material, as it is made of something (though the nature of that "something" is a later topic). From an Eastern perspective it is made from a something which forms the basis of reality where our individual iteration is merely an illusion of separateness from the greater connectedness.

Rather than approach reality with a dualistic either-or, this-that, mindset, another way is to understand reality, all of existence, as an interrelated whole. That which we consider an individual *whole* is actually an aggregate or plurality which is perceived, contingently, as a unity. Even the attempt to "breakdown" the elements of reality to a fundamental "simple"[2] is problematic. Plato and Aristotle, even granting their quite different scientific conceptuality of the world, would agree. For Aristotle substance is "within which we distinguish principles, causes, and elements." (*Physics*) Substance is not only matter but the source of all there is, tangible and intangible and yet substance cannot be understood apart from its qualities or manifestations, actualizations, and so cannot be reduced to a "simple."

Later, David Hume argued in *Treatise of Human Nature* that we have no idea of external substance, distinct from the ideas of particular qualities. We have the notion of mind only from particular perceptions the mind has of particular objects. These particular qualities are signs and roads backwards toward substance, as Aristotle held, tangible and intangible, scientific, artistic, religious, cultural. Nature, to Hume, therefore had multiple dimensions—aesthetic, physical, social, psychological, and so on, each essential and fundamental, none existing in isolation but in an interrelated, overlapping schema.

What exists cannot be understood apart from its qualities or manifestations, not to be broken down to a "simple," an irreducible jot, but seen as

---

2. A "simple" is anything that has no proper parts. The use of "simple" is not restricted to material objects. Anything, no matter what ontological category it is from, is a simple if and only if it has no proper parts. An atom (or "simple") was understood to be an entity with no proper parts, but we now know atoms to be much more complexly composed.

a complexity of potentiality and actuality. To try to reduce reality to some fundamental "atom," a singular "what," is perhaps misguided. There is no "simple" but a complex or complexity at the very root of reality.[3]

As scientific investigation has become more fine grained we have progressed beyond the atom to ever smaller "units" which seem to comprise what seemed elementary at first. Perhaps the search for a final "absolute" is wrong directed and not fruitful. Even such a conception as string theory as a "unified" explanation is itself intricately complex, a web of simple yet intertwined traits, properties, and powers. The universe itself, as has been the argument made here, is a network of relationships. Even from a quantum perspective, there can be no one simple and final universal perspective.

This is not to deny our present scientific understanding of sub-atomic particles, field theories, quantum mechanics and the like but only to point out that present knowledge and theory are always challenged and at the cusp of ever finer understandings of the workings of the cosmos.

The realization of the complexity and interrelatedness at the root of reality creates a new understanding for the conceptualities related to the metaphysical "divine," what is being termed here Spirit, and the associated (Christian, as that is the tradition from which I come) views of Jesus, and conceptions of life, death, sin and salvation, consciousness, and community.

In the dialectical encounter of "source" and "condition" are Spirit and self-world. But not in a dualistic "this or that," "one or the other" sense but in a deep interrelation which even as the two are essentially and qualitatively different from one another they are also inseparably connected with each other in the lived reality of human existence. We, as humans, as the world, live constantly at this intersection, experiencing the temporal and eternal, the physical and the metaphysical not in objectified phenomenological measurement but in existential encounter. This is what is meant in offering the Judeo-Christian-Islamic notion of the reality of the metaphysical "divine," or in Buddhist Śūnyatā.

We make a constant mistake when we objectify "God" or Spirit, thinking of the divine in an object/subject relationship, as a "thing." Spirit, or "God," is an activity, a motion, a word into which we try to pour the interdependent creative "nature" that describes Spirit and creation. How do you capture sunlight in a jar?

From this encounter, we might then understand that "belief in God is not a matter of believing in the proposition that he exists; it is an orientation in which the Highest One comes into view with salvific effect."[4] In properly

---

3. The reader is referred again to Buchler, *Metaphysics*.

4. Johnston, *Saving*, 16.

relating to Spirit a person awakens to a more fundamental point of reference for existence and is thereby saved.

What then of Spirit, this metaphysical "divine," the "new model God"? How should we understand how Spirit works, interacts, saves?

To begin, let's look at what the traditional view has given and how it fails to present an understanding of that "divine" for the modern world, for that notion of "God" and "divine activity" essentially removed the "divine" from the mundane, everyday world in which the believers exist.[5] What follows is framed around the defects Charles Hartshorne enumerated in *The Divine Relativity*.[6] In this work we are attempting to construct an understanding which allows reverence for, and seeks new ways to worship Spirit, the metaphysical pole or aspect to existence, not the doctrines of our ancestors.

The basic deficiency inherited, as has been argued throughout, is an otherworldliness which values flight from this world and the one common task presented to us in the Judeo-Christian-Islamic traditions: concern for the welfare of this creation, in favor of another "heavenly" realm divorced from the divinely created universe.

In Western thought and culture we tend toward labeling and abstracting to create universal but discrete formats for describing and interpreting things, events, and experiences. Perhaps this is a part of the human tendency to stereotype, produce a "shorthand" descriptor for those things, events and experiences.

But this abstraction, this creation of descriptor forms, can obscure our vision and experience, especially so when they are considered to be themselves actual and independent existents. This becomes problematic for language as we attempt to describe religious or spiritual experience.

In speaking about the "place" of our conscious experiences of knowing, feeling, willing, and reflection, just as in describing "Absolute Nothingness" of Zen as a "place" of the ultimate unification of experience—the "place" of religious consciousness—"place" (or "loci," "matrix," or other substitutes) does not point to a thing of location.

In this "place" all existences subjective and objective find their rest, of being-just-as-they-are in that "all existences reside as interrelated determinations of the place itself."[7] Such a "place" is both Absolute Nothingness (no subject-object dualism) and Absolute Unity. In this sense even "God" as an abstract "object" of worship or regard as "Other" falls away to reveal a deeper context. It is this deeper context, which Zen refers to as "Absolute

---

5. See Moltmann, *Theology of Hope*, 310–16, for criticisms on this point.

6. Hartshorne, *Divine Relativity*, 148–50.

7. Mitchell, *Spirituality and Emptiness*, 11.

Nothingness" and I refer to as "Spirit," which is the metaphysical context for the "cosmic demand," for the "divine" in life.

Not merely transcendent to everything else, this "place" or matrix, is also immanent, penetrating the depths of our everyday experience, embracing all creation. This is religious experience, the "place" of Spirit.

We have seen how the deficiency of divorced dualistic "realms" has led to a deadening of attitude toward others, toward the natural world, our climate. Of course there are exceptions and exceptional people who have prophetically strived to call us back to an awareness of these issues and the need to "repent," to change direction. But those voices have been just that: prophetic, calling for a return, against the overwhelming tide of hostility and, even worse, indifference which otherworldliness engenders.

Against this deficiency, this work argues for a different understanding of the relation of physical and metaphysical, of an inseparable interrelatedness of these two aspects of life. Not by positing a realm, transcendently unchanging and unconnected to the world. This latter has led to the convoluted mental exercises of trying to tie contradictory and exclusionary objects together. Instead the argument here has been for a naturalism that finds the heart of existence in the intersection of the metaphysical and physical within the existential experience of this world.

A second and related deficiency is a concern for or worship of power. This deficiency not only concerns the locus of agency but also the nature of what agency is in a dualism between influence and sensitivity. As in the previous, first deficiency ultimate power is understood as standing outside of the natural order, in a realm beyond the cosmos. Such agency is often characterized as the unlimited capability of overwhelming the natural order, imposing its own will—whether or not this power is actually, always, or everywhere used.

This deficiency has led to all sorts of mischief and conundrums for theologians and philosophers, not the least as mentioned previously the questions of theodicy. If "God" has ultimate agency why would "God" not put an end to suffering, pain, and tragedy? Such a capricious being, if a human, would and should be considered monstrous. No less for this conception of the divine. Ultimate, transcendent power to influence which allows unchecked the evils of the world is, in a very real way, what the story of Job is all about.

And in the end, Job's faithfulness in the face of Yahweh's immense and capricious power (and Yahweh's assertion of moral superiority in Job 30 and 40) makes such a cosmic interventionist power irrelevant. Job's faithfulness (like tested Abraham and tormented Jeremiah), his being morally better than his cosmic tormentor, shatters the need for such a being and provokes the possibility of something more spiritually developed.

This deficiency in the worship of power is also related to the issues (to be addressed later) of sin, evil, and prayer.

Understanding the dynamic of the intersection of metaphysical and physical as has been argued here allows both for the recognition of the validity of natural processes under the scientific method of investigation and also reinterprets "power" in terms of potentiality and actuality as available components or complexes in determining events. The confluence of Self/self in *expressive activity* in the outpouring of Self/self becomes the template for the ultimate intentionality of reality, a supreme power understood as supreme sensitivity to the other.

Related to this deficient understanding of power is what Hartshorne calls "Optimism," a denial that fundamental in the nature of existence, and thereby God or the divine, is tragedy. This recognition also finds expression in Buddhism's First of the Four Noble Truths: a recognition and acknowledgment of the presence of suffering. That suffering exists no one would deny but often the defects of contingent life are viewed as the "wages of sin," as the nature of "fallen creation," a cancellation of any relation the divine has with the world. In such understanding lies a denial of the reality of life as we know it by the dualistic division of the world into "good" and "evil"—the evil flesh and the good divine—by way of those prior deficiencies of other-worldliness and *supra*-power.

The new conceptuality espoused here accepts the world we live in as it is; there is or can be no other. This is not to deny suffering and defect but so that suffering and defect, the contingent, might be seen in a different way. Through a new understanding of the world, ourselves and our place in the cosmos, and the intersection of the metaphysical and physical aspects that frame all existence, we have an opportunity to examine what life is and recreate our understanding of our place in it in hope and a realistic acceptance of the nature of the contingency and especially tragedy we experience.

The next deficiency, again a result of the wholly otherness of the traditional understanding of the divine, is the related division of "physical" and "spiritual" into competing and incompatible valuations. Of course the terms themselves point to differing content but as argued previously the physical and the metaphysical or "spiritual" are inseparable aspects of a whole, neither complete without the other and both contributing to the other. The metaphysical or "spiritual" may be understood as having a broader scope, perhaps, than the physical in the encompassing of potentiality and actuality, but the traditional understandings of these have created a false choice.

The failure to bring together the values of the physical and the spiritual has led to a moral quietism, emphasizing the spiritual—seeking "heaven" and divine authority—to the detriment of alleviating human need. We see this failure in the problematic attitudes of religion in matters of marriage, sexual relations, and sexual orientation. But we also see such attitudes play out in other political and social arenas. At bottom, this failure has devalued not only creation as the experienced arena of value but also the spiritual aspect in denying a sensitive interrelatedness between the world and the divine.

Again, as argued above, the new conceptuality of Spirit seeks to remedy this deficiency by acknowledging the rightful inseparable interrelationship of these aspects of existence. In this new understanding comes an awakening to the salvific nature, to the new orientation toward life, this bond creates.

And, finally, the deficiency of moralism which flows from all the rest but is most acutely understood in the context of the false choice of "spiritual" over "physical." This deficiency centers around "the notion that serving God is almost entirely a matter of avoiding theft and adultery and the like, together with dispensing charity, leaving noble-hearted courageous creative action in art, science, and statesmanship as religiously neutral or secondary."[8]

This deficiency effectively deprives the world of agapeic interaction demanded by the cosmos by diverting the locus and the focus of both human and divine engagement to a disengaged realm of "spiritual" deeds and treasure. Such attitude also disallows the positive and conscientious engagement of others "outside" the circle of particular belief from having any efficacy.

In very simple terms, the "Golden Rule"—treat others the way you would wish to be treated—cuts across world religions and cultures, even if stated or understood in differing emphases. Found as early as Confucian times (551–479 BCE) this aphorism is found in Buddhism, Judaism, Christianity, Islam, Hinduism, Taoism, Zoroastrianism, and almost all ethical traditions. This is not an attitude cultivated by nor exclusively the property of a particular theism or religion, indeed one need not have a religious or theistic underpinning at all. And yet, the intention of other-directed service is clear.

Nor is such engagement limited to charitable acts. Such a universal aphorism points out, and the conceptuality argued here entails, the necessary involvement in world to the care and betterment of that world and the

8. Hartshorne, *Divine Relativity*, 149.

beings in it. This includes the messy and contingent activities of political and social engagement, discussion, and action. Not with a framework of rigid, transcendent "laws" but in a compassionate engagement of sensitive mutuality.

In summary, to quote Hartshorne at length:

> A wholly absolute God can provide no lasting good inclusive human achievement save by the dubious notion of an everlasting prolongation of individual or racial human existence, even then present human achievement is not intelligible integrated into the permanent achievement. A wholly absolute God is power divorced from responsiveness or sensitivity; and power which is not responsive is irresponsible and, if held to settle all issues, enslaving. . . . [A wholly absolute God is divorced from all human, physical or sensory value and experience, deriving nothing from Creation, uninfluenced or touched by tragedy . . .] and is a contradiction in terms.[9]

How then does Spirit operate? Spirit encompasses all of creation, its potentiality and actuality, returning that potentiality and actuality in the self-emptying outpouring, "influencing" by way of the interrelatedness of all things, working toward the kenosis of all things for all things as the highest awareness of creation's reality. In the same breath all of creation's potentiality and actuality as co-creator, as meaningful existent, is given back to, is sensitively incorporated into Spirit and so is woven the garment of creation.

9. Hartshorne, *Divine Relativity*, 149–50.

Chapter 22

Nowhere is that paradox, that "inscrutability," [that the gospel is "in" but not "of" the world] more evident than in the cross. A symbol of death and defeat, God turned it into a sign of liberation and new life. . . . But we cannot find liberating joy in the cross by spiritualizing it, by taking away its message of justice in the midst of powerlessness, suffering, and death. . . . The lynching tree is the cross in America. . . . The cross is a reminder that the world is fraught with many contradictions—many lynching trees.

—JAMES CONE[1]

We have journeyed quite a way in the quest to understand that Spirit, "God," is not an entity, not a person, but a word (among many human words) used to put a name to the basic mystery present in life: why am I here, what am I for, why do bad things happen and where is there justice in the face of the amoral, if not immoral, universe? But the word is not the thing, and is especially not that to which reverence is due.

Spirit names one of the poles at the intersection of the inseparable components of existence, and itself signifies integrated, interrelated non-duality. This word is one of the names we give to the power or force that enables a finite and broken humanity to draw life, something positive, out of the deep well of suffering which is the constant in existence. This power is transformative, that is we are enabled, if we are willing to surrender ourselves to that force, to affirm community, love, a solidarity of compassion, in the face of an unfeeling universe or others which take no notice, if not actively seeking to negate, our existence.

Created nature itself is not a state, though it would perhaps be considered a process. More to the point, "creation" as a term juxtaposes something

1. Cone, *Cross and the Lynching Tree*, 156–59.

actualized to a no thing, or unactualized potential. Created existence, because it involves living and changing is "finite," is "limited," is time-full, in flux. That finitude precludes a progressivity toward an ultimate goal, a utopia, within creation.

In that this finitude contains within it the very contingency and occasions of suffering which prompt our religious or spiritual quests, finite creation often becomes synonymous with "sin" or a "fallen" state contrasted to a transcendent and absolutely good "Other." We seek redress; we want rescue. In our confusion of deity and humanity in an attempt to create an infallible answer to our problems we jettison the time-full flux of creation for a self-declared, self-directed assumption of omniscience of the true "end of things," however well intended, to the detriment of other beings.

Looking at suffering and tragedy in a different, new way, as fundamental to the nature of existence, not as a sinful or fallen state, we find a way that does not deny or negate creation as an arena of redemption and spiritual understanding. We find that understanding the nature of our existence and the inseparable intersection of the metaphysical and physical creates a transformation, a new orientation, in salvific language—"redemption."

From the Christian perspective, the greatest symbol expressive of this state is the cross. The cross is a symbol of this transformative power, the tragic and the suffering out of which is drawn a dawn of life and solidarity and unity. This is the meaning of the redemptive power of God.

In suffering, in tragedy, we can react with anger, striking out, with withdrawal into ourselves, with negation of ourselves and those around us, or we can surrender to the transformative power of love, compassion, of holding one another closer in solidarity against the storm-tossed seas of Life. Unfortunately, the cross has become not the stumbling block that Paul described, pointing to the enigma of suffering and powerlessness becoming transformed to meaningfulness and life, but a symbol emptied of that power and presented as a club of obedience, a marketing icon of political agendas, and thoughtless sentimentality. To recapture the power in this symbol will require a redirection of understanding.

In twentieth and twenty-first-century America, the true cross has become the lynching tree, here referring to James Cone's *The Cross and the Lynching Tree*. This image, whether an actual tree or the lynch mob death of blacks, Indians, gays, captures the power the cross once carried for early Christians and clearly displays in graphic detail the anguish and despair the brokenness present in contingent life. But is it not also true that the transformative power of brutal death into life also takes place within, among, and through our contingent existence?

What is the content of this death into life if not a new understanding which, like the jettisoning of self-privileging and self-love above, does *not* seek reward but is an outpouring of love, a self-emptying of self, that looks for nothing in return. For the Christian, this kenosis and salvation, "death and resurrection of Christ," find its first fruits in a "new life," a transformed and new orientation toward existence.

All of us are capable of wrong-doing to one extent or another; we are like sharks in the sea of life—our voraciousness, our appetite for self-centered action to assert our being in the face of an amoral and unfeeling universe, in the face of annihilating Death, is but our nature. Against that world of contingency and self-privileging we have set government and civilization to restrain that "sharkiness," to keep that nature at bay. But we also realize that such institutions are also fallible and contingent. Thus, we find that "sharkiness" is part of the environment against which the cross / lynching tree symbolizes the transformative power of love, of life recreated in Beloved Community.

The argument here attempts to push the power of this transformative symbol of salvific grace, inch by inch, back from an exclusive (in the Christian tradition) emphasis on "the redemptive activity of God" to an understanding of this grace in creation, the goodness and loving-kindness of the divine in and toward creation, the fidelity and presence of the divine in all creation. Nature is continuous with Spirit and Spirit encounters humanity, all nature really, in the flux of historical passage. In so framing this transformative power the scope of such occasions of grace is enhanced throughout the entire creation.

Occasions of grace are found in the structures of family, society, economic order, indeed the whole world. Such a way of speaking about the action of Spirit invites participation in these structures as gifts and opportunities, giving hope to despair, strength to live and work in the ambiguity of our world, and a sense of freedom and partnership with Spirit in the process of "new orientation."

With all this in mind, let us look a little closer at suffering, tragedy, and sin from a different perspective.

Chapter 21 discussed the three poles or aspects in which we can view the world, the nonhuman and purely natural "scientific," the individual and collective moral/ethical, and the metaphysical/religious. The metaphysical/religious aspect, it was argued, is the more fundamental and wide-ranging of the three and so is the lens through which understanding is best delivered.

That suffering and tragedy exist is not disputed but how we understand the meaning of suffering and tragedy can make a difference in how we see our world, our place in it, and derive meaning.

The natural world, that first aspect discussed previously, is not corrupt, fallen, or a place of sin. It is the product of natural processes, which humans have been able to study about, theorize over, and establish meaningful knowledge about that has, for the most part, been of benefit to the world.

Has there been calamity, tornadoes, earthquakes, eruptions, meteor strikes, and the like with devastating consequences for life forms? Of course. But in and of themselves these naturally occurring events are not of good or bad valuations. They just are; valuation in terms of good and bad, positive and negative, comes with a judgment as to how such an event affects the "self." Probably not just the human aware "self" but that is at this point all that we can be sure of.

Therefore, if creation qua natural processes is not itself sinful and suffering caused by natural processes is a product of the judgment of "self," then the locus of understanding sin and suffering must be found elsewhere.

However, before moving on, a corollary of the deficiencies already mentioned needs specific emphasis. In the "self"-centered orientation, which I am arguing is at the center of much of the problematic conceptuality of the "divine" and of "sin" and suffering, lies the notion that the cosmos, created nature, is a mere stage upon which we, the "self-aware," conduct our lives. This idea of a passive nature that has no independent standing of valuation unless humans deem it so has permeated our religions and theologies, especially in the Western traditions.

From the Western Christian tradition this has meant that nature is a poor, secondary player, if at all. But if, as argued here, all creation truly is to be a part of this interconnected, interrelated web of inseparable metaphysical and physical, then the natural world should have equal footing in consideration with the "self-aware" human. Western Christian tradition has truly lacked a creation theology that values the world as the world for itself and not as merely utilitarian for humanity.

A true creation theology would take seriously the ecology of natural processes, value the natural world of processes for itself. Instead, we have been living with an exploitative understanding of "dominion" and "domination," using and then despoiling and throwing away. This has led to the current climate crisis which not only the "self-aware" human faces but large swaths of other living beings.

Though the production of such a theology is not the present task, the reader is directed to investigate how such might be done.[2]

2. Specifically, for the struggle to come to terms with a creation theology from the Christian perspective, the reader is urged, as a starting place, to look at Sittler, *Essays on Nature and Grace*; Cho, *Ecological Vision of the World*; Horrel, *The Bible and the Environment*; and authors such as John Cobb Jr. and Rosemary Ruether, as well as Pope Francis's

If the natural world as natural world (i.e., natural processes) is not where we locate our consideration of suffering, tragedy, and sin, where do we turn? This question leads us back to the second pole or aspect considered previously, the human or transhuman arena of activity, ethics, and morals.

Of course such natural phenomena as tornadoes, epidemics, earthquakes, asteroids and the like cause suffering and tragedy. As has been argued, these are natural phenomena caused by natural processes. They might be considered to have "positive" and "negative" effects on other parts of the interrelated whole of nature, but really "positive" and "negative" are only projections of human feelings and interests. The occasion of an earthquake is not any different than the blowing of the wind. The tiger devouring its prey is only a manifestation of its impulse to survive. To apply the label of "bad" or "evil" to such events in the nonhuman natural "dimension," if you will, is to view them through the lens of human valuation and not as they should be: through the lens of natural laws.

So, then, if the valuations of "good" and "bad/evil," "positive" and "negative," are products of this second aspect of our existential life, how do we move forward toward an understanding of these valuations and "sin."

In this second human aspect the value judgment, individual and collective, of actions takes place. Such valuation might be somewhat clearer in that ethically the qualities of honesty, kindness, responsibility, courage, integrity and the like are considered positive. In opposition, the qualities of lying, cheating, stealing, killing, betrayal, are considered bad or evil. In the sense of collective humanity peace is considered positive and war, famine, conflict as evil. However, even with this in mind, ethically the judgment falls more heavily on one's motive to do good than outcome especially when personal conditions might militate against such a motivation.

Humans, however, are complex to state the obvious. Our motivations are a mixture of altruism and self-desire. We do not always follow simple ethical and moral codes. Earlier in this work, Paul's Letter to the Romans was quoted to eloquently make this point, "For I do not do the good I want, but the evil I do not want is what I do. . . . For I delight in the law of God in my inmost being, but I see in my members another law at war with the law of my mind, making me captive to the law of sin that dwells in my members" (Rom 7:19–23). On a solely human level, we can perceive ethical and moral principles; we can experience and name suffering and tragedy that result from phenomena, especially those events and actions with origin in human activity. But here, too, we find ethical and moral dilemmas in the relative

---

encyclical on creation, *Laudato si'*. Numerous articles on the subject are spread across a wide variety of religious journals of various faiths and interreligious groups.

distinctions of good and evil, the complex entanglement of motivation and outcomes, which occur in a contingent, finite world.

Perhaps here we are closer to an understanding of what "sin" might be; for here lies the third aspect, the metaphysical inseparably interrelated but with a more fundamental basis in our existence. From this third perspective, the phenomena of the natural processes of the world can be seen more neutrally. From a traditional theistic perspective they might be viewed not as "good" or "bad" but as a manifestation of unfathomable divine "will." From the perspective of, say, Buddhism, the natural phenomena are also neither "good" or "bad" but just *are* as subjectively experienced.

Leaving the occurrence of natural phenomena aside and focusing more on the intersection of the metaphysical with human activity, we can immediately see the "linchpin." From the perspective of the Christian (again, from which tradition I come) "sin" is *not* just separate evil acts or the accumulation of individual acts. "Sin" is the disobedience of, the rebellion against, "God's laws." Throughout the Bible the emphasis is on the turning away from God by the willful "self." The Torah and the Prophets and so then too the Christian New Testament emphasize the right orientation of "self" toward the divine and how that "self" has turned away, justified "self-privileging," and even attempted to turn the divine "law" to the purpose of "self" desire.

What is the purpose, then, of these metaphysical "laws" however delineated and the biblical testimony directed toward the world? These "laws" define the correct relationship or orientation one ought have with the divine and toward creation, and the need for redemption, for a salvific change, a turning around.

For most all religions, the alienation from correct relationship or orientation, "sin," is considered universal and basic to the fact of being contingent and human. In nontheistic Buddhism the dualism of divine and secular, good and evil (in an absolute sense) drops away in favor of an ultimate interrelatedness and interdependency of everything; nothing independent or self-existing. In this *no thing* is true emptiness which is dynamically identical with true fullness. The salvific purpose in Buddhism is the realization of this Śūnyatā, subjectively and experientially.

Even though very distinct and different in ontological outlook, the point is that the nature of the salvific intent in both is directed toward a right understanding of or orientation toward this third, metaphysical aspect of existence. For the purpose here the significance is understanding "sin" as the lack of this orientation and the salvific message as the redemption, "new orientation," already present and "on offer" through the *expressive activity*, the outpouring of Spirit self-emptying to creation. For the Buddhist, the

salvific message lies in the awakening to the reality already present identified in the term *Śūnyatā*.

This new orientation or "new life," viewed from a *panentheistic* Christian interpretation, is by turn one that mimics the kenotic activity of Spirit
by the "self's" kenosis, self-emptying in agapeic interrelation with Spirit and
creation. In so understanding the divine, Spirit, in relationship to creation
we find a ground that goes beyond the "self" involved life. This Self/self-
emptying is not a projection of our common desire to control our lives that
eludes our physical powers. In this outpouring we might begin to recognize
or glimpse what a highest ideal of love and compassion might be, that emptying Self/self-gains or defines fullness of Self/self.

The problem inherent in viewing "sin" as individual acts or a collection
of such acts is that such a view ignores the wider dimension of the historical, social, and collective nature of this blindness to "self" privileging, "self"
interest, "self" love inherent in human existence. Recognizing my own personal place within this universal thirst for "self" thereby entails my share
and responsibility, in the deepest sense, in all such events from white or
male privilege, slavery, Jim Crow, redlining, the drug trade, gang violence,
up to even including genocide, war, and Holocaust.

The importance, here, of the three aspects described above becomes
clear. As a human, I participate in and share responsibility for the collective
defect inherent in being human at the most fundamental, metaphysical level. To be clear, in terms of a humanistic sense of justice (the second ethical
and moral aspect named above), the responsibility for individual historical
evils does not fall on the victim. The point to be made here is that within
the third, metaphysical aspect even an event relatively unrelated to me must
be grasped by nature as fundamentally a matter of my responsibility within
the interrelated, sympathetic nature of reality. Our, my, own deeply rooted
"self" oriented love bears a share as ultimate cause of even such a horrific
event as the Holocaust. We have to realize we either share in the common
human blindness to our "self" love and interest, in need of a salvific "new
orientation," or we continue in that blindness and ignorance of our plight.

So, if "sin" is the blindness to our "self" love in need of a salvific or redemptive "new orientation" which takes the form of kenotic, self-emptying
in the dialectic Self/self-outpouring, what then becomes of the actual historical consequences of such acts? How do we cope, on a human level, with
such events?

In the ethical, relative dimension of contingent human existence we
make judgments, make assessments of responsibility and consequences
for such historic, contingent events. The moral standards by which such
judgments are made have been topics of discussion since the beginning of

recorded history. An assessment of moral theory or ethics is beyond the scope of this work.

However, it can be said here that we need to recognize that the contingency and relativity of ethical judgment within the viewpoint of human existence, in other words "justice," will inevitably also engender counter-judgment and conflict. Because of this it is important to avoid the absolutization of particular historical good or evil which arises from the emotional attachment or involvement, the love or hatred, we as the "self" naturally tend toward.

This process of absolutization is problematic because it not only blocks a realistic view of the event, such absolutization removes the event from the human, moral dimension. Absolutization blinds us not only to the context of the event but the historical nature and character of that event. Removing the context and historical character of an event thereby creates an amnesia, an isolation from historical interrelation with other world events, which also becomes a denial of the fragile, contingent nature of existence and a forgetfulness which banishes events to an irrelevant past.

In the dimension of human existence, the second aspect, such events need to be dialectically ever-present even as they are past. We need, even as we are required to ethically and morally judge events, a humility, perhaps "compassion" in the Buddhist sense, in the realization of both the contingent nature of our decisions and understanding, and also the interrelated connections with the history of past events in which we exist.

"Sin," then, to return to the original topic of this chapter consists not in specific, individual acts or the collected body of acts but in the "self-will" which is the "self-privileging" and "self-love" of the *incuratus in se* self with its compromised conception of the good. What is the solution; where is the "redemption"?

The salvific solution lies in the *metanoia*, the transformational change of heart, the re-formation, in short—the new orientation offered through and present in the self-emptying of Spirit which invites us to our own kenosis, self-emptying (the Greek *metanoia* carries the sense of "turning around"). This self-emptying of Self and "self" is "*agapé*" which is itself both emptiness and fullness in giving, emptying in love and compassion.

How does this eliminate the pain, sorrow, and tragedy of the contingent world? It does not. Pain, sorrow, tragedy are all a part of contingent life. The lesson of the Passion of Christ lies not in a life revivified from an interlude of death. The lesson lies in the self-emptying faithfulness and love of Jesus even in the most horrifying and vilest of deaths. If a "resurrection" was the point of the Passion, would Jesus as "Son of God" dying from a snake bite in Gethsemane, no Passion, no Good Friday, be just as salvific?

Mark Johnston argues, and I agree, that it is this self-sacrificing faithfulness, a faithfulness unto a painful and horrifying death that is the difference.[3] All intercessory devices, every scapegoat, the very concept of reward and righteousness is destroyed in the self-emptying that seeks nothing in return but is only faithful unto death.

Spirit, the fundamental divine ground or matrix is that "compassionate unity" where the "self" is cast aside for loving merger with the other/Other . . . *agapé*.

Agapé is living through dying, not looking at or for God (Spirit) but rather Spirit living through us; we truly are alive through *agapé*, not in a "humanitarian love" sense—through human will or sentiment—but love and compassion even in the face of death, even as Jesus on the cross or Stephen praying for those who stoned him.

A redeemed life does not erase the contingent natural world where we exist. But in the *metanoia*, the transformed and reoriented self-emptying life to which are called we find a new perspective freed from "self-will." We can see the truth that self-love and self-privileging has blinded us to: the lengths we contingent beings are willing to go to protect our "self," our privilege, from our interrelation with the whole creation, and to project our (false) sense of righteousness.

There is truth, then, in the Johann Heerman (1585–1647) hymn translated by Robert Bridges (1844–1930), "Ah, holy Jesus, how has thou offended?" From the second verse:

> Who was the guilty? Who brought this upon thee?
> *Alas, my treason, Jesus, hath undone thee!*
> *'Twas I, Lord Jesus, I it was denied thee;*
> *I crucified thee.* [emphasis mine]

---

3. Johnston, *Saving God*, 166–74.

Chapter 23

But if such ideas [afterlife and resurrection] were not yet official doctrine, at least they were being contemplated as a necessary solution to the quandaries of monotheism [growing] steadily in significance from the fifth century BCE onward.

—PHILLIP JENKINS[1]

Quite apart from the question of what is meant by "sin" and "salvation and redemption," the pot goes from simmer to hard boil with the question "Saved for what?" which inevitably presents the issue of the afterlife.[2]

No religious or spiritual topic provokes more ardor, more polarized judgment, and more wishful and incoherent thinking than "afterlife." The basic answer is, "We don't know; no one has been there and come back with a chronicle detailing what happens next." Well, definitely there are religious opinions or speculations of various sorts based upon the beliefs and "reports" arising from respective religious proclivities from traditional religions to New Age spiritualities. But these frankly are more or less special pleadings based on acceptance of traditional, ancient beliefs and cosmologies.

Then there is scientifically established materialism which details that the mind is just a function of brain cells and nervous system functions and so cannot survive death. Other than being a flat, "Get over it!" such an answer is not much help in understanding the existential crisis death

---

1. Jenkins, *Crucible of Faith*, 16.

2. Such a massively intricate and important topic as the status of an afterlife requires much more space than is available in this volume to explicate. There are numerous theologians and philosophers who address a continued, historic existence of personality or self, including Charles Hartshorne. But I have found the most compelling case to be laid out by Mark Johnston in *Surviving Death*. Much of the reasoning set forth here follows Johnston's thought, though quite truncated for space, if not clarity.

poses, especially in light of materialism's denial of any sort of metaphysics as discussed earlier.

The crux of the afterlife issue is the underlying supernaturalist religious beliefs. Those beliefs, in their variety of incarnations in world religion, have sought to address the suffering and defects of contingent life, but more pointedly afterlife is most focused on death.

More than suffering and tragedy, death confronts us with the most basic of existential crises: the end of conscious awareness and presence with others. Death, too, signals the end of a possible positive resolution, in our favor, of grievance, wrong, and suffering. By promising a restoration to conscious life with others, especially in the positive and advantageous condition of a "heaven," afterlife seeks resolution of the threat death poses (with the added bonus of a "hell" for those who have wronged us).

Everyone, everything dies. Rich or poor, good and bad. "From dust you came and to dust you shall return" is the Christian Ash Wednesday call to remember in humility this truth. If this is so, that the saint and the evildoer, the wise man and the fool all ultimately perish, why then is good more important than the bad? Even the writer of Ecclesiastes found this profoundly unsettling, "since the same fate comes to all, to the righteous and the wicked, to the good and the evil. . . . This is an evil in all that happens under the sun, that the same fate comes to everyone" (Eccl 9:2–3).

Now there's a fine kettle of fish! What an existential conundrum . . . why be morally or ethically good if that good and I share the same grave with tragedy and evildoers? I need some assurance that I and the good I do will continue on!

Wait! Isn't that the same "self-privileging," the love of "self" we've been discussing for the past few chapters? Yes, but hold that thought for a bit.

Moral rationalists would argue that moral goodness is a normative property of certain acts, whether rewarded or not, just the same as moral badness is also a normative property attaching to certain acts, whether punished or not. Under this reasoning, self-interest plays no part in the goodness or badness attached to the act and in fact can override self-interest in the pursuit of the good. The problem with the argument of the moral rationalist is that reality, where we exist after all, cares not a bit for such distinctions and so the priority of the rational pursuit is compromised.

But even the argument from self-interest falls flat when my interest is compared to that of the vast universe, or just the billions of other humans on this planet, with their myriad of differing standards, customs, and beliefs. The threat of death would seem to invalidate, or at least render irrelevant, relative or contingent standards of good and bad—or at least the efficacy of making such a judgment. We see this all the time in the goodness punished and wickedness rewarded in states and cultures around the world, and close to home.

In the context of the religious and spiritual quest of humanity outlined in this work, such is the framework for the hope, the longing, for succor, for amelioration, for redemption, for an answer to the "evil under the sun." We hope that the plea for justice is not simply an empty message set adrift into the Void.

Thus the plea, this hope, gives rise amid the silence of existence in contingent reality for a place where the moral scales are balanced, where the right triumphs, where morally good actions are rewarded. If not in this world, then in another—the afterlife. In this the afterlife seems required by morality, as a guarantor of justice in the face of the multitude of injustices faced daily by people around the world.

The aim here is to suggest the possibility that there is something *within* existence, human life, which answers that demand regarding the importance of goodness since the whole argument of this work rules out any supernatural answers or means. The position taken here is emphatically *not* for some sort of "resurrection" of the dead, corrupt body, nor the continued "historical" existence of a personal essence, one's individual personality, disconnected from that physical body, a spirit or soul.

Rather, the emphasis will be on understanding what the "good" is, and how the importance of goodness can survive the threat of death. By concentrating on the meaning of the kenosis, self-emptying, of self already discussed we can discover that this already is a death of "self." This transformation or reorientation of life overcomes "self" death as what we experience as "self" is encountered in a nondiscriminatory equality with others. In that, true self becomes both empty and thus full, participating in the same kenosis of Spirit, truly empty and thus truly full, which encompasses the full dynamism at the intersection of the physical and metaphysical.

Thus "identity" for the "self" becomes something new and different. The agapeic identity, what might be labeled as "good" ethically and morally but is really something much more, has shed the "self" delusion, the superlative enduring "self," to find one's own distinctiveness within the interrelatedness of all things, truly empty and truly full.

But, it is objected, I don't want some sort of substitute "life"; I want my life, my own self, or better yet I don't want to die in any real, lasting sense!

Here again, we meet the "self" which desires self-privileging, which focuses only on self-interest, which finds only self-love most important. Which is completely understandable existentially, whether or not a factual basis in reality is to be found. But as argued previously, this "self" delusion is what actually separates us from understanding the truth and meaning of our existence.

In addition, addressing the issues surrounding death from a supernatural perspective certainly make sense in the ancient cosmologies and understandings in which they were formed. Even though we are viewing this issue from a different stage of intellectual and scientific developmental, this does not negate that these earlier approaches "spoke" to that culture, whether or not they may have been literally false.

Doctrinal and theological issues need to be separated from exegesis, the critical explanation of interpretation of the biblical texts. However, one ought, from a practical standpoint, consider the "worldview" of any biblical passage, let alone any theological interpretation, and its problematic nature for contemporary understanding and utility.

The problem of not moving beyond such a developmental stage is that the understandings of that stage (in this case the supernatural explanation of death, afterlife, soul, and so on) carry a dissonance into the world in which we now find ourselves. Such dissonance distorts the truths that lie behind "salvation," "redeemed life," "goodness," "the divine," "death" and thereby stunts spiritual growth that enables us to see the world in an appropriate way, to discover what *agapé* and goodness require of us.

The notion that we survive death, that our individual personality lives on past our mortality and the corruption of our bodies has taken on a number of directions in religious and spiritual communities but mainly center around the "resurrection" or reanimation of a physical body or the release of an "immaterial soul or spirit" substance. These result in the survival of an individual personality, through a physical, mental or spiritual substance that carries the individual's identity to heaven. Amongst those various scenarios are differing arguments as to when this takes place for the "immaterial" substance, immediately upon death or at some future *Parousia*, second coming or end times.

Much of the argument, philosophically and theologically, has centered around the distinction of "mind" and "body," and the meaning this might hold for these conceptualities. Thinkers from Aristotle and Plato to Descartes to Luther to Locke and Kant have arrived at doctrines or conclusions that differ quite widely. In the end, however, the question revolves around the issues of the persistence of either a bodily or "spiritual"/"immaterial" substance and the related problem of consciousness or the psychological connection that makes the conveyance of consciousness ("personal identity") forward possible.

Where did the basis for such ideas come from? Are these ideas "biblical" in the sense that they are an integral part, for the Western Judeo-Christian tradition, of the received testimony of the Torah, Prophets, and/or the New Testament canon?[3]

In reality, much of the spiritual universe that the Judeo-Christian-Islamic traditions take for granted today came about in what is now called the "intertestamental times," that is the period between the closure of the "Old" Testament canon and the "New" Testament events of the Gospels and Letters. In the two to three centuries prior to the Common Era (300 to 50 BCE) new images, symbols, and worldviews were taken up into the religious imagination: angels and judgment, heaven and hell, apocalyptic visions, messiahs, demons and Satan. These were the forces of darkness and light that were contending over the world, much like the contemporary, historic political, cultural, and social forces and chaos that characterized life in those years.

The religious conceptual world that was being built during this time was not drawn by literary whim but by encounter with and transformation by the collision of differing cultural thought as the religious and spiritual chroniclers sought to make sense of the tumultuous times engulfing them. The Hellenistic dynasties that ruled much of the Mediterranean brought the conceptualities of Greek thought. The Jewish encounter with not only Greek culture but also the Persian and Mesopotamian religions, especially Zoroastrianism, resulted from the expansion of trade and cultural exchange taking place over wide ranging empires.

But the incorporation of "foreign" conceptualities into what became a Judeo-Christian-Islamic conceptual inheritance was not so much the fact of the encounter as it was the need in that intertestamental Jewish community for new ways to interpret or understand contemporary events in light of traditions that did not quite "fit." In many ways, the reconstruction that took place then is not so different from the present necessity of reconceptualizing our understanding of faith.

Contrary to how popular culture often views this inheritance from some two thousand years ago, there was not widespread agreement over exactly what even the new concepts or reinterpretations even meant. Two good examples are the Jewish factions within this time period: the Pharisees, the Sadducees, and Essenes, and the early Christian conflicts between the followers of Peter and Paul. What exactly was the content of these ideas, how wide-ranging could or should the beliefs extend? It is only in retrospect, in the passage of time and the contingent decisions of religious authority that certain ideas became tradition or canonical and others were

---

3. For an extended discussion of the origins and growth of many of the "biblical" themes we now take for granted as a canonical part of religious conceptuality, see Jenkins, *Crucible of Faith*, already cited above.

relegated to the heretical and dismissed. But at the time, the stew of ideas bubbled energetically and caused no end of friction and chaos itself.

"Resurrection" is a conceptuality without much traction in the canon of the Hebrew Bible, contrary to Christian back-readings or interpretations from a "New Testament perspective." Those few psalms (49 and 73) that seem to imply differing destinies for good and bad after death seem outliers and are problematic as individually directed. Even Ezekiel's "valley of dry bones" (37:1–14) that are raised from their graves is more indicative of Israel's restorative destiny than any individual revival.

Only in the book of Job, written most likely during Persian rule of the area, does a view of afterlife become prominent in its consideration of theodicy (God's culpability for evil and suffering). Confronted with the destruction of all he has Job contemplates how such events can be reconciled with the goodness of God. Yet even in the face of calamity Job remains faithful, going so far as to meditate on a hope for individual survival after death, a resurrection (Job 14:13–15 and 19:25–26).

By intertestamental times with apocalyptic visions of angels and demons, heaven and hell, however, such a viewpoint became a widespread solution to the theodicy problem of monotheism. The book of Daniel written in this time suggests a raising of the dead. The Mishnah, the basic text for Rabbinic Judaism collecting existing traditions and teaching especially Pharisaic from the period of the Second Temple and redacted after the fall of the Second Temple, indicates the acceptance of resurrection as a necessary belief.[4]

By the time of the New Testament events and their later chronicling, the idea of resurrection of the dead in the context of the Apocalyptic Day of the Lord was prominent, though there was dissension from the Sadducees who pointedly denied a resurrection as not scriptural.[5]

Likewise the idea of a "soul," a surviving individual personality, is not necessarily found scripturally, indeed as mentioned above Luther and others hotly debated how such survival of the individual post death would take place. The ancient Egyptians were quite interested in the fate of individuals after death but those concepts probably, again, did not enter into the conceptualities of the Hebrews until the Ptolemaic period.

The Greeks themselves were intensely interested in afterlife as evidenced by the variety of mystery cults that arose during the intertestamental period. The cultural interaction with the Persians and Greeks most likely

---

4. Mishnah Sanhedrin 10:1.

5. Matt 22:23; Acts 4:1–2; Acts 23:6–8. The Sadducees are explicitly listed as not believing in resurrection in Mishnah Sanhedrin 10:1.

influenced the afterlife portrayed in Daniel (Dan 12:2). Indeed the judgment scenes in Daniel find corresponding mention in the New Testament, especially in Revelation. What is important here is the dualism, light and dark, angel and demon, that permeates the literature in the intertestamental times through the New Testament canon (and many noncanonical books of both the Hebrew Bible and the New Testament).

This dualism was not a thread that ran through the Hebrew Bible and into the New Testament of Christianity. This dualism was a product of the period of upheaval, politically, socially, culturally, occurring during that period from roughly 300 BCE through 70 CE. The conceptual categories thus present were a reaction to those events and the attempt to understand the (Hebrew) monotheism which tradition we in turn have received.

This dualism, which is a departure from the tradition received in the Hebrew biblical canon, drew a radical distinction between the material world (material creation, plants, animals, people)—physical matter, and the spiritual, the realm of truth and light, the right and virtuous. With this framing it was an easy step to the separation of the corrupt flesh from the eternal soul or spirit (Romans 7 and 8). The Greek, Platonic influence is visible in the depictions of the invisible soul imprisoned within the physical body, in need of liberation, release to a more authentic existence in a higher reality.

By the time of Martin Luther the idea of the immaterial soul was an accepted part of doctrine. Luther's argument was that the soul "sleeps" until the End of Days, which sort of contradicted the Parable of Dives, or even the thief on the cross who would be with Jesus today in paradise (punctuating comma not withstanding).[6] The English moralists insisted that the soul was destroyed by death. The argument still raged on through Locke, who sidestepped the issue by pointing to the psychological connections that produce consciousness as the repository of judgment. Even today what is to be saved, what persists, is a source of conflict.

The point to be made by this short, thumbnail, excursion into the historic and cultural context of the ideas of "resurrection" and "soul" is that neither is necessarily basic to the foundational message from the Hebrew Bible. Rather as found in the later texts in that canon and in the New Testament those concepts derive from the wider cultural, social, and political context of the Ptolemaic and Roman regimes in the eastern Mediterranean and were incorporated, piecemeal and not with universal

---

6 The point about the comma is merely a semantic argument of whether Jesus' promise to the "Good Thief" is what is said "today" or if the promise is "today you will be in paradise."

agreement, into belief systems in an effort to understand the monotheistic faith in a turbulent world.

So, then, what can we say about "resurrection," afterlife, and the soul? How is "resurrection" to be understood in relation to the salvific emphasis on the kenotic, self-emptying, Passion of Christ?

Chapter 24

Beyond promising eternal life, these new doctrines elaborated on the nature of survival. What, exactly, could or did survive death? This question was of paramount importance in distinguishing among the Jewish sects, as each followed a doctrine born of its role in the conflicts of these years.

—PHILLIP JENKINS[1]

At the root of this discussion we are confronted with the inherited conception of the "afterlife." From religious texts, from literature, fine arts, and other media—especially movies and pop culture, we receive a variety of messages and images about the "afterlife." All carry, albeit often in very differing ways, a moral message either of reward, recovery, or fulfillment.

Set against the contingent world in which we reside our eager acceptance of this sharp contrast with the contemporary defects of life we experience is understandable. We all seek a "wellness" in this life; we all desire fulfillment and meaning, justice amid chaos and suffering; we all fear the loss of "self," or the pain in the loss of the presence of a loved one.

We have seen how the concept of "afterlife," already a part of the intertestamental cultural stew in Middle East Judaism, grew in the Christian community from encounter with such Greek and Zoroastrian concepts, taking on supranatural content especially as the faith community sought to understand "messiah" or "christ" within the apocalyptic interpretation of the times. There is also the wider world context of "afterlife" ideas from ancient Egypt to the native peoples of the Americas to the conceptions of reincarnation.

An "afterlife" promises an answer to all the losses in life, a reward and fulfillment, an everlasting happiness after this "veil of tears." However, as

1. Jenkins, *Crucible of Faith*, 129.

painful and frightening as the prospect is, we must seriously question the reality of such a concept.

Generally, the "afterlife" has two differing modes, each with their own "subsets" of how such an event might take place. "Afterlife" is taken to be either resurrection of a dead body or the escape of an enduring, independent, immortal, and immaterial "soul" for a continuation of the "self" in some "next world."[2] Centrally problematic for each case is how personal identity, the personality associated with consciousness, is understood to exist, if at all, and how such identity could be thus transmitted.

The "resurrection" conceptuality argues for the reconstitution by God of mind and body at the End of Days, thereby seeking to bypass the question of whether the mind is dependent on the body. There are a variety of nuanced stances on this point, such as Luther's "soul-sleeping" or a neo-Lockean materialism, but ultimately the status of identity is the paramount issue.

In the enduring immaterial "soul" or "spirit" conceptuality, the question of the seat of consciousness, of mind, and how it is carried forward, in distinction from and without a bodily entity is foremost. In other words, how is "soul" in a "spiritual body" identical with, as transferred from, "soul" in a physical body? Again, the question of what constitutes personal identity is fundamental.

The objection that "with God, all things are possible!" might be, and indeed usually is, raised to obviate the need for examination of such fundamental questions. But I counter that such objection is only "special pleading," ignoring unfavorable evidence and seeking special treatment—"self-privileging," in extremis. If such would be the case, then there could be no stable understanding with which to view this world, negating the possibility of any trustworthy scientific examination of phenomenon; such a "God" would truly then be a God of chaos and not the biblical God. If, as even a traditional theist would argue, this is God's creation and it is in this creation we might glimpse the nature or order of God, then such a chaotic notion must be rejected as problematic for knowledge itself.

So, then, how to understand the "person" and whether a "person" can somehow survive death in one of the methods noted above—bodily

---

2. To do justice to the topic of "afterlife" would require a whole volume of its own to explicate the various historical, philosophical, and theological strands that encompass the schools of thought. The following discussion borrows from and is indebted to Mark Johnston's *Surviving Death*, as noted above. If my abridgement of his lengthy and necessarily complex and technical arguments leads to misunderstanding then the fault lies with my summation and not Johnston's reasoning.

resurrection or the separation of an immaterial "soul/spirit" for continued personal historic existence in whatever actual format.

Now Paul denies the posthumous existence of the same body (1 Cor 15) in favor of the "spiritual body" that arises from the sowing of the corrupt, dead, natural body. However, the inherited bodily resurrection is a product of the Gospels, such as the story of Lazarus, the post-crucifixion appearance of the dead in Jerusalem, and the Easter story. Two different traditions of "afterlife" even in the Bible should give us pause to consider that perhaps this idea of "afterlife" is not quite so settled, that "resurrection" might actually mean something different than what we traditionally have been taught.

If we consider that the person, with all her or his identity and consciousness, is dependent on and identical with the body, then when the body perishes any "soul" that might exist would presumably also die. To exist again—to be numerically the same and only such person, a given body's pre-death state would need to be re-created, reproduced in its matter and organization as it was at that time.

There are a number of technical problems here, not the least of which is the continual loss and re-creation of body cells that sustain a physical body over time. Our body at one year old is not the same as the body at twenty or fifty or ninety, and neither are our thoughts and feelings. So if a mere organism is what is being revivified, which one is it?

In addition, we should consider the conditions of both somatic death and cellular death. Somatic death is the death of the organism as a whole, the failure of all the vital organ functions—heart, lungs, muscle, and brain activity. This is a systemic event of the physiology of a body. Cellular death happens on a much smaller scale—the biochemical processes of the cells which make up the various organs of the body lose functionality. When the body dies the process of cell operation and re-creation ends and the cells die, one by one, not to be replaced. That corruption or deterioration continues to the extent that no information is retrievable beyond basic non-personal cellular and genetic data, like DNA.

Cellular death occurs later than the somatic death of a body, which makes organ transplantation from one body to another even at distance possible. Specific organ cells themselves die at different rates, ranging from ten to forty minutes though freezing, or at least "putting them on ice" might prolong this deterioration, again allowing for transplantation of organs at distance when kept cold. Some organs themselves can be kept alive through mechanical means for a period of time, but without the total functioning of the biological system these, too, will break down and die.

By the onset of rigor mortis, some five to ten hours after somatic death, massive cellular organ failure has occurred. None of the body's organs are capable of regeneration much less sustaining physical life. This is the dissolution of natural, bodily life without recourse to any sort of natural intervention.

At this point, even a "miraculous" revivification of a dead and dissolute body would not produce the same, numerically same and only such, person from a pre-death state. This sort of "reactivation" would not be in any way a continuation of the natural processes that exemplified life. If one bases "resurrection" on God's miraculously breathing life into a corpse, activating the very atoms collectively present, this would need to be considered a "new life" and not a continuation of the former life. In addition, how would such a miracle of revivification operate for a body that has literally been blown to bits or burned to ashes? That body cannot, by definition, be brought back to its particular life.

There have been a number of tortured explanations of how God might create the conditions for a "resurrection" of the body, but, honestly, these really don't make much sense, particularly to a Christian faith from which the "resurrection" concept comes, but which also presents itself as "the crucial response to the undeniable fact of bodily death."[3]

At bottom, a body has essential organic components. However, for a body, a person, to exist is not just that these pieces exist in and of themselves, scattered as it were. To make up a life they need to be functionally organized in such a way as to mutually sustain a whole organic form or existent over time. To propose that such a descriptive condition can happen twice identically, in natural life and in "resurrected" life, contradicts that this is one life, the numerically same and only such person, and denies the dynamic unity over time that defines a persistently existing body.

"Resurrection" as it is commonly viewed does not appear to be viable. The identification of the "person" with a physical, biologic body doesn't "work" for such a concept. Nor, really, does it agree with most of the arguments from the New Testament which views death as the destruction of God-created life in all its meanings.

Rejecting a bodily criterion for "resurrection" and "afterlife," we are left with the Platonic inheritance within Christianity of the immaterial "spirit" or "soul." And just at this point, as Johnston points out in *Surviving Death*, we are confronted with belief in a metaphysics of ancient Greece as being a fundamental element of creedal faith. A metaphysics, by the way, as has been pointed out in previous chapters, that is not sustained by the Hebrew Bible texts. The grounds for this metaphysics is in the encounter with and attempt to fashion a religious understanding of the turbulent intertestamental

3. Johnston, *Surviving*, 107.

wars and upheavals of empires, in the mélange of Jewish/Greek/Persian and other cultural thought, by what became the biblical witness.

If, as we might suppose, in the end faith in the importance of goodness, mercy, compassion, *agapé* is fundamental to all religions, independent of particular beliefs, ought we consider certain temporally, historically conditioned doctrines as more fundamentally required? More to the point, is Paul correct in admonishing the Corinthians, "If the dead are not raised: 'Let us eat and drink, for tomorrow we die'" (1 Cor 15:32)? Is the basis of a moral or ethical life wasted unless predicated upon belief in a particular metaphysic? Or, is the moral or ethical life coherent without such a belief?

The argument here is the latter. The ethical and salvific coherence of the "redeemed" life is not dependent upon the doctrine of a "resurrection" so understood, whether bodily or of an immaterial "soul." Does this satisfy the profound sense of tragedy and loss in life in the way belief in an "afterlife" does? No. The defects of this world are evident and no doctrine or creedal belief can remove the anguish and suffering.

> There is something both childish and obscene, and I would add irreligious, about the attempt to put an otherworldly frame around such things so they seem not to be the tragedies or horrors that they manifestly are. Sometimes things are so horrible and tragic that nothing that subsequently happens can diminish the tragedy or the horror; anyone who tells you otherwise is just making it up or relying on someone else who just made it up.[4]

Continuing on and examining that second mode, then, what of the "soul"?

What we know of our mental functions, even at the highest levels, is that they are connected to and conditioned upon operations within the brain itself. We have found that impairment in specific areas of the brain due to damage or disease can lead to certain cognitive problems. Such findings indicate that problems with our mental capabilities are dependent upon the operation of the brain as an organic process and from a neurophysiology perspective the mind seems to be just a function of the operation of the brain and nervous system.

Often at this point the "out of body" experience is presented as a counter to this fairly materialist perspective. This experience is characterized by the sense of leaving one's body in a near death experience, often "looking down" and observing from a third person perspective the immediate goings on, traveling through a tunnel toward a "white light," a feeling of peace and contentment, and so on. There is obviously some sort of phenomenon happening that is called, "out of body experience." Investigations into these

---

4. Johnston, *Surviving*, 130.

events have not discovered any evidence that could point to some kind of distinct disembodied knowledge of the event.

In addition, even these experiences seem to be culturally conditioned. The "near death experience" or "out of body experience" described above finds different expression in Japan. In many Eastern cultures there is a different emphasis on the mind-body due to particular philosophical and religious outlooks, for example of Buddhism, Confucianism, and Taoism. The result, in Japan, is *embodied* connection to the "ground of being," expressed in imagery of rivers, trees, flowers, the Tori Gate (symbolic of the connection with the transcendental).

Beyond these considerations, there are psychoactive drugs that themselves produce "out of body experiences" within living, conscious people. Ketamine in particular produces such an outcome but other psychedelics also induce "mind altering" effects with similar outcomes.[5] In such cases "out of body experience" occurs while the person is manifestly still alive and "in body," though possibly incoherent.

The evidence for an immaterial "soul" or "spirit" that carries off our personal identity is ambiguous at best. From the best medical data we have on the function and impairment of brain activity, the presence of an immaterial "soul" does not find support and the mind as a function of the brain seems all the more obvious.

Creedal claims of supernatural revelation aside spiritual substances and bodily revivification do not appear to be viable understandings of reality. This is a rather large aside, but the claim to supernatural revelation, an extraordinary claim, requires extraordinary evidence, beyond creedal or doctrinal belief systems. Otherwise such claims are "special pleading," a "self-privileging" of particular religious belief.

Religious faith that clings to the past of created dogmas, absolutizing them, turns such tenets into idols, created works that, finished, have nothing further creative to express. "Sin" is to be devoted to such idols, to "self-privileged" works. Authentic faith calls for devotion to creative acts not their products. To miss this is to wander blindly in a wilderness.

The stark reality is that death is the end, the annihilation of presence, the cutting off of life with other beings. The concepts of bodily revivification and the immaterial "soul" or "spirit" flying free of bodily constraints is really in the end no more than spiritual pride.

> Is it not another case of false dichotomy to insist that after death
> I must live forever or find no immortality at all, that the universe

---

5. Though there is quite a body of literature here, a recent publication addresses this brain, mind, drug connection: Pollan, *How to Change Your Mind*.

must conserve all value forever or none at all, that there must be
a universal human-like Purpose or no meaning?[6]

We are after all speaking about the metaphysical "divine" which encompasses the entire universe, of which our planet is but less than a miniscule portion. To own up to this reality is to allow just how fragile, precious,
and fleeting our lives are, and the need to care for, respect, and enjoy all life.
For when that opportunity is wasted that loss is forever.

Given this, perhaps we might find another way to address the stark
reality of death. Perhaps, though the road through bodily revivification and
immaterial substance flying away might be closed, the destination might
not even be what we thought or expected. Perhaps "resurrection," "afterlife,"
means something entirely new and unexpected, at least in our Western, Pla-
tonized cultural understanding.

6. Milligan, "Limits of Conventional Religious Language," 314.

Chapter 25

I submit that both paradoxes [of the mind's "identity" or "identities"] will be solved . . . by assimilating into our Western build of science the Eastern doctrine of identity. Mind is by its very nature a *singulare tantum*. I should say: the over-all number of minds is just one.

—ERWIN SCHRÖDINGER[1]

Without the supernaturalist elements of religious belief, how then are we to find any efficacy in such terms as "new life," "afterlife," and "resurrection"? As alluded to in earlier discussions these terms have new meanings once we recognize the "self-love," the "self-privileging," that underpins much of our belief systems. The very concept of "self" has some rather dubious or shaky underpinnings, particularly when we look at what "personal identity" might mean.

Birth and death are bookmarks that delineate our existence, especially in the Western and traditional Christian understanding, with "the soul" or "afterlife" being the answer to the defects and suffering of the experienced world. But looking at the matter from a different perspective, what if the dualism of birth/death and the existence of an independent, sufficient "self" are illusory? Going further, beyond the monotheistic Western traditions, what if the dualism of samara (everyday world and its suffering) and nirvana (the cessation of such suffering) themselves, of Buddhism, is itself illusory? This is the sense of Buddhist spiritual thinkers Nāgārjuna and Dōgen's understanding of the matter.

We often define our lives through distinctions, polarities, and dualisms. Wealth and poverty, pure and impure, and so on. But in doing so we find that both poles must define the content of our lives. In other words, to

1. Schrödinger, *What Is Life?*, 134–35.

seek the "pure" life we must also be preoccupied with impurity, guarding and discriminating lest impurity invade our lives. We thus find ourselves discriminating life situations and responses into "pure" and "impure." Hawthorne's *The Scarlet Letter* provides a narrative of how such an orientation plays out, as does our communal life in general.

The dualism of life and death presents the same problem. We live our lives in the constant shadow of death, defining every moment by our mortality, that we shall one day cease to exist.

Transcending the dualism of life and death, living in a way that recognizes the interdependency of life and death, and also that life is life, birth is birth, and death is death, is possible when we understand that the true nature of our dilemma is the symbolized entity of "self." An awareness of death is only possible as a function of the delineated "self"—

"If death exists, then I will die. . . . Since I was born and thence will die, 'I' must exist."[2]

If there is no delineated ego-self (non-self) then the dilemma of externalism or annihilationism is resolved. Both birth/life/"self" and death are deconstructed to reveal the true nature of things, the interrelatedness and interdependency which is at once full and "empty," immanent and transcendent, Śūnyatā—what I call "Spirit."

Previously I discussed Johnston's "arena of presence and action" as the actual source of what we call "self" which is an illusion. Life, and death, though real enough in an experienced world of constant change and flux, is illusory as related to such a "self." They are illusory as "a way of thinking projected on to the world, one of the conceptual structures with which we organize and structure our world—including ourselves."[3] We can deconstruct this illusion.

Rather than the consolation of a pure heavenly realm or other immaterial, transcendent dimension of escape, we can radically reengage the world, liberated from the fear of death, to realize our agapeic relation with all creation.

Birth and death are opposites. Birth is birth; death is death. We need not desire one and avoid the other nor grasp at birth/life and try to evade death. When life is lived, not in fear of death, we can fully live. This is the message of John 10:10, "I came that they may have life and have it abundantly." Filled up, packed in fully, and overflowing to others in joy and strength. This is *agapé*.

2. Loy, *Engaging*, 83.
3. Loy, *Engaging*, 84.

How does this happen? By "forgetting yourself," letting go of the illusory dualism of life and death in the psychological construct of "self." Let go of the separate "self" thought to be doing the birthing, living, and dying.

In birth, the infant has no sense of "self" as a discrete being undergoing a process distinct from itself. If there is no "I" being born, then there is only the action or process of birthing, complete in its moment. The same is true of death if no "I," self-sufficient/self-subsistent, exists.

We exist, the world exists, not as discrete objects in time, but as confluences of temporal processes which we identify as objects. I, and the world, do not exist in time; I and the world are time. What I do, what happens to me are not events in a container called "time" external to me. They are forms that my existence, my "arena of presence and action," takes in the flux of the ever-changing world.

Thus I am actualized by the myriad things when I forget the insecure, illusory, and impermanent psychological construct of "self." I "forget" myself to awaken to my true nature—not inside my head looking out at a world outside of "me" but "I" am one of the variety of ways in which the cosmos expresses itself, in constant motion and change. This is the myriad of things of *Śūnyatā*, "emptiness," Spirit that do not die as having not been born.

By letting go of this "self" in a kenosis, "self" emptying, for other-directed love and compassion, not only does such a "reorientation," a "resurrection" in the fullest sense of a Spirit filled life, occur but the "self" finds its own fullness within that world of other and itself changes the kenotic Spirit which enfolds creation.

To understand what this means, we need to examine what we actually mean by "self," "human identity," "consciousness," "mind," and how that understanding connects with a reconceptualized "resurrection" as a salvific "reorientation."

When we think of personhood, of personal identity, we usually consider identity as fixed within bodies, personalities, or souls. Only within those categories do we then think of aspirations, influences, projects, and a drive to live. However, from a practical standpoint, these latter actions and thoughts are the concrete reality from which what we mean by personhood or identity actually emerges. This consciousness, this unified arena of presence and action, as Mark Johnston terms it, is "a fundamental context for the worldly happenings that make up the details of one's life."[4]

There is no separately existing entity at the core of our mental life, a "soul," which constitutes our personal being and which persists through time. No such entity exists in distinction from our body and brain. Our

---

4. Johnston, *Surviving*, 138.

personal identity is actually secured through concrete patterns of activity—aspirations, influences, projects, and a drive to live—which describe our identity by pointing to our future self. This "special *self*-concern is just this pattern of special concern directed toward a person one takes to be oneself."[5]

Thus we have been looking at the situation backwards, so to speak. There is no "self" behind our mental function. Rather than an independently persisting entity determining who we are, the pattern of self-concern, the concrete patterns of activity, are the elements of what we deem "personal identity."

What we have been calling "consciousness" is not an independently existing "entity" but rather a perspective, a fundamental context through which the world of events is filtered. This is the "arena of presence and action" presented earlier. In this arena of presence and action we live our lives and through this arena the details of our lives take shape in activity within the events of the world.

We structure this arena around its "center," a "here," which becomes the boundary for "my" thought and experience, and which we identify with "me," our "self." This position of "here" is juxtaposed with "there," meaning the world, everything else not "me." And it is the "here," the "me," the "self," which takes precedence in position over all else, especially when considering the end of the presence "here," death.

The realization that, from the world's perspective, this central position of "here," of the fountainhead of reality—"me," is peripheral can be jarring. We cannot believe that the central position in the universe can end. Until we understand that there is no "central" position, there is no center, or perhaps that the center is everywhere, the salvific import of a reconceptualized "resurrection" and "redemption" will be hidden from our awareness.

In this "arena of presence and action," what is being perceived by "me" at the "center" is a perspective on modes of presentation. These things, events, or items are sensed from a particular position of viewing the world's events. That "me" or "center" is apparently focused on my head, as part of my body with all its sensory data presented to "me." Actions emanating from "me," willed activity, also appear to arise from this "center" as do the higher-order mental acts such as contemplation.

As far as each of us can discern, there is one and only one such "center" that is "me" from which all this occurs. All thoughts, feelings, will to activity, are bound into this "center," the arena of presence and action, in which the "stream of consciousness" flows. This bound arena, this intentional "object"

---

5. Johnston, *Saving*, 184, italics original.

as it were at the center of our attention, is structured around a "center" which in reality does not exist in the external world. Nor does it exist in the mental world. The apparent unity of this "center" which is the arena in our mental life results when the various modes of presentation become available to us and are attended to.

The realization of this is the essential point in contemplative meditation and mantras. The "here" of the center is emptied of everything except the "there" of the mantra or object of contemplation. As the "there" fades away, the "here," then, also slips away to the "centerless" experience in which the "self" drops away. Once thought, attention, reappears so the arena returns.

Descartes reasoned that because he reasoned, therefore he existed. But the prior introspective question not asked was whether anyone or anything was actually doing the thinking. Thinking can be going on in a centered arena without the need for anyone at that center.

To be at the center of the arena of presence is in the most important sense what being "me" is. This is where I experience "myself," my activity, my thoughts and feelings. Not someone else, not something else, just "me" "here" now.

I am really, really attached to "me." My death is not just the ceasing of "me" but the annihilation of the thing that made me "me"—this "center," this arena of presence and action. More profoundly distressing is realizing that this "center" was never, ever the center of reality. For the cosmos continues on, closing around this illusory "center," the "I" or "self" that was itself only defined by its relation to the phenomena of the world. "You are dust, and to dust you shall return" (Gen 3:19).

There is an egocentrism, a self-referential concern, that is familiar to all of us. Whether or not we exhibit an impersonal concern for others' well-being and their interests, this core remains even as we altruistically expand that circle of special concern. The one for whom self-referential concern holds no more special consideration than concern for any other is the case that gets noticed—the citation for bravery, placing another's safety or well-being above their own, giving one's life for another. Those seem the exceptions.

There are two differing modes to what we mean by "I" at work here. One aspect of "I" is referential in the context of, say, my name tag at the neighborhood block party. "I" in this sense is context dependent, and there are many "I's" present, though only one refers to "that one" sitting in the lawn chair. The other aspect of "I" is subjective and is bound up in the thought that "I" am "me," the one at the center of this arena of presence and action. *This* is the one to whom the self-referential, egocentrism comments are directed, as distinct from the context referential human body "I."

Why is this important? In the context of the argument of this work, the contextual referential "I" is the physical animal body that is present at the block party. We recognize as a finite and contingent being this body will at some point succumb to death and decay, as do all finite objects sooner or later. This has occurred, as it happens, billions of times in the past and will continue in the future. "Ashes to ashes," as the saying goes.

The biologic death of referential "I," the human being, is a part of a continuing process of the cosmos. In a sense, the truly subjective "I" at the center can think of that event dispassionately as a natural part of the life of the human species. In the same way the others "there" in the world can, from their own arenas, safely consider my death, consequential for my family and friends I hope, but even in grief certainly nothing to incite a personal existential terror. "He was after all over one hundred . . ." (One can hope.)

But for the "I" at the center of the arena, this is calamitous. What then counts as the property of "me"? Everything that is/was valued "here" is suddenly indistinguishable from what is/was valued "there" with the collapse of my center! No wonder death, read as "my own death," is incomprehensible to me and must obviously be a major defect of this world!

Still, there were times and places that actually existed without "me," and there will be such times and places to come.

These past chapters have been about understanding the "I" behind the curtains, the truly subjective "I," the one who confronts the end of the arena of presence and action. Such an end is important to "*me*," not in some abstract way but in the sense that "I" am at the center of that arena. That "I" at the center is an asymmetric special concern that, in a very basic way, I want to protect, unlike my concern for the other, "there."

Understanding this true nature of "self" will enable us to find a salvific meaning to life in a comprehensible way. The "self" regard that lies at the root of our arena of presence and action, at the root of human nature, is the concern for "self," ourselves—himself, herself, over the "other" which is *not* "here." This is the "self-privileging," the "self-love," that lies at the heart of what religious faiths term "sin" and "evil." It is a disposition of our "self," in the very structure of our consciousness, to favor the "here" over the "there." And it is in the reorientation of "self" that salvific meaning becomes apparent.

The foregoing has attempted to tease apart the important difference between a "self" identity and "personal" identity. "Self" identity is the more basic identity that carries the continuity of one's arena of presence through time. "Personal" identity is that identity through time of the publicly available, contingent human being which is now the center of that arena. This latter ages, is injured, perhaps becomes impaired in some way, and thus changes physically over time so that indicators of the "personal" change over time. Self-concern follows "self" identity like one watching the movie of the "personal" unreel over time.

What is at stake here is the difference between the end of "personal" identity and the ultimate disposition of "self" identity. The fear of death is most acute in the idea that at some point there will be no one at the center of this particular arena of presence and action, the property of being "me." No longer is the issue the survival or non-survival of the "personal" identity publicly known as "me." More basic is the desire for the continuation in some centered way of the property of "me" in the subjective, "self" identity of the arena of presence and action. But as we have seen, even this "self" at the center of the arena of presence and action is insubstantial, not connected to a characterizable substance, such as "my soul," which is carried forward distinctly in time from moment to moment.

In the simplest terms then, "I"—the "self"—am located not by the physical body which seems to contain "me." This biological organism is "my" physical identity "bookmark" in the phenomenological events which create the world. "I"—the "self"—seem to be located at the confluence of the perceptions or perspectives of these events, along with the processes of thought and will. "Self" never appears without a companion perception and so is never to be captured as the "self's" "self."[6]

All of these interrelated and interdependent elements dynamically create what we call "the mind," the "self," much like the elements of a reel of film, individual frames dynamically interrelated, create a whole movie. This dynamic convergence appears to be focused in our head, within our brain, that is a part of our "bookmarked" personal identity.

But unlike a reel of film, this dynamic convergence is illusory, it has no physical object nor is this "self" anything substantial, anything beyond mere appearance. There is no persisting mental self at the subject center of our mental acts. The "mine-ness" of these thoughts, feelings, and perceptions are the result of their integration and availability for reflection and not the result of the awareness of some intrinsic constituent "ego." These thoughts and experiences seem to fit together, appear as an integrated whole, as a result of the functioning of our brains.

There is no mental "third person" in our mental acts, just the operation of the brain and nervous system accessing the bundle of occurrences which make up the structure of reality. The "self" is perspectival and

6. This at least seems to be David Hume's point about self and perception. Hume, "Of Personal Identity," in *Treatise of Human Nature*, 533.

interdependent with that structure, which includes all other "selves," intimately connected in reality.

This sounds weird, but consider the comments above about contemplation and mantras. The aim through those exercises is to experience the true mode of existence, the experience of "self-less-ness," the emptiness of self, the "center-less-ness" of actual existence. In this recognition comes the realization of our "own" interrelatedness, our interdependence with creation. The "self" falls away, emptying, self-emptying into Self, Spirit which empties Self creating, incorporating, and sustaining existence.

One might respond that at least there is "something there" in the identification of a human being who is reported as the site for this "self," this "consciousness." That external "here" has a physical bookmark that can be picked out as distinct from other physical bookmarks in the phenomenological world.

But, as has been argued, this particular first-person pronoun, though a particular human being, is one biological entity among billions that have gone on before. That personal identity will die as all other biological things do. The "self," where special concern lies, is not the same as that bookmark. Indeed, there does not seem to be anything that adequately ties together both the bookmark of personal identity and the egocentric special concern of "self."

We are left, then, with the startling idea that, in the most relevant sense, "self" does not exist, that there are no objective facts concerning identity that justify the "self-concern," the "self" love and privileging which has organized the trajectories of our lives.

In essence, "my" death, the one most relevant to me as the lack of temporal continuance of "my" center, the arena of presence and action, though I can acknowledge it as a mental conceptuality, is impossible to imagine. Quite simply, consideration of such a continuance or lack thereof of "self" concern has no basis for determination; there is no substance carried forward and with the lack of substantial "self," the loss of "self" has no definition. And, to be honest, we won't be aware of it.

Where then is the comfort? How then can we understand these terms of "redemption," "resurrection," "new life" in a way that is affirming of our lives in the world as it is? In what way can this knowledge, instead of increasing our despair at the world, increase our love and compassion? What then is the "Love of God"?

Chapter 26

Are not five sparrows sold for two pennies? Yet not one of them is forgotten in God's sight . . . you are of more value than many sparrows.

—LUKE 12:6–7

What has been said so far should not be taken to diminish the value of life, especially that of an individual, nor the love and compassion owed to the world around us. The sense of the passage from Luke (also present in Matthew) is not the diminishment of the natural world, sparrows or otherwise, either. The point is the very real and present value that contingent life has, even in its most trivial elements, "the hairs on your head." Everything has importance and value.

So understanding death, as has been argued for the past chapters, is not meant to devalue the suffering and tragedy, the sense of loss, death brings. The understanding presented underscores the presence of that suffering and tragedy and the preciousness that we humans too cavalierly dismiss with "self" centered attitudes which result in greed, poverty, hunger, hate, conflict, and war.

The focus for these chapters has been how the "self" in self-centeredness, self-love, self-privileging, has blinded us to our true nature, to the true calling of the cosmic demand. Especially in the United States the emphasis on the "self-made" man or woman, the "rugged individual," the go-it-alone person, has driven us in the direction opposite the compassion, *agapé*, to which we are called.

This cosmic demand has been called "Spirit" in this work; other religious and spiritual communities, theistic or not, have other words designating the understanding of such a call. This work has tried to put this call and the encompassing Spirit engendering this call in a naturalistic, *panentheistic* framework, as incomplete and unfinished a product as it might be so far.

The biggest obstacles in the way of defining or shaping a new conceptuality, in finding a new direction for our understanding of life and metaphysical meaning, are how we have understood Death and "Self." These two issues are intimately bound together in our minds, as we have seen. The effort of the past chapters, and really the whole book, has been to tease these apart, to see them in a different way and so confront them at first individually and then as a complete whole.

Death, as has been argued, is certainly very real and final in the physical sense. There is no denying the loss and suffering there; it is a part of life and has been for billions of lives and billions of years. But if death is very real and final physically, the notion of death in the sense of the end of "self," that center in the arena of presence and action, is more problematic.

There were two notions presented in the last chapter regarding the use of "I" in referring to "self." In the first, "I" stands as a "bookmark" for the physical, contingent human being, the one to whom certain facts and events of the physical world refer and which signifies a particular person, "personal identity." The second "I" refers to the subjective unity at the convergence of the various experiences of the world, and of our thinking or mental processes, which appear as the center of a persisting arena of presence and action, or consciousness, "self-identity." This latter notion, as the focus of "self" concern, was deemed to have the more important status of the two as being "who I am."

It is in this latter, subjective, "self-identity" that we encounter the issues of "self-privileging" and special concern, what is considered in this work to be the basis the religious term "sin," the suffering and defect of the world as we experience it. But, as has been argued to this point, this "self," this center, has no real substance. As a cross-time unity of experiences this "self" is a perspectival confluence of those various modes of experience this "entity" is an insubstantial illusion. When we speak of "mind" or "consciousness" or "self," we are referring only to an "entity" that is "constituted by the things that successively occupy the center of a persisting arena of presence," but with all the substance of the wind.[1]

This arena—this first person and individual perspective—and not what is passing through it, is what is meant in speaking of "consciousness." A mental "construct" made up of informational fields (visual, auditory, bodily, thought) that appear about an implied center, our brain, this center incorporates real and unreal (dreams, imagination, etc.) things but has no objective reality outside the intentional acts within its range.

---

1. Johnston, *Surviving*, 111.

Being a confluence or convergence emphasizes the interrelated nature of both this "mind" and the rest of the world being experienced. As a non-substantial "entity" that is part of a greater interdependent reality, we can find the ceasing of such a non-substantial center less threatening. At the same time we can realize that the "empty self" is actually full of interconnected reality, encompassed by and incorporated into Spirit.

Death still has its sting. Life is precious. But our "being," that "self" and "not self," is already a part of a greater and interdependent whole. What have we to fear? Bodily death is sad; but it is also a function of life, happening billions of times over since the beginning of time. The loss of "self," "self-identity" is really an illusion and we are, in any case, a part of a larger agapeic "Self"—Spirit—which emptied into reality is also taken up in encompassing fullness.

So, "resurrection" is the emptying self finding completion in the full Self, our loving guardianship of the beings around us rippling into the onward rush of the interdependent creation, encompassed, filled, and incorporated into Spirit.

This is not the preservation of identity, of the good over evil, of value, which is the "heaven" of traditional imagery or movies. This world is messier than that. But what this change of focus does is to radically center us, as I think the thrust of the core message of the Judeo-Christian-Islamic traditions and possibly many of the Eastern spiritualities do, on *this* world. Rather than concerning ourselves with what comes after death, we are called in all of these traditions, by the cosmic demand, to compassion and love and care of *this world*, and the beings in it!

The framework for this outlook can be found in both the Christian concept of *agapé* and the Buddhist *anatta*. The basic concern of *anatta* is that there is no persisting self, or no persisting self worth caring about. In the same way, *agapé* is self-emptying love, "self-denial," for compassion in the service of others.

"And whoever does not take up the cross and follow me is not worthy of me. Those who find their life will lose it, and those who lose their life for my sake will find it" (Matt 10:38–39; see also John 12:25 and parallel passages in Mark and Luke). This is the well-known call, for the Christian, to deny the "self," pick up "the cross," and follow Jesus. If one removes the transactional sense of reward that has been woven into these and like passages, the agapeic message is clear.

From a Christian perspective the idea of "kenosis" creates a dynamic for expressing the Trinitarian idea (as expressed in previously referenced work).[2] In First Article terms, God as Creator, creation and everything in it are an expression of the Emptying God. God and creation are relational, all creation is interrelated, interdependent, as being the Self-Emptying expression of Spirit (God). The "self" is only meaningful when considered as enfolded in this Emptied Self which is Nothing and Everything.

The "fall" is a reverse or negative kenosis in the freedom of humanity/ creation which issues from and is implicit in that Self-Emptying expression. The "fall" signifies the "self-love," "self-privileging" of ego over and against the interrelated and interdependent nature of creation in Immanent Kenotic Spirit (God). This is, in Buddhist terms, the source of suffering—*duḥka*. Looked at from this perspective the Eden Story, the story of Adam and Eve, is less about a "sin" of "disobedience" and more about the "self" awareness which creates the "self-love," "self-privileging," that is the real "sin"—the denial of interrelated reality for a "self" curved in on itself.

From a Christian perspective the sign of redemption, Second Article, is the self-emptying, kenosis of God in Jesus Christ. The existential meaning of the cross for us is in the reorientation, *metanoia*, that is repentance and return to the original nature expressed in the First Article. This "change of heart" is the emptying of "self" into Self, the kenotic Spirit which is Nothing and Everything.

Recognition of the "collectivity" or interrelatedness of creation, which itself reflects Immanent, Self-Emptied Spirit, leads to kenosis in a communal, agapeic relationship of social transformation—the body of Christ in the world, the church or spiritual community.

We err when we attempt to locate or "concretize" the divine. In this "place," or "homeground" per Keiji Nishitani,[3] also called "Emptiness," "Absolute Nothing," "Buddha nature," here Spirit, "True Self" is found, which is what we share with all other things as the "ground" for the contingent existents or expressions of Spirit Self-Emptying.

Thus, "Emptiness" is not nullity but the interrelatedness of all things, all embracing Spirit. Each thing is a unique expression reflecting the interdependent, interrelated whole—paradoxically selfless in unity and in that selflessness uniquely itself.

Similarly, many Jewish scholars have also called attention to the radical Torah message of care and concern for others in Scripture. In Islam, *zakat* speaks to this service of care and compassion, not just individually but collectively, as an obligation of faith and piety. Looking at other spiritualities

---

2. See Mitchell, *Spirituality and Emptiness*, 11. Nishida Kitaro makes much the same point in *Last Writings* and more specifically, the two-part article "The Logic of 'Topos.'"

3. Nishitani, *Religion and Nothingness*.

from Hinduism to Confucianism to Taoism to Buddhism and on, we find the same spiritual message, the call to heed the cosmic demand of love, care, and compassion.

This is not to confuse the various religions or say each of these religious or spiritual communities are the same. They each have unique histories, particular messages, and differing ways of "seeing" the world. But what is unique can also have commonalities. The point here is a shared common interest in the compassionate care such spiritualities are called to.

What then of "the good"? Is our orientation, then, a life-denying asceticism? No. *Agapé* here as "self" emptying, understanding the insubstantiality of that center, is not "self" denying but recognition that the world is full of such centers. Such "self" emptying is actually the promotion of the fullness of self/Self in the embodiment of compassionate service toward others, love, the character and condition of the good.

Does this orientation guarantee success? We can't say. But this would seem to be what "hope" would look like, as a future outcome. Nonetheless, such is out of our hands, not within our control. We, though, are called to a faithful, hopeful service, to *agapé*, not to transactional behavior based upon reward.

In the end, "redemption," "resurrection" comes down to this: that the "new life," the "redeemed" life, is one that is "reoriented" life in the truest sense of *metanoia*, the transformative change of heart, the changing of life direction, "repentance," spiritual conversion. What is this "reorientation," this *metanoia*? It is the "self" emptying, the outpouring of "self," in *agapé*.

How does this take place? What is it, practically, that is being described? Before that discussion, the dualism of "faith" versus "works" needs to be extinguished. That dualism is the argument over whether "faith" (in the Christian perspective, in the "saving grace of God through Jesus Christ") alone is salvific, or if "works" (sometimes called "works righteousness"), that is "good works" are the needed ingredients to "earn" salvation.

This is, admittedly, a rather abbreviated description lacking the various nuanced descriptions of each pole and the debate that has raged for millennia. It also ignores that part of the argument that turns on whether "works" are the visible "signs" of "faith."

Such debate turns ultimately on the "freely offered grace of God," available to all without terms other than "only believe." This dualism, I think, has colored so much of our thinking and activity around salvific conceptualities that we often dismiss anything we might do with regard to a salvific offer as suspect, as "trying to earn salvation." This argument ignores those mystics, especially within Christianity, who themselves found no such dichotomy in their meditative experience of the "divine" and of loving gracefulness.

I think it time to journey beyond these two boundaries, these markers on the trail, to set a new path toward our goal.

Along this new path is the fundamental reconsideration of our religious orientation toward the "inner," toward how we behave or think in regard to "self," to "self-identity."

The "outer," the "personal identity" as described previously, will be where the fruits of this movement will appear. The "outer" sense of identity is necessary to our functioning in the world. But the distraction of the physical, the "personal identity," can blind us to the actual conflict of "self" privileging, "self" love, arising from the "inner" "self" of "self-identity," that arena center, the ego.

We have been accustomed to think of "salvation," "redemption," and so on in one way. Our thoughts and feelings are all oriented along this path. But, to take a new, different path we will need to change our pattern of thought.

Chapter 27

Know that when you learn to lose yourself, you will reach the Beloved.
There is no other secret to be learnt, and more than this is not known to me.

—ANSARI OF HERAT[1]

What is on offer is what was there all along, the kenotic outpouring of Self into self, the "self" emptying of self into Self, namely the fundamental agapeic relationship, the cosmic demand—which is reality, which is Spirit. That reality is there; it "costs" us nothing and yet "costs" us everything. That seeming contradiction is resolved by the actual emptiness of "self," as has been argued through these past chapters. It is in the realization of this "emptiness" of self/Self that emptiness and fullness fall away, that such categories no longer have meaning.

The kenosis of Spirit is not a onetime event but continually unfolding immanence in creation. In glimpsing the dynamic interrelatedness of nature, we thus glimpse the movement of Spirit's Self-giving and uniting love (*agapé*) in and through creation.

We have become so accustomed to thinking in terms of the evolution of things (not in the physical, scientific sense but in the psychological sense as follows)—that I can or will become something, should know more, control more, and so on—that it is difficult to halt, to stop time so to speak, to become quiet and so allow for the realization of the emptiness of "self" and its fulfillment, to realize the self freed both from attachment to ego-self and also from nihilistic notions that define "empty" as "no-self." This would be "true self" based on the equality and interrelatedness with others.

This does not deny the real distinctions of the physical sociohistorical dimension of life (see chapter 21). Without such distinctions our world

1. In Huxley, *Perennial Philosophy*, 276.

would be chaotic and interdependency would not be possible. The focus here is on that metaphysical dimension, the religious/spiritual, in order to clearly realize the nonsubstantiality of the world, which in its interdependency creates its fullness. This is similar to the Buddhist "ending of attachment." Looking at "self" or "ego" not as an objective entity but as a perspectival convergence of experiences and reflections on the world—thoughts, memories, responses, knowledge over time—we can realize the possibility of an ego-free response. Within such a response, even "self"-emptying becomes ego-free in accepting our immersion in the world's existential experience. This is true compassion, true love, true *agapé*.

How does this happen; what do I need to do to participate in the "re-orientation," to accept this salvific offer?

First is to realize that agapeic interrelatedness already exists, without any work or effort on our part to bring it about. Second is to recognize the need to allow "I" to fade away; "I" need do nothing. In fact, participation is ego-free, without a particle of endeavor, without trying to "become" something, as noted above. If we are trying to negate something, in other words "trying to be something" or "to gain something," then ego or self is still striving for something, still consciously trying to reach a goal, and interfering with this journey.

In following this path of self-emptying, we are only rediscovering something which has been a part of various religious and spiritual traditions for millennia. The practice of self-examination or self-reflection is a thread that runs through both Eastern and Western religious faiths, albeit in differing ways and with differing emphases.

In the West, we find Christians such as: Julian of Norwich, Meister Eckhart, and Catherine of Sienna back through John Chrysostom, Gregory of Nyssa, Augustine, and Priscilla. There are the Jewish mystic traditions which stem mainly from the Kabbalah, interpreted through scriptural Prophets, Second Temple period (200 BCE to 100 CE), and through rabbinic teachings—such as Rabbi Akiva, Moses Maimonides, to modern age Martin Buber and Abraham Heschel. In Islam, the Sufi tradition predates much of what we consider Middle Eastern religions and which also had spillover into Judaism.

In addition, other spiritual communities have similar elements. The Hindu *karuna* which is a love based upon ideals of showing mercy and compassion even to those without mercy or compassion. The Sikh's *khalsa*, "path of love," and *seva* which is selfless, loving devotion and service to fellow humans. This latter, like *agapé*, is grace in action. Even for Socrates the truth was found in grasping every moment, transforming the brute fact of this world's sorrow and suffering to "the great, loving peace which opens the soul . . . [in pursuit of] a life toward the good."[2]

Perhaps one of the most telling examples from the Hebrew Scriptures is the story of Job. Here is one who is truly emptied in every way but who, in the end, exemplifies unconditional love, not of the divine for human, but human for the divine. Even though beaten down, tested, in every way by a capricious God, Job nonetheless remains faithful, loving God even in questioning divine motives.

What all have in common is practice aimed at a spiritual transformation of the ego-self, at an awareness of or participation in the transformative presence of the "divine," not "my will but thine," "God," Spirit becoming present in our inner acts. As we have seen, much of the Western faiths still had a conceptual basis in a worldview much different from today's understanding and influenced how such transformative realization was accomplished.

The path proposed here differs in ways from some of those Western mystics and is akin with an Eastern understanding of the dynamics present in examining the ego, "self." *Agapé* especially is detached from the later Greek conception which made it the property only of the gods. Although the various Eastern cultures certainly had their own "worldviews," to a very large extent the content of Buddhist, Taoist, and Confucian spiritualities are more pragmatic or practical in their outlook. That is, they do not depend upon an overarching cosmology for the spiritual understanding they engender, or the salvific practice they offer.

What is needed, in this I can only address the faith tradition from which I come, is a transformation of our understanding and practice. The traditions which have carried faith for millennia no longer are able to express themselves in an intelligible way, if they ever truly did, as has been argued previously. The conceptualities held over from previous millennia and ancient cultures need reexamination and either reformulation or rejection if they no longer suit. The issues and arguments in the previous chapters regarding death and the "self" are the focal points in constructing a new path forward.

The beginning in this transformation occurs in accepting the world as it is. Even if one is not inclined to agree with the arguments put forward above regarding death and the nonexistence of "afterlife," the best I believe one could argue would be for Socratic "nonknowledge." Frankly, no one knows what happens once we die; no one has been there and back with any veracity nor is there a scientific or philosophically logical basis for something beyond the close of life here on earth. Ultimately, "life after death"

---

2. Jasper, *Socrates, Buddha, Confucius, Jesus*, 15.

is not something we can do something about; our "answers" are all only speculation and gesture. There is nothing to be done to stop that finitude we share. And what follows is what follows, whatever our understanding, rumination, philosophy, or religion.

We do not live and act "unto death," that is to justify ourselves toward that end point. That is, in fact, a truth that we can derive from the teachings of Jesus, and others. Those teachings direct us not to concern ourselves with "afterlife" so much as direct us to live and act in the present moment, entering into the web of life, to realize/actualize the connectedness of the world around us, not the least of those being our neighbors. Therefore, the emphasis on the meaning of living here and now, on openness to human experience, and cultivating a passionate heart seem to be the most appropriate beginning point for this new journey.

The basis of understanding or realizing this transformation is contemplation or self-reflection. Engaging in the practice of self-examination or meditation is not the pursuit of a navel-gazing escape from the world, a denial of the suffering of life. In fact, just the opposite is true. The practice of self-examination or reflection reorients us from "self-love" and ego-self-privileging to a self-emptying *agapé*.

This practice enables us to move away from such dualism to greater single-mindedness, an unselfconsciousness. In this state of mindfulness, in a life awareness, the equality and interconnectedness of all things is present in thought and in deed. In this awareness we see the indivisibility of existence, how deeply complex and interrelated life is. Every thing has absolute value and is worthy of respect, animate or inanimate. They are not objects to satisfy our egocentric needs, to insensitively use heedlessly, wastefully, or destructively.

For example, mindfulness even in the simple act of eating will help us realize that in wasting food, in the food we throw away, we show indifference and inequality toward not only the value of that object but the server who brought the food, the cook who prepared the food, the storekeeper who sold the food, the trucker or shipper who brought the food from producer to seller, the farmer who grew the food, and plant or animal that provided the food . . . and so on. Interrelatedness appears when we are not in the "center."

Self-reflection and meditation can bring about an awareness of this "center-less" form of consciousness from which mindful attention and compassionate action flow. As described in a previous chapter, in such contemplation, first the "there" drops away then the "here" which seems at the center of our being disappears until the arena of presence and action has no locus, no center where thought, sensation, or intention are found. Nothing appears, until thought again intrudes and that "center" once again appears.

Here we come to the awareness of what the lack of "self" and the focus on interrelatedness and equality can be like when the mind is no longer separated by "ego" from the rest of the world.

Not that this awareness or realization is a "one and done" type of activity. This is a transformational process that ripens or enriches as it is revealed through living a life of deepening awakening to this "reorientation," to the agapeic rich life. Our spirituality and theology go wrong in seeing judgment in this process rather than compassion for the plight in which all find themselves.

Instead our awareness can find this "Word" of God (Spirit) draws absolute and contingent together and discover the embrace of one to the other, recognizing that redemption has already happened, is found, is present in Spirit's outpouring even if the contingent does not acknowledge or accept it. This is the "already but not yet" of Christian faith.

Being single-minded in awareness of what you do not just in a meditative activity but in everything; that is an expression of a self-reflective life. Even the work of daily life can be an occasion for meditation or self-reflection. In so doing we touch Spirit, which is the beginning of the world and its end, its emptiness and its fullness.

Leading a life of self-reflection, we can not only awaken spiritually, we can recover our basic humanity—especially in the awareness of the true nature of things we can see our moral responsibility toward the world. The "self"-love evident in our concern for our own "redemption" or "salvation" and our "afterlife" is a fundamental human blindness. From a Christian perspective that concern runs counter to the gospel's "grace-filled" message of "God's love" prodigally and freely given to all so that concern over oneself can be transformed into love and compassion for your neighbor.

Practicing self-reflection enables us to clarify our experience of things without trying to change or control them. Even with practice though we still will experience turmoil, the return of "ego." The mind's activity does not cease and the ego-self is always present. Perhaps this is another way of understanding what Martin Luther meant by *simul justus et peccator*, simultaneously righteous/saved and sinner. Our thoughts are full of possibilities but we can use that vitality to deepen our awareness and practice. We all have earthly needs to survive. But the issue before us is whether we are bound to those needs and possibilities or not. The ego-self creates desires and objects of gratification and the world encourages us in doing so. But freeing ourselves from such "hooks" by self-reflection allows us to enjoy the unfolding of life before us in freedom and contentment.

Such thoughts, feelings, and attitudes are fleeting, are only part of the natural activity of our arena of presence and action. Allowing them importance just affirms that illusory "self" and makes them real, rather than the impermanent and transitory things they are. Realizing their insubstantial nature allows such expressions to unfold into emptiness, bringing peace. Such is the nature of continuing practice.

Self-reflection, as advocated in these chapters, is nothing new in human history. There is a long history in both the West and the East of practiced awareness. Even with a Western tradition, however, the Eastern path toward such understanding is less dogmatic in many ways and better "fits" the transformational trail forward I believe we need to blaze.

Chapter 28

Fear cannot be got rid of by personal effort, but only by the ego's absorption in a cause greater than its own interests. Absorption in any cause will rid the mind of some of its fears; but only absorption in the loving and knowing of the divine Ground can rid it of all fear.

—ALDOUS HUXLEY[1]

A ll of this must seem strange and foreign when first encountered. Even heretical when compared to the beliefs and conceptualities that have shaped our religious and spiritual thinking and faith. Changing our ideas about death, accepting its finality without the reward of a continuing personal history, is terrifying at first. Reflecting on meaning in our life in light of this will be difficult. More so, perhaps, is the change in perspective on what "repentance," "redemption," and "salvation" might mean in terms of letting go of "self" for a "reorientated" life of service in *agapé*. But these are struggles that we must endure in order to realize a faith that is meaningfully transformed to meet not only the modern world but also the cosmic demand of Spirit.

In a contingent world things are constantly changing. Even our minds, perceptions, and thoughts. Everything is transitory. Even us. But we don't want to recognize that. Our "ego," our "self" privileging doesn't want to admit that we are not permanent in some way.

Because of our belief in a substantial "self" we misinterpret the world in order to preserve our "self." This *incurvatus in se* "self" only produces more suffering in a mistaken view of reality rather engaging in acts of benefit to all. Every living being exists in this predicament.

1. Huxley, *Perennial Philosophy*, 163.

Freeing ourselves from ego as the primary reference point of life, the transformed understanding of "repentance," "redemption"—"reorientation"—allows for a new way of experiencing life. This is the purpose of self-reflection.

Following this "trail" on our journey of self-reflection may seem simple. Examine your thoughts, see what you are thinking, change your thinking. But in practice this is not so easy. There are many "trail maps," guides or teachers that can direct us on this path. Having someone with experience to guide us, just like most endeavors, not only reward us by the benefit of their knowledge, we also have someone to be a "mirror" held up to us, to point out those aspects we overlook. My task here is not to instruct readers on the process of self-reflection and meditation. There are many helpful publications that can provide such instruction and transformation without the need for adherence to a particular sectarian or religious belief system. No single instructional path will fit all circumstances and be suitable for every person. To be effective instruction must fulfill that person's needs and characteristics of thinking.[2]

The temptation is to feel at some point that we have "arrived," that we need go no further in self-reflection. This is merely the "self," the "ego," once again asserting its privilege and dominion. The path of self-reflection is a continual one, always seeking a deeper awareness of what self-emptying, *agapé*, means for us.

As we journey not only are "maps" and "guides" helpful, having traveling companions is necessary for support and encouragement. This is our community, for Christians the "body of Christ," for Mahayana Buddhists the *Sangha*, and so on. That support and encouragement can sustain confidence in our journey and understanding comfort in fearlessly freeing our vulnerabilities and difficulties.

The potential that arises in this self-reflection spills over into our everyday experience, too. The awareness we gain through spiritual and meditative practice directly impacts how we live our daily lives.

By this point there are a few raising the objection that all this sounds like Eastern, Buddhist jargon. And indeed many of the points made here find a genesis in Buddhist (and Confucian and Hindu) thought. But the

---

2. I have found books and authors particularly helpful over the years: Thich Nhat Hanh (esp. *Zen Keys* and *The Miracle of Mindfulness*), Masao Abe (in Cobb's *Emptying God*, *A Study of Dōgen*, and *Zen and Western Thought*), Francis Cook (*Hua-yen Buddhism: The Jewel Net of Indra*), Fung Yu-Lan (*The Spirit of Chinese Philosophy*), Shunryu Suzuki (*Zen Mind, Beginner's Mind*), Philip Kapleau (*The Three Pillars of Zen*) Dzigar Kongtrül (*It's Up to You: Self-Reflection on the Buddhist Path*). Details are in the bibliography.

practice of mindfulness, being aware of how we think, how we act, is not limited to a particular spirituality. In fact, such mindfulness is of value to the wide range of human religion.

Mindfulness focuses our attention on our thought and action to enable us to see reality clearly—in our body, in our feelings, and in our mental processes. Mindfulness is not just an intellectual process but encompasses the whole being, in everything we do. We don't leave our mind behind in daily living, for the ground of our practice is in that direct experience of ours.

This discussion may seem to have strayed from the topic of a new understanding, a "reorientation" or "redemption." However, the point is that redirecting our lives toward the cosmic demand of *agapé*, the true nature of reality, and ultimately of Spirit, is a process in which we participate, in which we are an integral part, like the molecules of water that make up the rushing river. We are a part of an interrelated, interdependent whole. To realize this in our lives necessitates some effort on our part. Not the effort of monkish solitude, though many religious traditions espouse such a course.

The aim here is for this process to permeate all aspects of our life, a mindfulness vision and agapeic life. To reach truth is not to accumulate knowledge nor is it found in concepts or abstractions but in awakening to the concrete reality that surrounds us. This is because ego-self grasps absolute beliefs and is closed to new ideas. Likewise, even religious beliefs and practices can prevent us from seeing life clearly, can obstruct spiritual insights that others have that may transform our own understanding.

In making the arguments that I have thus far, the understanding needs to be clear that Buddhists are not Christians and Christians are not Buddhists, in the same way other world religions are not interchangeable. Each has their own unique history and conceptualities, some of which need to be addressed in the light of the modern world we live in; that is for each to decide. However, we should not close ourselves off to mutual transformation that come from the spiritual insights of others.

Chapter 29

Reframing our perspective or concept of the "metaphysical divine," as this work argues, has been necessitated by the cosmology of the modern age radically different from our forebears and the consequent need to transform our understanding of reality and the cosmic demand to which religion bears witness.

As has been argued in these chapters, the word "God" especially as used by the monotheistic religions has been meant to denote an Ultimate Reality from which everything flows and to which everything returns. To this power all prayers, supplications, and offerings are directed as the ultimate power which is the beginning and the end of all reality.

But, as David Tracy points out, as we come to understand this power, we discover a deeper, more complex reality that engenders

> the pluralistic and ambiguous reality of the self, at once finite, estranged, and needing of liberation by a power not its own. There are many models of religious enlightenment, sometimes complementary, more often conflicting: a radical enlightenment to emptiness as the Ultimate Reality in many of the Buddhist ways; an enlightenment to "Thou art Thou" (Atman and Brahman are one) in much of Hinduism; an enlightenment to a compassion so great that we become willing to postpone our own final enlightenment to work for that of others in the Bodhisattva traditions of Buddhism, an enlightenment to a sense of our precarious but necessary relations to the whole through the civic order in the civil religions of the Greeks, the Romans, and the Confucians; an enlightenment to our relations to all living things in Taoism and in the primal, archaic religions; an enlightenment to God's law as delineating the way in Judaism; an enlightenment to a life oriented by radical faith, hope, and love in Christianity; an enlightenment to political and historical

responsibility in the prophetic strands of Judaism, Christianity, and Islam. Despite their often radical differences . . . all these ways do demand a singular transformation of self: from self-centeredness to Reality-centeredness.[1]

Tracy acknowledges that it does not follow that these enlightenments are "different expressions of the same religious position" or "practice the same way of liberation." However, the argument of the present work seeks to go beyond a passive pluralistic response to actively seek to engage with the meaning both of the Christian tradition and the insights from other spiritual traditions, especially Mahayana Buddhism for a constructive transformation in both communities.

In this engagement it is just as easy to misconstrue the content of other spiritual traditions as it is to mistakenly create equivalencies where none exists. The dialogue between Christian and Buddhist has been decades long and fruitful for both mutual and self-understandings. Taking seriously the product of such dialogues and the various religious insights presented in this work will, I believe, necessitate a transformation of spiritual self-understanding such as argued here.[2]

The aim of this work has been for a radical reorientation away from salvific reward in a personal "afterlife" which is, I have argued, flawed scientifically, philosophically, and spiritually. Beginning with the acknowledgment of the insubstantiality of "self," the illusory "center" of our arena of presence and action, we can find salvific "redemption" in our kenotic, self-emptying, response to the cosmic demand of love and compassion—*agapé*—which is already present to us in self-emptied Spirit encompassing all creation. We have this ability to be free of the "ego-self" just by virtue of being born and the willingness to be present.

With the foregoing arguments in this book one might conclude I am rejecting *in toto* the Christian tradition. Nothing could be further from the truth. Yes, the conceptual framework inherited from ancient times and elaborated over centuries needs to be examined, reconstructed, and in some cases rejected as obscuring truth. Yes, the argument in these pages is for a new understanding of and relationship to fundamental concepts, to deal forthrightly with metaphor.

1. Tracy, *Plurality and Ambiguity*, 89.

2 The fact that I have not here addressed those issues that arise in Buddhism from this engagement should not be taken as a dismissal. Others such as Masao Abe and John Cobb (in works such as *Emptying God* quoted throughout this work) have sought just this mutual transformation and instruction.

But the Judeo-Christian tradition also carries, along with such baggage, a spiritually strong imperative of humanistic compassion and care not only for others but for the world. This message too often has been hidden behind our all too human tendency to "self-love" and "self-privileging." That such a wall might even find its way into the scriptural writings of that tradition should not be surprising, nor in anyway devalue the critical demand, the cosmic demand, evident in the Torah, the Prophets, and the Gospels.

There is a subtlety in negotiating between what I have set forth in the chapters above, which borrow heavily from Buddhist tradition, and the Buddhist tradition itself. This subtlety is most clear in the meaning of the moment of selflessness in meditation, in the meaning of "emptiness" and "fullness," and how illusory even these words are. This subtlety, however, indicates the continuing need for dialogue and mediation over these differences.[3]

In making the arguments I have, I want to push the reader to consider that having "an ear to hear" and "an eye to see" in a different way might bring fresh insight, a new "trail map" for our human journey.

The Western emphasis, in Greek philosophy and the Judeo-Christian tradition, on a teleological view of existence has in many ways caused much of the crisis in religion today. Rather than a teleological divine plan progressing from a beginning to an "end time of fulfillment," the argument here is for a non-teleological perspective or, perhaps, bringing that "end" into a beginningless "present" in the same way "self" is emptied and becomes full in a dynamic process. The "end," so to speak, is the resultant kenosis and agapeic outpouring already present to us now in reality. The inner dynamism of the universe is preserved as a given and our part in the interrelated and interconnected web of existence is made clear.

Is this reconstituting of our understanding a completed task? Not in the least. There is still much to understand and we live with the constant struggle with the "ego-self." We live in a contingent world in which the evolving process of coming to wisdom and compassion is just as much beginningless as it is endless. The dynamic relationship of "self-emptying" and "fulfillment" are embraced in each moment as we realize the relationship of inter-being and deep responsibility to others which constitutes the cosmic demand of *agapé*.

---

3. This point is made in a book, now in its third edition, which I found in my seminary days in its first edition, William Johnston, *Christian Zen*. Johnston's book was my first introduction to Zen Buddhism in the context of the dialogue with Christianity after having previously been exposed to Buddhism and Hatha yogic meditation while in college.

In this "egolessness" we are letting go of grasping and fixation, of hopes and fears, the tendency to hold on to worldly objects as ends in themselves, as objects for the "self." In "egolessness" or "emptiness" we don't crumble to dust or disappear or isolate ourselves from the richness of the world. On the contrary, by letting go we can enjoy what we have, can appreciate the world for what it is, can recognize true pleasure from pain—a heart filled with joy, love, compassion, and contentment.

Life on its face, even with the beauty we can find, has a harshness, an impersonal, cold, and uncaring nature, like the storm tossed seas or the might of a hurricane or tornado. The truth to be teased out is that in the face of this existential darkness, there is a way of seeing, a strategy of knowing, a technique of empowerment to endure if not surmount the challenges we face. Not "pie in the sky," but ever-present moment to moment.

When we perceive the two-sidedness of our lives we can understand the opportunity, and the peril, before us and so be motivated to action. On the one side, we have the incredible good fortune to be born, to be here in this moment. On the other, we are also reminded that we "are dust, and to dust [we] shall return."

If we forget the good fortune of our birth, no matter the circumstances, it is easy to find life meaningless and full of rage or cynicism or depression. If we forget our impermanence we too easily become complacent or arrogant or callous to the precious gift we hold.

Life is precious; this moment is precious in its precariousness and easily slips away. In remembering our impermanence we are called to act now, for time is fleeting.

To what are we called then? First, we are called to remember that we are human and rightly understand our movement through the world. Second, we are called to remember our impermanence, that each moment passed never comes again. Third, we are called to remember that all our actions have consequences that will ripple through the world. In these ways we are ultimately called beyond "self" to "empty self," that is to a life which stands in an interrelated and interdependent relation with the world, *agapé*.

Will we perfectly and completely fulfill our calling? Most probably not. But even in imperfection, the impermanence of the world allows repair to the damage our ignorance (willful, sinful, neglectful . . .) has done. This does not deny the consequences or effects of our actions. But without a recognition of impermanence we also fall into the despair of the possibility of change, the unawareness of repentance, which is also ignorance. The biblical God of Eden in Genesis called out to Adam, "Where are you?" not to physically locate Adam but to call Adam to recognize himself "where he was," to return, *metanoia*, to reenter the path of a right relationship.

This is the self-emptying world filled with Spirit which is self-emptying to and for us and for the world.

The task before us is to rebuild our sense of spirituality and community. In this, the argument I have tried to make is that there is a need to find new ways to honor and to voice our spiritual traditions, exploring both Western and Eastern experiences, to make sense of the spiritual dimension of life and also respect the understanding of the world that modern science can provide.

We have become so technologically and individually focused that, instead of this spiritual task, we find ourselves engaged only in conflict, consumption, suffering, and death. We have neglected the insight that true happiness only comes in the reawakening of our humanity, in rebuilding community toward a recognition of interbeing and responsibility to our neighbors. This is the sane and healthy life to which we are called by the "cosmic demand."

It is a bit ironic, as a last word, after all these pages filled with concepts and conceptualities that the final word is, in reality, to not get lost in concepts, phantoms of the mind. Life is more than concepts. Life and our experience of selflessness are found in the living reality of daily life and our relationships. Our awareness of the self-emptying of agapeic "re-orientation" is not to be found in the abstractions of the mind but in the concrete lived experience of each moment, in this world, with everything that surrounds us.

Postscript

Without concrete signs of divine presence in the lives of the poor, the gospel becomes simply an opiate; rather than liberating the powerless from humiliation and suffering, the gospel becomes a drug that helps them adjust to this world by looking for "pie in the sky."

And so the transcendent and the immanent, heaven and earth, must be held together in critical, dialectical tension, each one correcting the limits of the other.

—James Cone[1]

My intention in this book is the reconception and reorientation of religious and spiritual thought, mainly as it arises from the Christian tradition. Using Buddhist concepts in such a reworking, I know I open myself to the charge of abandoning my "faith," as a Lutheran if not a Christian. I would, however, reject such a characterization as fettering the "divine" to a narrow and challenged traditional range of understanding. I assert that clarity and integrity in the faith journey necessitates raising provocative questions and being willing to take theological risks in order to discover, or perhaps uncover, truths about oneself and one's own tradition.

In so doing, I am not declaring a final understanding of "God" or "ultimate truth" common to all humankind. Such a declaration would be cultural and religious imperialism. However, the fact that a diversity of religious and spiritual traditions exists does not thereby create rigid and separate cantons which are incapable of communication. In contrast, the search for similarity and unifying communication affirms, even while acknowledging differences, an abiding interconnection within and among religious and cultural

---

1. Cone, *Cross and the Lynching Tree*, 155–56.

communities. In this I find myself among those trust that Spirit is one and that religions should learn from and challenge each other.

The result has been a deeper appreciation of the Christian tradition from which I come, but also liberation in clarity of spiritual vision from engagement with Buddhism. This challenge, though at times uncomfortable and unnerving, has helped me to realize that these two traditions have a normativity for me, but in different ways.

My understanding, or rather reconceptualization, of the Christian claims regarding "God" and Jesus are more guided by Buddhism than by traditional theological categories. Although I retain the content of my Christian tradition it is from a Buddhist perspective that I find an intelligible understanding of creedal categories of the divine, Jesus as the revealer of faith, life, death, and resurrection. I won't repeat the arguments made earlier regarding "self," the emptiness of death, and the resurrection as "reorientation" regarding the "self." At the same time I want to acknowledge that conceptualities expressed here, in particular "kenosis," are not necessarily only from an Eastern tradition.

Kenosis has a European strain separate from the Buddhist interpretation that does not necessarily follow from Paul's Letter to the Philippians but concentrating on the Gospels. Even the early Christian church councils are much more ambiguous on their formulations. However, those formulations, and the European strains, are dependent upon a Greek philosophical format that constrains their positions and thinking, not to mention a more anthropocentric, anthropomorphic cosmology that does not have the benefit of more astronomy and physics.

Even within the Christian tradition itself we find Spirit ("God") is the "place" of all things in nature; all things reflect in a multitude of ways Spirit within their being (Bonaventure, Aquinas). As all forms reflect Spirit we can glimpse in this dynamic interrelatedness of nature the movement of Spirit's kenotic creative love, the creativity of Spirit which is love, kenosis, *agapé*, and the effect of the kenosis of love, creation. (Aquinas, 1 John, and so on).

With this creative and kenotic immanence we can not only perceive Spirit in creation but can further contemplatively "find" Spirit innermost in each being and most deeply inherent in all things. This is not something external to our existence, added on, but foundational—the "ground," "place," or "matrix" of our being. Our participation in this ground, Spirit, "merges" us in the "vanishing of ego" with all creation, especially other humans in compassionate love as brothers and sisters in God (Spirit).

However, I do want to emphasize what I believe is a significant shift in understanding the Christ-event for Christian belief and life. This is a shift away from the normatives of sovereign power and lordship toward an emphasis on the cross. Such a move, I think, is very much Christian and Lutheran. The central and defining image, as indicated previously in this book, ought to be Christ's suffering and death. This really is the metaphor for all of life as we know it. As I described earlier, an emphasis on Jesus' self-giving, "self-emptying," faithfulness in love to the end is the reference point and context in terms of which the ultimate is understood. Hence the explicit references to Śūnyatā or emptiness and the profound point of contact between Christian and Buddhist interpretations of human life.

In this way, too, we can find a nondual, if asymmetric, reciprocity much like Buddhist "Form" and "Emptiness" in Christian "God" and "World." There is, in fact, only one reality, God-world, Emptiness-Form, that exists in a dynamic interrelatedness. There is no other place for these to exist than right here, right now.

Though this understanding may be more Buddhist, I am no less a Christian for it. I believe Buddhism helps to reclaim the reality expressed by the more traditional, and largely unintelligible, language of faith. The images in the Gospels abound—the oneness of Jesus and the Father, that offer of oneness to us, vines and branches, one body, Paul's statement that to be a Christian is live a life rooted in Christ (Col 2:6). How different, in this context, is the Spirit's indwelling from the achievement of enlightenment in Buddhism?

On the other hand, Christianity has normative priority ethically for me, especially in terms of social ethics. Though this discussion is a continuing one, even the Buddhist scholar Masao Abe among others acknowledged the need to engage with this area of discernment especially with regard to suffering due to social injustice. This is an area that should be trod upon carefully as critical discernment carries the responsibility of careful and respectful understanding of both positions. I claim no expertise as a Buddhist scholar nor an ethicist. From my position within the Christian faith tradition, I find the following ethical issues of consequence to the spirituality presented in this work. As further consideration and formulation is necessary, this is not a "final word" on the subject, but a work in process as we seek to reconceptualize and live out our faith.

We live in a world of suffering, a world of large-scale defects. The message or call to fix this world, present in Judaism and clearly proclaimed by Jesus, is much more overt in Christianity. That structures of oppression need be confronted is not contrary to Buddhist teachings but also does not play a central role in the same way. The motif of God's rule, present in Judaism and Christianity, has a clear pointer toward how the world should look, how the world would work, if this message was heeded. This is not only an individual call but a call to corporate conversion, for social justice, a new social order.

Such a message or demand is unsettling, disturbing, and ultimately dangerous for the messenger. In this instance, the tie between individual and social conversion, "reorientation," has a significant and normative status.

Both Christianity and Buddhism share a compassion for suffering and the desire to do something to transform this state of human existence. Compassion and love play basic roles as necessary conditions for change. However, from the Christian perspective, systemic, structural sin and injustice are obstacles that compassion alone cannot adequately address. The source of these obstacles may be "self-centeredness" or "self-love" or "self-privileging," as Christians and Buddhists can agree. But these "individual" poisons take on corporate lives of their own within the structures of human society, independent of the individual, and function in a sociopolitical way that requires a social "mindfulness" to transform such "powers and principalities" as Paul terms them.

This is not to say that Buddhism does not recognize the social or corporate aspect of the world's suffering. Far from it. Vietnamese Zen master and author Thich Nhat Hahn rightly notes the "spiritual bankruptcy" of both East and West in pursuit of material development and industrialization, of a system that overtakes us. But even in acknowledging the efficacy of struggles such as Gandhi's, the emphasis tends toward the "awakening" of the individual, or perhaps of individuals in community, to become a spiritual force for a "new civilization." "Churches must work to rebuild communities in which a sane and healthy life can be lived, realizing that true happiness does not rest in the consumption of goods paid for by suffering, famine, and death, but in a life enlightened by the insight into interbeing and the recognition of our deep responsibility to be true to ourselves and to help our neighbors."[2]

The most delicate balance in finding normativity between Christianity and Buddhism is the very overt Judeo-Christian-Islamic embrace of the poor and oppressed as the privileged focus of God's love. Although this privileged status often falls by the wayside in practice when taken as a basis for action this preference can easily become ethically problematic. The Buddhist perspective would remind Christians that God's love embraces all, oppressed and oppressor, equally and unconditionally. This is a practical reminder that love of the poor does not thereby engender hatred of the rich.

Yet the voice of the poor, marginalized, and oppressed ought to have a privileged status in terms of our need to listen and learn—how poverty affects the structure of family and individuals; the role structural discrimination plays in health care, employment, education, and more. Of course,

2. Hahn, *Zen Keys*, 161.

such privilege does not convey exclusive or inerrant judgment—people make mistakes, err in judgments—and other thoughtful voices ought to be heard. But such messages, most often excluded, make real the suffering and the need for action, and are an essential first step for mindful understanding of suffering.

The task before us, then, is to continue to engage with other faith traditions, to understand ourselves by understanding others, knowing that Spirit encompasses all. We must build out from new understandings of Spirit-world-self so that the expressive nature of the "cosmic demand" fills our lives and our activity in this world with the presence of Spirit, to love Spirit with your whole heart and soul, and to love your neighbor as yourself.

Bibliography

Abe, Masao. *Zen and Western Thought*. Honolulu: University of Hawaii Press, 1985.

Abe, Masao, and Francis Cook. "Response to Gilkey." *Buddhist-Christian Studies* 5 (1985) 67–101.

Armstrong, Karen. *The Case for God*. New York: Knopf, 2009.

———. *A History of God*. New York: Ballantine, 1993.

Baeck, Leo. *The Essence of Judaism*. New York: Schoken, 1948.

Berger, Peter. *A Far Glory: The Quest for Faith in an Age of Credulity*. New York: Anchor/ Doubleday, 1992.

Bonhoeffer, Dietrich. *Letters and Papers from Prison*. London: SCM Press, 1967.

Braaten, Carl. *Christ and Counter-Christ: Apocalyptic Themes in Theology and Culture*. Philadelphia: Fortress, 1971.

———. *Eschatology and Ethics: Essays on the Theology and Ethics of the Kingdom of God*. Minneapolis: Augsburg, 1974

———. *The Future of God: The Revolutionary Dynamics of Hope*. New York: Harper and Row, 1969.

Brown, David. *Divine Humanity: Kenosis and the Construction of a Christian Theology*. Waco, TX: Baylor University Press, 2011.

Buber, Martin. *I and Thou*. Translated by Walter Kaufmann. New York: Scribner, 1970.

Buchler, Justus. *Metaphysics of Natural Complexes*. New York: Columbia University Press, 1966.

———. Review of *Man's Vision of God and the Logic of Theism*, by Charles Hartshorne. *Journal of Philosophy* 39 (1942) 245–47.

Capra, Fritjof. *The Web of Life: A New Scientific Understanding of Living Systems*. New York: Anchor Doubleday, 1996.

Carroll, Sean. *The Big Picture: On the Origins of Life, Meaning, and the Universe Itself*. New York: Dutton, 2016.

———. *From Eternity to Here: The Quest for the Ultimate Theory of Time*. New York: Dutton, 2010.

———. *The Particle at the End of the Universe*. New York: Dutton, 2012.

Cho, Hyun-Chul. *An Ecological Vision of the World: Toward a Christian Ecological Theology for Our Age*. Rome: Gregorian University Press, 2004.

Cobb, John B., Jr., and Christopher Ives, eds. *The Emptying God: A Buddhist-Jewish-Christian Conversation*. Maryknoll: Orbis, 1990.

Cone, James. *The Cross and the Lynching Tree*. Maryknoll: Orbis, 2011.

Cook, Francis H. *Hua-yen Buddhism: The Jewel Net of Indra*. University Park: Pennsylvania State University Press, 1977.

Cox, Harvey. *The Secular City*. New York: MacMillan, 1965.

The Dalai Lama. *The Universe in a Single Atom*. New York: Morgan Road, 2005.

Dunne, John. *The Way of All the World*. New York: MacMillan, 1972.

Gilkey, Langdon. *Blue Twilight: Nature, Creationism, and American Religion*. Minneapolis: Augsburg Fortress, 2001.

———. "Cosmology, Ontology and the Travail of Biblical Language." *Journal of Religion* 41 (1961) 194–205.

———. *Naming the Whirlwind: The Renewal of God-Language*. Indianapolis: Bobbs-Merrill, 1969.

———. *Reaping the Whirlwind: A Christian Interpretation of History*. New York: Seabury, 1976.

Gleiser, Marcelo. *The Island of Knowledge: the Limits of Science and the Search for Meaning*. New York: Basic, 2014.

Goldstein, Rebecca. *Incompleteness: The Proof and Paradox of Kurt Gödel*. New York: Norton, 2005.

Gottschall, Jonathan. *The Storytelling Animal: How Stories Make Us Human*. New York: Mariner, 2013.

Greene, Brian. *The Fabric of the Cosmos: Space, Time, and the Texture of Reality*. New York: Knopf, 2004.

Greene, Robert Lane. *You Are What You Speak*. New York: Delacourt, 2011.

Guardini, Romano. *Sacred Signs*. Translated by Grace Branham. St. Louis: Pio Decimo, 1956.

Hahn, Thich Nhat. *Zen Keys: A Guide to Zen Practice*. New York: Doubleday, 1974/1994.

Hartshorne, Charles. *The Divine Relativity: A Social Conception of God*. New Haven: Yale University Press, 1984.

———. *A Natural Theology for Our Time*. La Salle, IL: Open Court, 1973.

———. *Omnipotence and Other Theological Mistakes*. Albany: State University of New York Press, 1984.

———. *The Zero Fallacy and Other Essays in Neoclassical Philosophy*. Chicago: Open Court, 1997.

Hartshorne, Charles, and William Reese, eds. *Philosophers Speak of God: Readings in Philosophical Theology and Analyses of Theistic Ideas*. Chicago: University of Chicago Press, 1969.

Hawking, Stephen. *A Brief History of Time: From the Big Bang to Black Holes*. New York: Bantam Dell, 1988.

Heisenberg, Werner. *Across the Frontiers*. New York: Harper & Row, 1974.

———. *Physics and Beyond: Encounters and Conversations*. London: Allen & Unwin, 1971.

———. *Physics and Philosophy: The Revolution in Modern Science*. Amherst, NY: Prometheus, 1999.

Heschel, Abraham. *God in Search of Man: A Philosophy of Judaism*. New York: Farrar, Straus & Cudahy, 1955.

———. *Man Is Not Alone*. New York: Farrar, Strauss & Giroux, 1976.

Hick, John, ed. *The Existence of God*. New York: Macmillan, 1964.

Holt, Jim. *Why Does the World Exist?* New York: Liveright, 2012.

Horrel, David G. *The Bible and the Environment: Toward a Critical Biblical Ecological Theology*. Oakville, CT: Equinox, 2010.

Hume, David. *Dialogues concerning Natural Religion*. Part 9. London: Scott, 1875.

————. *A Treatise of Human Nature.* Vol. 1. London: Longman, Green, 1874.

Huxley, Aldous. *The Perennial Philosophy.* New York: HarperCollins, 2009.

Ingram, Paul O. "Buddhist-Christian-Science Dialogue at the Boundaries." *Buddhist-Christian Studies* 31 (2011) 165–74.

Jasper, Karl. *Socrates, Buddha, Confucius, Jesus.* New York: Harcourt, Brace & World, 1962.

Jenkins, Phillip. *Crucible of Faith: The Ancient Revolution That Made Our Modern Religious World.* New York: Basic, 2017.

Johnston, Mark. *Saving God.* Princeton: Princeton University Press, 2009.

————. *Surviving Death.* Princeton: Princeton University Press, 2010.

Johnston, William. *Christian Zen.* 3rd ed. New York: Fordham University Press, 1997.

Kaufmann, Walter. *Critique of Religion and Philosophy.* New York: Harper, 1958.

Kitaro, Nishida. *Last Writings: Nothingness and the Religious Worldview.* Honolulu: University of Hawaii Press, 1987.

————. "The Logic of 'Topos' and the Religious Worldview Part I." *Eastern Buddhist,* n.s., 19 (Autumn 1986) 1–29.

————. "The Logic of 'Topos' and the Religious Worldview Part II." *Eastern Buddhist,* n.s., 20 (Spring 1987) 81–119.

Kongtrül, Dzigar. *It's Up to You: The Practice of Self-Reflection on the Buddhist Path.* Boston: Shambala, 2005.

Lee, Bernard. *The Becoming of the Church: A Process Theology of the Structures of Christian Experience.* New York: Paulist, 1974.

Lewis, C. S. *The Discarded Image: An Introduction to Medieval and Renaissance Literature.* Cambridge: Cambridge University Press, 1994.

Look, Brandon C. "Gottfried Wilhelm Leibniz." *The Stanford Encyclopedia of Philosophy.* Summer 2017 ed. Edited by Edward N. Zalta. https://plato.stanford.edu/archives/sum2017/entries/leibniz/>.

Loy, David. "*Shushogi* Paragraph 1." In *Engaging Dōgen's Zen: The Philosophy of Practice as Awakening,* edited by Jason M. Wirth et al., 81–87. Somerville, MA: Wisdom, 2016.

Meyer, Michael A. "The Thought of Leo Baeck: A Religious Philosophy for a Time of Adversity." *Modern Judaism* 19 (May 1999) 107–17.

Michael, Helen. "Abraham Heschel's Concept of God." *European Judaism: A Journal for the New Europe* 30 (Autumn 1997) 131–50.

Milligan, Charles. "The Limits of Conventional Religious Language for Contemporary Meaning." *American Journal of Theology & Philosophy* 17 (September 1996) 295–316.

Mitchell, Donald. *Spirituality and Emptiness: The Dynamics of Spiritual Life in Buddhism and Christianity.* New York: Paulist, 1991.

Moltmann, Jürgen. *Theology of Hope: On the Ground and the Implications of a Christian Eschatology.* New York: Harper & Row, 1967.

Moor, Robert. *On Trails.* New York: Simon & Schuster, 2017.

Musser, Charles, et al. *The Whirlwind in Culture: Frontiers in Theology; In Honor of Langdon Gilkey.* Edited by Joseph Price. Bloomington, IN: Meyer-Stone, 1989.

Nagel, Ernest, and James Newman. *Gödel's Proof.* In *The World of Mathematics.* New York: Simon & Schuster, 1956.

Nishitani, Keiji. *Religion and Nothingness.* Berkley: University of California Press, 1982.

O'Dea, Thomas F. "The Crisis of the Contemporary Religious Consciousness." *Daedalus* 96 (Winter 1967) 116–34.

Pascal, Blaise. *Pensées: The Thoughts of Blaise Pascal*. Translated from the text of M. Auguste Molinier by C. Kegan Paul. London, 1885.

Pollan, Michael. *How to Change Your Mind: What the New Science of Psychedelics Teaches Us about Consciousness, Dying, Addiction, Depression, and Transcendence.* New York: Penguin, 2018.

Raymo, Chet. *When God Is Gone Everything Is Holy*. Notre Dame: Sorin, 2008.

Ricard, Matthieu, and Trinh Xuan Thuan. *The Quantum and the Lotus*. New York: Three Rivers, 2001.

Robinson, J. A. T. *Truth Is Two-Eyed*. Philadelphia: Westminster, 1979.

Schermer, Michael. *How We Believe*. New York: Holt, 1999.

Schmidt-Leukel, Perry. *Buddhism and Christianity in Dialogue: The Gerald Weisfeld Lectures 2004*. London: SCM, 2005.

Schrödinger, Erwin. *What Is Life? With "Mind and Matter" and "Autobiographical Sketches."* Printing of the 1944 ed. Cambridge: Cambridge University Press, 2000.

Shariati, Ali. *The Hajj*. Costa Mesa, CA: Jubilee, 1978.

Sittler, Joseph. *Essays on Nature and Grace*. Philadelphia: Fortress, 1972.

Snook, Lee E. *The Anonymous Christ*. Minneapolis: Augsburg, 1986.

———. *What in the World Is God Doing? Re-imagining Spirit and Power*. Minneapolis: Fortress, 1999.

Tillich, Paul. *Systematic Theology*. Vol. 1. Chicago: University of Chicago Press, 1967.

Tolstoy, Leo. *War and Peace*. Modern Library ed. New York: Random House, 1994.

Tracy, David. *Blessed Rage for Order*. New York: Seabury, 1975.

———. *Plurality and Ambiguity: Hermeneutics, Religion, Hope*. Chicago: University of Chicago Press, 1994.

Whitehead, Alfred North. *The Concept of Nature*. London: Cambridge University Press, 1920.

———. *Religion in the Making*. New York: Meridian, 1960.

Williams, Daniel Day. *Essays in Process Theology*. Edited by Perry LeFevre. Chicago: Exploration Press of the Chicago Theological Seminary, 1985.

———. *God's Grace and Man's Hope*. New York: Harper & Row, 1949.

———. *The Spirit and the Forms of Love*. New York: Harper & Row, 1968.

Wittgenstein, Ludwig. *Tractatus Logico-Philosophicus*. New York: Harcourt, Brace, 1922.

Yu-Lan, Fung. *The Spirit of Chinese Philosophy*. Translated by E. R. Hughes. Boston: Beacon, 1962.